CHALLENGING
ENVIRONMENTAL ISSUES

Middle Eastern Perspectives

INTERNATIONAL STUDIES IN SOCIOLOGY AND SOCIAL ANTHROPOLOGY

Editor

S. ISHWARAN

VOLUME LXVIII

JOSEPH G. JABBRA
AND
NANCY W. JABBRA (EDS.)

CHALLENGING ENVIRONMENTAL ISSUES

Middle Eastern Perspectives

CHALLENGING ENVIRONMENTAL ISSUES

Middle Eastern Perspectives

EDITED BY

JOSEPH G. JABBRA

AND

NANCY W. JABBRA

BRILL

LEIDEN · NEW YORK · KÖLN

1997

This book is printed on acid-free paper.

Library of Congress Cataloging-in-Publication Data

Challenging environmental issues : Middle Eastern perspectives /
    edited by Joseph G. Jabbra and Nancy W. Jabbra.
        p.   cm. — (International studies in sociology and social
    anthropology, ISSN 0074-8684 ; v. 68)
        ISBN 9004108777 (pbk. : alk. paper)
        1. Environmental management—Middle East. 2. Middle East-
    -Environmental conditions.   I. Jabbra, Joseph G.   II. Jabbra, Nancy
    Walstrom.   III. Series.
    GE320.M628C43 1997
    333.7'137'0956—DC21   97–16210
                                                                              CIP

Die Deutsche Bibliothek - CIP-Einheitsaufnahme

Challenging environmental issues : Middle Eastern perspectives /
ed. by Joseph G. Jabbra and Nancy W. Jabbra – Leiden ; New York ;
Köln : Brill, 1997
    (International studies in sociology and social anthropology ; Vol. 68)
    ISBN 90–04–10877-7

ISSN 0074-8684
ISBN 90 04 10877 7

PRINTED IN THE NETHERLANDS

To Michael and Mary

May they live in a pollution-free environment

CONTENTS

Challenging Environmental Issues
Middle Eastern Perspectives

JOSEPH G. JABBRA and NANCY W. JABBRA*

ABSTRACT

This is an introductory chapter which reviews some of the most challenging environmental problems currently confronted by Middle Eastern countries, particularly in the areas of water, air and agricultural pollution. It also summarizes the eight articles included in this volume and concludes by proposing a number of policy changes which might help Middle Eastern governments and societies in their endeavor to protect their environment.

Introduction

THIS EDITED volume is the result of our keen interest in better understanding the problems faced by our global ecosystems. It is also the result of our deep commitment to urge, continuously and tirelessly, both citizens and leaders the world over to work together for a better protection of the environment so that our planet may be saved for us and for future generations. We know that human activities and behavior will determine the fate of our environment and indeed the survival of the human species. Therefore, we can no longer dismiss major environmental disasters with insouciance. Scholars, experts, artists, and environmentalists in general, have been documenting, vividly and graphically, the ravages visited upon the environment by the modernizing drive of both developed and developing societies. At the risk of destroying the fragile balance between all forms of life and their environment, states have ruthlessly pursued economic development, and citizens and corporations throughout the world have been consumed by the urge to make profit and amass huge fortunes.

In our drive to improve human standards of living, we have paradoxically paid scant attention to environmental threats to all living species, the need for clean air and water, the impact of acid rain on agriculture, lakes and rivers, the effect of pollutants on the ozone layer, the safe disposition of hazardous waste, and the

* Marymount College, 7900 Loyola Blvd, Los Angeles, CA 90045-8316, U.S.A.

relationship between population growth and the environment. It seems that every time governments are faced with an apparent choice between economic development and jobs on the one hand, and the protection of the environment on the other, priority is always given to the former. Short-term plans dictated by canons of political survival and expediency always seem to take precedence over long-term strategies with politicians and decision makers deftly relegating environmental concerns to the realm of rhetoric.

The United Nations Conference on Environment and Development held in 1992 in Rio de Janeiro, Brazil, was hailed by the international media as "Earth Summit." It was meant to be a major milestone in the march of humanity toward sensitizing world leaders to environmental issues and securing their genuine commitment to a better and safer environment. Unfortunately, the greener future promised in Rio seems to have receded into the background of ruthless trade expansion and intractable regional, ethnic, and religious conflicts. Thus, the degradation of the environment continues unabated the world over.

Nowhere is this situation more serious than in the Middle East, which faces a major environmental threat. There, geography and arid and semi-arid climatic conditions have led to a concentration of people in coastal zones and little valleys with ensuing major environmental problems, acute water shortages, increasing soil erosion, and intensifying desertification all creating serious environmental challenges. According to Mustafa Tolba, acute underdevelopment and massive drives for industrialization have accentuated environmental deterioration (Abu Fadil, 1991: 33), and increased air and water pollution to an all-time high, particularly in the oil-producing countries. Pollutants of all kinds, including highly acidic sulfates and nitrates, have emerged as a major environmental challenge for Kuwait, Qatar, Iran, Saudi Arabia, Iraq, and other Middle Eastern countries. The Arabian Gulf is seriously polluted due to the devastating 1980 Iran/Iraq War, and the 1990-91 Gulf War. Naval war destroyed oil facilities and vessels causing large amounts of petroleum to spill into the Arabian Gulf water, threatening the elimination of all fish species. Mustafa Tolba declared in an interview with Middle East Magazine (quoted in Abu Fadil, 1991) that in the Middle East "there is also a misuse of land, and that's almost symptomatic of any Middle Eastern country which has agricultural land." He further explained that the construction of roads, airports, housing, and prestige projects on agricultural land is robbing many Middle Eastern countries of valuable assets and causing a major environmental crisis. According to a joint study by the United Nations Environment Program and the US Environment, if the greenhouse effect leads to a further expansion of the seas, a rise in the Nile Delta could flood one-fifth of Egypt's agricultural land causing a crisis of major proportions. Furthermore, any change in weather patterns will likely add to the aridity of areas in the Middle East and thus speed up land degradation.

The concentration of population along river banks, and sea and gulf coasts, and the unchecked drive for economic development have had a major environmental impact on water, air, land, and agriculture in the Middle East.

A. *Impact on Water*

The Tigris River is one of the two main water sources in Iraq and is the only water source for the city of Mosul in northern Iraq. As it inches its way from Turkey through Iraq all the way down to Shatt Al-Arab, it receives untreated domestic waste water and waste from factories and commercial centers, adding pollution to the already polluted Arabian Gulf (Khalaf, 1990: 406). Increasing production and use of plastic in the Arabian Gulf countries compounded by unregulated shipping and waste disposal practices, have contributed enormously to the concentration of plastic particles on the sea surface and beaches of the United Arab Emirate (Khordagui and Abu-Hilal, 1994: 327). The same phenomenon has been observed on Beirut beaches in Lebanon where tar, plastic pellets and large plastic objects have posed a serious threat to marine life, eliminating altogether some fish species, while making others a health hazard and therefore unmarketable (Shiber and Barrales-Rienda, 1991: 17-30). As a consequence of land-based polluted discharges, the Black Sea is becoming a cesspool. Turkey's land-based pollution load, including all municipal, industrial, and rural discharges, is estimated to increase significantly by the year 2020. As a consequence the Turkish Ministry of Environment and the Middle East Technical University initiated in 1993 the three-year field measurement program to update the database on the major pollution sources located on the Turkish Black Sea Coast (Soypak, Oguz et al., 1994: 31).

Although environmental issues in Egypt, as in most other developing countries, have received limited attention in the past, with increasing human activities and the seriousness of water pollution in some parts of the country, protection of water resources is becoming a priority consideration. Moreover, some experts have claimed that a large percentage of untreated waste water is discharged into the Nile, irrigation canals, and drainage ditches. In addition to the raw sewage, significant proportions of fertilizers and pesticides continuously threaten to contaminate ground water. This is a major concern in Egypt because ground water is used extensively for drinking purposes and is more vulnerable than surface water to fertilizer contamination. Mahmoud Abu Zeid (1992: 82-83) concluded that increasing water pollution from industrial and domestic sources, if allowed to go unchecked, will reduce the amount of drinking water available. Clearly, this is not in Egypt's long-term interest. Furthermore, the total economic and health costs due to unchecked water pollution will continue to increase substantially.

In the environmental session that followed the 1993 diplomatic breakthrough, Arabs and Israelis immediately recognized the importance of protecting the Gulf of

Aqaba's fragile coastal ecosystems, its sandy beaches, its warm lagoons, sea grass beds, and coral reefs. Both sides agreed that they should invest jointly in technology that would prevent oil spills. Such pro-active arrangements would not only save money, but also protect each country's tourist industry. Both realized that pollution prevention is especially critical in the Gulf of Aqaba because of its small size and limited absorptive capacity. It is noteworthy to mention that in Israel, where national law requires that sewage not be dumped into the sea, the mayor of Eilat has been facing criminal charges for months because his municipality has failed to divert its waste water from the Gulf of Aqaba. Ironically, the City of Aqaba, which is less than two miles away from Eilat, has complied with a similar Jordanian law by using Israeli technology (Sachs, 1993: 6-7).

Although much attention has recently been paid to the problem of oil-caused pollution in the Arabian Gulf, more efforts are still needed to minimize the pollution stress on that ecologically special area. The Arabian Gulf is one of the busiest oil transport water arteries. Half of the world's oil passes through its bottleneck, the Hormuz Strait. In 1980, the eight Gulf oil-producing countries began to refine crude oil for their own consumption, adding refined petroleum wastes to other pollution sources, including those resulting from oil exploration, production, transport, and natural seepage. For example, along the approximately 1800 kilometer coastline of the Sultanate of Oman, all petroleum activities are concentrated in a restricted area at Mina Al Fahal, 17 kilometers northwest of Muscat. In this zone, all the oil produced in Oman arrives through pipelines, is stored, refined in part, locally marketed, and exported abroad. As a consequence, 304 tons of oil waste is estimated to be added annually to Mina Al Fahal waters. This problem is compounded by illegal discharges of ballast waters from tankers traversing the Hormuz Strait (Awad et al., 1990: 91-99; Emara, 1990: 399-401).

Before the discovery of oil and its exploitation in 1946, the Kuwaiti marine environment was a relatively pristine ecosystem, impacted only by the waste of a small fishing and training community. By 1940 (Bonine, 1980), the swift growth of the oil industries resulted in rapid urbanization of from 70,000 to 1.9 million in 1988 (CSO, 1988), and in an accentuated industrialization that created multiple sources of marine pollution. In a recent study, Al-Muzaini et al. (1991: 181-189) showed that Kuwaiti liquid waste has grown, and will continue to increase considerably. Moreover, the collection, handling and treatment practices of local sewage and its dumping into the local marine environment, exert different negative impacts on the Kuwaiti marine environment, including the elimination of certain fish species and an increase in microbial pollution. According to a 1992 report published by Israel's Ministry of Environment, thirty to forty percent of the water wells in that country exhibited microbial contamination.

The Egyptian National Environmental Action Plan identified the Manzalah and Bahr El-Baqar drains as two of the country's "Black Pots," which are examples of areas so polluted by heavy metals and other wastes that Egyptians are skeptical about the safety of consuming fish from those areas. If the situation is to be corrected, action must be taken soon (Siegal et al., 1994). In a recent article, Massoud et al. (1992: 755-772), pointed to the lethal effect of pollution on the western harbor of Alexandria, which is under stress because of the excessive increase in population and the amount of waste dumped in it.

The Israeli Government is seriously concerned about sewage pollution in Lake Kineret. This lake, the only fresh water lake in Israel, contributes 35% of the nation's water supply and is also heavily used for recreation and commercial fishing. This is compounded by the fact that the Jordan River, which enters the lake from the north, brings in with it sewage pollution too (Bergstein-Bendan and Koppel, 1992: 1457-1469).

B. Air Pollution

In a recent article, Kamal Hindy (1991: 273-279) studied the degree of alluvial soil contamination with heavy metals due to air pollution in Cairo. Turkey is trying to control air pollution by focusing on the textile industry and its polluting characteristics (Germirli et al., 1990: 265-275). Frederick Warner (1991: 6) described the environmental disaster that followed the setting on fire of Kuwait's oil wells by Iraqi troops. The fires increased the threat of severe local pollution, heightened by Iraq's discharge of oil into the Arabian/Persian Gulf. This environmental disaster was predicted at the 1992 World Climate Conference in Geneva, Switzerland, where King Hussein of Jordan presented the conclusions of his country's scientists: that if half of Kuwait's 50 million barrels of oil reserves were to go up in flames, the increase in atmospheric carbon dioxide could cause global warming and lower food production. The same was predicted at a conference in London organized by Greenpeace and the Campaign for Nuclear Disarmament: a decrease in sunlight and temperature as a result of the smoke, was sufficient enough to influence monsoons and reduce agricultural production.

In his analysis of the distribution of nitrogen oxides in Jiddah, Saudi Arabia, Sabbak (1990: 257-265) pointed to the fact that air pollution is a major concern in developed and developing countries as well. He added that attention must be given to air quality which is threatened by increasing numbers of automobiles, incinerators, factories, refineries, and other chemical industries. He warned against disposing of solid wastes by burning them in the open atmosphere. He added that Saudi Arabia needs to set up air pollution standards to protect human health and the environment, since factories have no emission control policies. This has led to concentrations of nitrogen oxides in Jiddas's air during the daytime. Cognizant of this problem and starting in 1985, the Saudi government began its crusade against air pollution by enforcing a vehicle inspection law which requires checking vehicle engines against any defect for the air to fuel ratio. The inspection, it was hoped, might help lower Jiddah's air pollution. In another project, Sabbak (1993: 41-49) studies the distribution of the hazardous hydrogen sulfide in Jiddah's atmosphere. The objective of Sabbak's article was to supply background information for city air quality standards, reduction of pollution in urban areas and advice for the public about the potential health hazards resulting from air pollution.

Raveendran and Al-Mahmood (1992: 1097-1100) traced metals floating in the atmosphere of Bahrain during the Kuwaiti oil fires. In their introduction, the authors spoke of metal pollutants emitted into the atmosphere by automobile exhaust, metal smelters, cement manufacturing plants, industries, and incinerators. They also pointed to the fact that metals and metallic compounds exist in three different forms: solid particulate matter, liquid droplets and vapors. They also added that populations living in industrial areas and near highways having high traffic density have relatively high concentration of toxic metals.

Air pollution has also been a serious problem in Lebanon and is caused by vehicles, power stations and heavy industry. Although the traffic situation is desperate, especially in Beirut and its suburbs, the number of imported cars continues to rise dramatically. What makes the situation worse is the ever-increasing consumption of leaded fuel which is rich in toxicity (Slim, 1993). The toxicity of the air in Lebanon has reached such a critical point that its impact has already manifested itself in a variety of health ailments (e.g., brain abnormalities, adverse reproductive outcomes, hypertension and anemia). Unfortunately the Lebanese government does not have strict and stringent rules in place to protect the quality of the air; and whatever semblance of rules exists is not enforced by the government and more often than not ignored by Lebanese citizens.

The quality of air in Iran is not any better, with the main sources of air pollution being automobiles and heavy industry. With no major public transportation system, private cars are the main means of transportation in the overcrowded cities contributing enormously to air pollution. In Oman, sulfur dioxide and carbon monoxide have increased air pollution. This alarmingly deteriorating air quality forced the Omani government to enforce special guidelines to stem the tide of air pollution from industry, transportation, oil and gas production. In Jordan, automobile imports have risen increasingly since 1970, and all vehicles operate on leaded gasoline creating a major source of air pollution (Tell and Yaser, 1997: 51). According to Israel's Central Bureau of Statistics (1996), emission of pollutants, especially from automobiles, is increasing at such a rapid pace that some experts (Luria et al., 1994) have predicted that air pollution in Jerusalem will exceed present levels in Mexico City by the year 2010.

C. Pollution and Agriculture

It is generally accepted that an increase in the use of pesticides, fertilizers, and many other industrial activities, will certainly cause an increase in environmental pollution. In the Wadi El Raiyan area in Egypt, where two lakes were formed from agricultural drainage, the concentrated effect of various pollutants is feared to pass into the biotic elements of the ecosystem to various degrees. Thus, due to their chemical persistence, unbiodegradability and tendency to accumulate in the biological systems, many inorganic pollutants have long detrimental effects on the ecosystem (Wilson and Saleh, 1990: 776).

Several studies have been published on the accumulation of heavy metals around highways and in urban and industrial soils (Ali, 1993: 251). Vegetation can accumulate residue from the soil and pass it on to the food chain. Vegetation grown in polluted areas or atmosphere can show severe damage. The effect of air pollution on plant growth and the symptoms of visible damage have been researched for several years. The use of plants as prior indicators have also been studied. More recently the effects of air pollution on plant growth and the use of higher plants as bioindicators in industrial and urban areas have attracted the attention of researchers. For example, mango trees were found to be sensitive to air pollution, and have therefore been considered as bio monitors for air pollution around industrial areas in India. The region of Shoubra Elkheima, to the north of Cairo, is one of the largest industrial areas in Egypt, where industries use all types of fossil fuels and emit air pollutants into the atmosphere. The soil is polluted with several heavy metals. In fact, lead was found in lettuce, carrots and other vegetables grown in this area. Symptoms on clover in Egyptian mallow plants grown in Shoubra El-kheima region include necrosis, red pigments and clorosis. These symptoms were found to be related to pollutants which are prevalent in the area (Ali, 1993). In Israel, where pesticides are used heavily and indiscriminately, ten percent of produce contains heavy doses of pesticide residues in excess of national standards.

Kamal Hindy (1991: 273-279) reported that the recently introduced extensive use of nutrients and pesticides in Egyptian cultivated land may play a large part in alluvial soil pollution by heavy metals. For instance, it has been reported that the use of some zinc and copper compounds as inorganic pesticides has led to the presence of poisonous elements in agricultural soil and harmful dust deposits in both urban and rural areas. Hindy's study showed that non-heavy metals accumulated in the alluvial soil distributed to the south of Cairo.

The devastating effects of pollution on agriculture in Lebanon has been well documented (Doueiri, 1996; METAP, 1995). The unregulated use of pesticides and other hazardous agricultural chemicals has caused serious damage to the soil and to the health of both human beings and wildlife. A similar situation prevails in Iran (Karimi, 1994).

About this Volume

In *Environmental Management: The Will and the Way in Jordan*, Professor Jreisat points to the superficial, even disjointed, way in which Jordan addressed its environmental problems before 1995. The author adds that, while in 1991 the Jordanian government identified in a well articulated statement, National Environmental Strategy, the criteria for the protection of the environment in Jordan, it did not begin to pass and implement important environmental legislations until 1995. As a result, the Public Agency for Environmental Protection was established under the aegis of the Ministry of Municipal and Rural Affairs. This agency began immediately to operate on the domestic, regional and international level providing information about and securing funds from a variety of sources for the protection of Jordan's environment. The author adds that one important asset of the Jordanian experience is that organized citizen groups have been active in inducing national awareness of environmental problems and promoting public demands for their solutions. He concludes that Jordan, like any other developing society, unfortunately suffers from a lack of essential human and financial resources, which makes the lofty goals of the National Environmental Strategy extremely difficulty to implement. Moreover, he adds that major development projects continue to be implemented without any reliance on impact assessment. Professor Jreisat's conclusion is not encouraging: the effective implementation of a sound environmental policy in Jordan is continuously hampered by excessive urban congestion, water shortages, automobile exhausts, legal pesticides, nepotism, favoritism, lack of skilled human resources, acute shortage of funds, and above all, by a weak national will to change attitudes and put in place effective policy for the protection of the environment.

In *Emerging Environmental Concerns: a Perspective from the Sultanate of Oman*, Dr. Joseph E. Kechichian explains how Oman, while in the throes of major development projects, was always concerned about the protection of its environment. He adds that Oman's Sultan Quaboos has always emphasized to his government and people, the need to preserve their environment and carefully protect the quality of life in their country. As a result, the Omani government has taken the necessary measures to protect their scarce drinking water resources and pristine coastal strips. Moreover, several specific areas were identified by the government for further attention over the long run: air pollution, non-toxic solid waste, liquid and solid toxic waste generated by industry, as well as other hazardous materials. In his drive to respond to environmental needs, the Sultan of Oman relied on four governmental units: the Council for the Conservation of the Environment and Prevention of Pollution, which was created in 1979 with the original responsibility to monitor marine pollution and later on (1984) to oversee the prevention of pollution in general; the Ministry of Regional Municipalities and Environment, which was vested in 1991 with full governmental responsibilities for the protection of the Omani environment;

the Office of Advisor for Conservation of the Environment, which was established in the Royal Court in 1974 with a focus on the Conservation of Nature and Wildlife Resources; and the Planning Committee for the Development and Environment in the Southern Region of Dhuffar. All four agencies are directed by capable Omani leaders who are fully conscious of the importance of the quality of life for Omani citizens, and fully aware of the Sultanate's continuous need to be vigilant about the quality of their environment.

In *The State of the Environment in Iran*, Dr. Seid Zekavat states that since 1953, until the fall of the Shah's regime in 1979, Iran witnessed accelerated industrialization, rapid population growth, urbanization, improved standards of living, and significant expansion in modern technology. The author adds that Iran's impressive economic development was counterbalanced by environmental deterioration which replaced the once spacious, serene, clean and healthy environment. In early 1970, the Shah's government began to adopt serious measures for the protection of the environment. It required that a program of pollution control and environmental protection be integrated with economic development planning to ensure that environmental problems were not isolated from national development activities. Unfortunately, by 1978, three years after the adoption of the Environmental Control Strategies, only a handful of regulations were enforced. The reasons for this failure stemmed from budget constraints, limited resources made available to environmental control programs and encroachment by industrial development and military preparedness measures, which were in progress when policies for the protection of the environment were adopted.

The author provides us with useful insights regarding the environmental policies of Iran's Islamic Republic. In accordance with the Constitution of the Islamic Republic, which succeeded the Shah's regime, Iranian citizens have the obligation to protect their environment, so that present and future generations may be able to realize their potential growth. At the 1992 Earth Summit, Iran presented its Comprehensive National Environmental Report, which focused on the status of Iran's land, water, human resources, and the sources of environmental pollution. A number of projects designed to improve the quality of the environment were embarked upon; they related to public awareness, research, pollution control and surveillance, and environmental protection projects. The author concludes by pointing to the ineffectiveness of Iranian environmental protection laws because of lagging technology, budgetary constraints, and just simple, general non-compliance. The author adds that in light of the overwhelming and interrelated problems of environmental degradation, Iran's hopes for a brighter future seem dim indeed. Unemployment, poverty, population growth, ecological degradation, and depletion of the country's national resources have been undermining sustainability and quality of life at the cost of future generations.

In *Environmental Challenges in Lebanon,* Rania Masri begins by placing Lebanon in its historical setting. She states that massive deforestation in Lebanon resulted in loss of timber resources and contributed to wildlife endangerment and extinction. It also caused dramatic soil erosion and loss of agricultural potential. Moreover, Masri adds that the 1975 Civil War had a devastating impact on the environment and currently protection of the Lebanese environment is something to be addressed after development. This outlook is held more strongly by the Lebanese government, whose main objective now is to secure economic development and rehabilitate Lebanon as a major economic and commercial center in the Middle East. The author adds that deforestation, land abandonment, and agricultural mismanagement have led to the intensification of water costs, soil erosion, as witnessed by the considerable amount of alluvial soil carried by the rivers from the mountains. The loss of soil productivity from erosion and pesticide residues, the over use of agricultural chemicals, the misuse of water and over grazing of livestock, as well as the abandonment of soil terraces, have posed serious long-term threats to the environment and its fragile ecosystems. Furthermore, most ground and surface water, springs, wells, and numerous rivers, and most drinking water, are contaminated. In addition, Lebanon's Mediterranean territorial waters suffer from significant coastal pollution and contamination, caused by a lack of solid waste treatment. The author also tells us that air pollution has not been the subject of any regulation with the exception of the prohibition of the importation and use of diesel vehicles and quiet condition for vehicle engines. However, both of these regulations have, for all practical purposes, been forgotten. In fact, there is no authority in Lebanon which is directly responsible for air quality protection. In her analysis of the Lebanese government's response to environmental concerns, Masri states that the establishment of the Ministry of Environment has not been effective and the new reconstruction plans are still not based on serious environmental assessment. The author concludes that despite some attempts on the part of the government to protect the environment, a closer examination of public policies and legislations clearly reveal that the government's will to protect the environment is weak, its Ministry of Environment lacks a strong and specific mandate, and no significant human and financial resources have been committed to provide a safe environment.

In his paper on Israel, Dr. Alon Tal describes how Israel's rampant economic development has had a serious environmental impact on its environment. He tells us that since the 1970s, emission of conventional air pollutants has doubled every ten years, largely due to the burgeoning number of automobiles. Moreover, the water flowing in most of the country's streams and rivers is poorly treated. Furthermore, green open spaces are being gobbled up by the insatiable desire of Israelis for automobiles, backyards, and villas. Other disturbing trends clearly point to toxic and municipal solid waste, which is growing in volume with no comprehensive policy for source reduction or treatment. Pesticides and fertilizers are used almost indiscriminately leading to an alarming deterioration of ground water. The author quotes a leading Israeli journalist and author, Amos Canaan, who said that "Jews have caused more damage to the Holyland during the last 50 years than that cumulatively produced by a litany of conquerors during the past 2000." But how did the Zionist adventurers, who were steeped in an ideology that adored the land of Israel, produce such degradation? The answer lies in rapid industrialization, massive economic and population growth and lack of effective government environmental policies. Although planning for nation building existed, the strategies for national development had no mechanism for integrating environmental considerations.

Present commitments to encourage ready access to automobiles as the primary form of transportation, is yet another example of the government's inability to confront the new ecological reality. Moreover, the Israelis' concern for nature preservation and conservation, although quite successful, betrayed very little environmental monitoring during the first four decades of Israel's existence.

Israel's attitude toward the environment underwent a drastic change during the 1990s, which manifested itself in the creation of the Ministry of Environment, the expansion of environmental activism within the non-governmental sector, and a dramatic expansion of an environmental education in media coverage.

Given Israel's population growth and economic boom, such an approach is long overdue. Already much damage is irreversible and to stem the tide, Israel must confront the following environmental challenges: integration of environmental considerations into economic planning; serious assessment of population growth and its impact on the environment; and promotion of environmental values through education.

In *Rape of Nature: The Environmental Destruction and Ethnic Cleansing of the Sudan*, the late Dr. Majak presents a gripping and graphic description of environmental destruction through unmonitored killing of wildlife, devastation of trees and forests, and the massacre and execution of people who would have been major players in the drive for the Sudanese environment's protection. He reveals to us that the villains in the rape of nature in Sudan are the greedy hunters, fishermen, and woodcutters, most of whom come from northern Sudan. He adds that the few southern Sudanese who took part in the environmental destruction had northern connections. It is clear from Dr. Majak's article, that there is no end in sight to the ravages visited upon the environment in Sudan, ravages which are compounded by bloody clashes among ethnic and religious groups, and fueled by major political and military conflicts between the North and the South. ·

In her article, *Regional Instruments for the Protection of the Marine Environment in the Arabian Gulf*, Dr. Badria Al-Awadhi states that mounting concern led leaders of the Arabian/Persian Gulf countries to adopt a series of collective protocols to prevent the pollution of the Gulf's marine environment. In 1978, they approved the first collective instrument at the Kuwait Regional Convention for Cooperation on the Protection of the Marine Environment from Pollution, and in 1989, the Emergency Protocol for Regional Cooperation in Combating Pollution Caused by Oil and Other

Harmful Substances. They also established a regional organization to oversee the protection of their marine environment (ROPME), and ratified in 1978, the marine emergency protocol to respond effectively to marine pollution emergencies. In 1989, they added a protocol to regulate marine pollution resulting from exploration and exploitation of the Continental Shelf, and in 1990 another protocol for the protection of the marine environment against pollution from land based sources, which came into effect in 1993. The author hastens to conclude, however, that in order for the Gulf marine environment to be protected effectively, the recently adopted protocols must be entrusted to and implemented by strong regional and national agencies working together harmoniously. Without capable implementing agencies, the regional anti-pollution instruments will be weak and ineffective, dashing hopes for a better protection of the Gulf's marine environment.

In her article on Syria, Gloria Saliba begins by describing the emerging Syrian interest in conservation and the protection of the environment. She adds that the status of Syria's environment is seriously undermined by natural as well as human-made factors. Population increase, urban sprawl, desertification, and dwindling natural resources are some of the challenges which threaten Syria's environment and its attempts to develop. The author also discusses the conflict that Syria is facing between expanding its agricultural development projects and the impact that this expansion is having on its environment and natural resources. Syria must meet the increased needs of full security for its growing population. To achieve this goal, Syrian policy makers are attempting to increase the productivity of the agricultural sector and to accelerate the pace of development by expanding the use of its land and water resources. However, this development drive, if not carefully monitored, could have a negative impact on environmental policy and damage Syria's environment and economy. The author also examines the integrated policy that Syria has recently adopted to achieve a balance between development aspiration and environmental protection. This challenging situation is complicated further by traditional social attitudes and foreign political pressures. The author also analyses the cooperation of Syria with many international organizations to achieve its environmental objectives.

Conclusion

It is clear from this collection of papers, that serious and challenging environmental issues confront government and society in the Middle East. Both must realize that they ignore the protection of their environment at their own peril. Therefore, I submit that the ethos that governs the attitudes of citizens in the Middle East toward the environment must be revisited and reassessed. The inherent drive of human beings to control nature at any price, their insatiable materialism, their blind devotion to science and technology, and the uncontrolled momentum for growth and development cannot go unchecked forever and without seriously damaging the environment.

To do so would sooner or later wreak havoc in the beautiful constellation of Middle Eastern ecosystems, havoc that might deprive the human species and all living organisms in that part of the world of their chance to survive and perpetuate themselves.

What might help Middle Eastern governments and societies in their endeavor to protect their environment, and provide their citizens with the quality of life they deserve, is a number of proposed changes worthy of their consideration and adoption both collectively and individually.

A change of attitudes of Middle Eastern people and governments exhibiting profound respect for the integrity of their environment, must take place. Such a change can be brought about and nurtured by taking seriously the rich cultures and religions of that important part of the globe. A return to a Judeo Christian perspective would constitute a powerful source of environmental protection. In Mark's (24: 15) and Luke's (19: 13) Gospels, we are enjoined to put to work faithfully that which God has put in our trust. We are directed to establish a harmonious relationship between ourselves and our environment. In that part of the world, Islam also provides guidance to Muslims for the protection of the environment: "humanity has been given the guardianship over God's heaven and earth, but no outright ownership" (Dwivedi, 1992: 363-380).

Governments in that part of the world must consider the environment as a valuable natural resource and learn how to manage it in a more rational way, and to reach that objective, they must integrate the environment and the quality of life in their development plans. They can no longer ignore with impunity deforestation, desertification, soil erosion, and air and water pollution which are threatening the very health of their citizens. They must realize that each individual has a right to a healthy environment, and no one can deprive any human being of that fundamental right. As to how this objective can be achieved, the first draft report on world conservation strategies for the 1990s provides us with some hints:

a. people should respect nature, for like all creatures, we are an integral part of nature and its users and consumers as well;

b. every life form is unique and warrants respect regardless of its worth to people;

c. all persons should take responsibility for their impact on nature;

d. people should ensure the means of survival of all other life forms; and

e. people should treat all creatures humanely and protect them from cruelty and avoidable suffering (IUCN, Second World Conservation Strategy Project, 1989, p. 3-4).

An environmental code of conduct must be seriously explored by Middle Eastern governments. Although rules and regulations may not guarantee the protection of the environment, they are, nonetheless, needed and can be implemented effectively, with strong support from governments and people. This support can emerge swiftly when concern for the protection of the environment and the quality of life has been internalized. In this regard, education can prove to be an important tool.

Concern about the protection of the environment should not only be expressed by non-governmental organizations and green groups, but also be included in the schools' curriculum. Establishing research institutes to provide objective data on the state of the environment can also be helpful. Professor Dwivedi tells us that "the role of a code is to provide incentives so that individuals may act in a way which is conducive, not only to their self-preservation, but also to the well being of the environment which sustains them. Such inner incentives become necessary when the external inducements, in the form of governmental directives, laws, or regulations are either unenforceable or not altogether workable. Another function of the code is to act as an adaptive instrument that encourages our obligation towards nature, which is seen as provider and sustainer of our life support system" (Dwivedi, 1992: 371). Professor Dwivedi provides us with a series of basic principles which are to govern the proposed code, ranging from our obligations to be good stewards of the planetary system to acknowledging our responsibility individually and collectively, and sensitizing our fellow humans concerning environmental protection and conservation. The principles provided by Professor Dwivedi are complemented by a series of tenets which he exclusively addresses to future generations and their rights to a healthy environment. Professor Dwivedi's principles and tenets are graced with many features, ranging from the moral commitment of all individuals to protect and conserve the environment to the promotion of responsible environmental journalism and the creation of a core of environmental volunteers in each society to help monitor and maintain a healthy and sustainable environment.

In conclusion, it is important to state that those who treat nature with disrespect must pay for the consequences. Nature does not forget and forgive the over exploitation of its resources (Dwivedi and Jabbra, 1995: 23). Consequently, "... at a minimum our activities be such that these must not endanger the natural systems that support life of all organisms on earth, including the atmosphere, the waters, the soils, and the living beings. Until compatible limits in our prevailing ethic of acquisitive materialism, unending growth ethic, and resource use are set, continued global ecological damage is unavoidable... there is no reason as to why the current emphasis on eliminating economic and social justice among individuals and nations cannot be expanded to include environmental injustice" (Dwivedi, 1994: 61).

This statement is applicable in any environmental situation, including the one prevailing in the Middle East.

REFERENCES

ABU FADIL, Magda
1991 "Ecocrisis in the Middle East." *Earth Island Journal.*

ABU ZEID, Mahmoud
1992 "Water Resource Assessment for Egypt." *International Journal of Water Resources Development,* Volume 8, No. 2, 1992.

ALI, A.E.
1993 "Damage to Plants due to Industrial Pollution and Their Use as Bioindicators in Egypt." *Environmental Pollution,* 1993, Vol. 81, No. 3.

AL-MUZAINI, S., O. SAMHAN and M.F. HAMODA
1991 "Sewage-Related Impact on Kuwaiti's Marine Environment—A Case Study." *WAT.SCI.TECH.* Volume 23, Kyoto (printed in Great Britain).

AWAD, H. Omanian, M.A. AL MOHARAMY and S.A. AL EISSA
1990 "Land-Based Oil Inputs to the Gulf of Oman." *Oil and Chemical Pollution,* 6.

BERGSTEIN-BENDAN, Talya and Fidi KOPPEL
1992 "Indicator of Bacteria for Fecal Pollution in the Littoral Zone of Lake Kineret." *Water Research,* Volume 26, No. 11.

BONINE, M.E.
1980 *The Urbanization of the Persian Gulf Nations. In The Persian Gulf States.* A.J. Cottrell, Ed. Baltimore, Maryland: The Johns Hopkins University Press, pp. 225-278.

Central Statistical Office
1980 "Annual Statistical Abstracts." Kuwait: Municipal Planning.

DOUEIRI, D.
1996 "Towards a Comprehensive Understanding of the Agricultural Policy in Lebanon." Ph.D. dissertation. Department of Islamic Studies, University of California at Los Angeles.

DWIVEDI, O.P.
1992 "An Ethical Approach to Environmental Protection: A Code of Conduct and Guiding Principles." *Canadian Public Administration,* Volume 35, No. 3.
1994 "Our Karma and Dharma to the Environment: An Eastern Perspective." *Environmental Stewardship: History, Theory and Practice.* Mary Ann Beavis, Ed. Winnipeg, Canada: University of Winnipeg.

DWIVEDI, O.P. and Joseph G. JABBRA
1995 "Environmental Protection in Central-East Europe." *Managing the Environment: An East European Perspective.* Dwivedi and Jabbra, Co-eds. Ontario, Canada: de Sitter Publications.

EMARA, Hosni I.
1990 "Oil Pollution in the Southern Arabian Gulf and Gulf of Oman." *Marine Pollution Bulletin,* Volume 21.

Environmental Protection Agency
1992 National Report. Iran: Publication Tehran (Farsi).

GERMIRLI, F. et al.
1990 "An Overview of the Textile Industry in Turkey—Pollution Profiles and Treatability Characteristics." *Water Science and Technology,* Volume 22.

HINDY, Kamal T.
1991 "Study of Alluvial Soil Contamination with Heavy Metals Due to Air Pollution in Cairo." *International Journal of Environmental Studies,* Vol. 38.

Israel Central Bureau of Statistics
1996 *Expenditures of Public Services for Environmental Protection,* 1992, No. 46.

KARIMI, B.M.
  1994 "The Extent of the Use of Agricultural Poisons and its Effect on the Environment." *The Scientific Journal of the Environment*, Vol. 7, No. 1. (Farsi).

KHALAF, S.A.
  1990 "Bacterial Pollution of the River Tigris." *Journal of Environmental Science and Health*, A25 (5), 495-503.

KHORDAGUI HOSNI, K. and Ahmad H. ABU HILAL
  1994 "Industrial Plastic on the Southern Beaches of the Arabian Gulf and The Western Beaches of the Gulf of Oman." *Environmental Pollution* 84.

LURIA, Menahem et al.
  1994 "Forecast of Photochemical Pollution for the Year 2010." Israel: Proceedings of the Twenty-Fifth Annual Conference of the Israeli Society for Ecology and Environmental Quality Sciences, 26.

MASSOUD, A., H. SAAD and I.M. Hemeda ENGIE
  1992 "Effect of Pollution on the Western Harbor of Alexandria: II Nutrient Salt." *Science of the Total Environment, Supplement*. Amsterdam: Elsevier Science Publishers.

METAP
  1995 Mediterranean Environmental Technical Assistance Program, Lebanon: Assessment of the State of the Environment. (Financed by the Commission of the European Communities, United Nations Development Program, European Investment Bank, and World Bank.)

RAVEENDRAN, E. and A.M. AL-MAHMOOD
  1992 "Trace Metals in the Atmosphere of Bahrain during the Kuwait Oil Fires." *Environmental Technology*, Vol. 13, No. 11 (November).

SABBAK, Ali Omar
  1990 "Distribution of Nitrogen Oxides in Jiddah Atmosphere." *Environment International* 16, No. 3.

SACHS, Aaron
  1993 "The Aqaba Paradigm: A Shared Oasis." *World Watch*, November-December.

SHIBER, J.G. and J.M. BARRALES-RIENDA
  1991 "Plastic Pellets, Tars and Megalitter on Beirut Beaches, 1977 through 1988." *Environmental Pollution*, 71.

SIEGAL, F.R., M.L. SLABODA and D.J. STANLEY
  1994 "Metal Pollution Loading, Manzalah Lagoon, Nile Delta, Egypt: Implications for Aquaculture." *Environmental Geology*, 23, pp. 89-98.

SLIM, K.
  1993 "The Current Status of the Environment in Greater Beirut During Reconstruction." The National Seminar on Environmental Awareness. AUB-UNESCO.

SOYUPAK, S., Mustafa OGUZ et al.
  1994 "Planning and Design Strategies for Marine Outfalls on the Turkish Black Sea Coast." *European Water Pollution Control: Official Publication of the European Water Pollution Control Association*, Vol. 4.

Sultanate of Oman
  1992 "Final Report and Main Conclusions and Recommendations of International Symposium on the National Conservation Strategy of Oman, Muscat: Ministry of Regional Municipalities and Environment," 6-9 December.

TELL, Sufian and Sarah YASER
  1987 "The Condition of the Environment in Jordan." (A study sponsored by the Department of Environment of the Ministry of Municipal and Rural Affairs, Jordan, in Arabic.)

WARNER, Frederick
1991 "The Environmental Consequences of the Gulf War." *Environment*, 33: 5.
WILSON, Bobby L. and Mahmoud A. SALEH
1990 "A Physical and Chemical Analysis of Egypt's Wadi El-Raiyan Man-made Lakes." *Journal of Environmental Science and Health* (Part A), Vol. A25, No. 7.

Environmental Management
The Will and the Way in Jordan

JAMIL E. JREISAT*

ABSTRACT

As a small country, Jordan is not a major factor in the production of products that are potentially dangerous to environmental quality or to citizens' safety such as toxic chemicals, hazardous waste, and herbicides. Yet environmental management in the country has recently acquired new importance and a greater visibility as a public policy as illustrated by a newly enacted law and a new organization to administer it. Difficulties remain, however, in the way the law is enforced. The environmental management system in place is profoundly constrained by lack of funding, weak enforcement capacity, and lack of a technical and scientific base for setting standards and measuring compliance.

THE CRUCIAL JOB in managing policies for protecting the environment in Jordan has been to define strategic and operational goals, and then to find ways and means for achieving them. Government officials in Jordan continually convey a sense of urgency in dealing with present environmental problems, which appear to defy political and territorial boundaries.

Universally, environment degradation has largely been the result of persistent proliferation of problems at the nation-state level, such as the production of environmentally unfriendly products and using up too many of the earth's resources. In developing countries, population growth and urban sprawl as well as surging poverty have compounded the problem of environmental degradation. Moreover, we know now that the early policies of industrial nations generally failed to accord environment protection a priority, slowly building the world ecological crisis (Rich, 1994: x). Over the years, without legal accountability or moral responsibility on behalf of both the public and the private sectors, deterioration of environmental quality has been escalating.

Environmental data convey clear but unsettling messages. Now we realize that over the past 200 years, mankind has consumed more natural resources than during the entire preceding known history of several thousand years. We now also recognize that current energy consumption alone accounts for most of the air pollution: 55%

---

* University of South Florida, Tampa, Florida 33620-8100, U.S.A.

Journal of Developing Societies, Vol. XIII, 1

of carbon dioxide, 90% of sulfur dioxide, and 85% of nitrogen dioxide (Rudel, 1995: 13). Until recently, few effective national or international laws existed for combating chemical and industrial pollution, recycling materials, improving the efficiency of using exhaustible resources, and so forth. Thus, people today have to contend with numerous inherited problems such as ozone depletion, soil erosion, desertification, acid rain, air and water pollution, traffic congestion, noise, population growth, global warming, and urban decay.

Many new national and international policies and laws have been consigned the task of managing countless intrusions in the "balance of nature" that have already resulted in serious negative effects on the health and well-being of people everywhere. Realistically, to arrest the general decline of environmental quality, and eventually to reverse it, has become a global demand requiring universal commitment for action. Actually, damage to the environment has instigated more than reconsideration of public policies at various levels of authority, worldwide; it is causing a rethinking of methodological issues of valuation employed in measuring economic progress.

To illustrate the magnitude of the problem in economic terms, consider that Gross Domestic Product (GDP), currently used for measuring economic and political activities, does not take into account social and ecological costs. A more accurate yardstick, critics say, is to use a "Genuine Progress Indicator"[1] that attempts to take into account social costs (crime and social breakdown) and costs of ecological damage (pollution).

Walter Rudel (1995: 14) provides an example from Germany. Defensive environment costs (the abatement costs), he points out, increased from 7% of GNP in 1970 to 12% in 1990, but did not include long-term damages such as ozone depletion, the greenhouse effect, increasing health hazards, or deforestation (for purposes of the present discussion, GNP "Gross National Product" will be treated as equivalent to GDP). The full "Eco-Costs" are estimated between 600 and 1000 billion marks (nearly $400-$666 billion) per year in Germany alone. If they were to enter the balance sheets, Germany's GNP would no longer indicate a growth rate, but rather a huge loss. In fact, if similar accounts are followed, most industrial nations would also end up in a negative growth mode. Thus, according to such estimates, today's national claims of profit and productivity are simply eroding the accounts of future generations.

This conclusion is certainly correct for Jordan and the rest of the Arab world. Over almost two decades, there has been a negative GDP growth rate in this area. Data from the World Bank and from authoritative sources within the Arab world convey this unsettling result. Expressly, statistical data from the annual United Arab Economic Report[2] indicate that development efforts over the past two decades actually increased the gap between population growth and economic expansion. "The Arab population in the period 1980-1994 grew by 48 percent, from 165 million to 245 million, while total Arab gross domestic product (in current prices) during that period grew by only 15 percent, from $437 billion to $502 billion. This means that over the last decade-and-a half the per capita gross domestic product of the entire Arab region declined by 22 percent, from $2612 to $2048."[3] These data would be more dismal had the calculations accounted for costs of destruction of environmental quality. Although Arab industrial sectors are weak and consist of mostly small-scale production and conversion of materials, their effects on the environment have been drastic. Industrial and chemical wastes are regularly dumped without treatment in rivers, gulfs, and on seashores. Automobiles, using leaded gasoline and increasing in number at a very rapid rate, have also become major pollutants of the air in cities throughout the Arab world (Awad, 1996: 23-35).

The Law and The Strategy

Laws are critical instruments for planning and managing environmental protection. Before 1995, Jordan dealt with environmental problems "in either a superficial or fragmented way," according to a former Prime Minister.[4] During this time, eight statutes dealt with water issues alone. A Jordanian lawyer has identified "more than 187 environmental articles in 19 laws and by-laws as well as numerous defense orders dating back to the early fifties " (Al-Omary, 1994: 131). In all these legal instruments, he points out, the environment is only treated casually in the context of other, often unrelated subjects, such as agriculture, public health, or antiquities (Al-Omary, 1994: 131).

Jordan's Environment Protection Law of 1995 considerably changed the situation and provided a comprehensive approach to the issues. This law is considered a milestone legislation for enhancing general awareness of the need to protect the environment and for elevating related activities to higher prominence among many competing public policy issues. "Environment," in this law, is defined as "the habitat where living humans, animals, and plants exist—it encompasses water, air, land, and all that affects this habitat."

Jordan's 1995 Law provides a clearer focus than before on the development of necessary institutional capacity for the country's environmental management. Issues of organization and methods, decisive for policy implementation, are delineated in general terms. Most significant of its provisions is the establishment of the Public Agency for Environmental Protection (referred to here as the Agency), a relatively small, independent administrative unit within the Ministry of Municipal and Rural Affairs. The Agency evolved from a previous small unit, established in 1980, within the same Ministry. Now, this unit is an independent agency with its own general director, a separate staff, and designated financial allocations in the public budget. The Agency is guided by an overall policy-making Board of Directors of fifteen senior government officials and seven non-governmental organizations (NGOs). The Board is chaired by the Minister of Municipal and Rural Affairs, meets bimonthly to establish general policies, approves the annual budget, issues instructions and regulations, and considers whatever matters are brought to its attention by the Minister.

In addition to a director general,[5] staffing consists of about fifty men and women, few of whom hold any particular, professional expertise in environmental affairs.[6] The budget is meager (little over $3 million annually), forcing the Agency to devote significant efforts to seeking grants and donations from within and outside the country. Almost all budget allocations are spent on the salaries of permanent staff and very little is left for anything else. The Agency is housed in a separate building on the outskirts of Amman, reflecting its new magnified and autonomous status. Except for the director's desk, which appears perpetually crowded with files and papers for his signature, the rest of the staff seems to have little to do. In fact, on each visit, I found most employees with empty desks, engaged in either eating, drinking coffee, or socializing.

Functions stipulated in the 1995 Law are sufficiently comprehensive to permit the Agency to do nearly whatever it deems necessary to protect the environment. The Agency is entrusted with solidifying relations between Jordan and other countries and with regional and international institutions concerned with the environment. This is a flourishing responsibility for two reasons: first, Jordan has entered into more than 23 multi-lateral and bi-lateral international agreements on the environment.[7] These affiliations generated a curious workload for the Agency with unique opportunities for international travel by the Minister and other senior officials. Second, environmental management in Jordan is fast becoming a continuous search for outside donors or lenders to finance a collection of projects of uneven merit. The Minister,[8] who also chairs the Board of Directors for Environment Protection, declared in 1996 that a plan of action has been approved by the Board, consisting of 37 projects slated for funding from international sources.

In addition, the Agency is entrusted with a significant legal mandate, empowering it to issue rules and regulations for achieving its objectives. Its functions include setting specifications for acceptable levels of air pollution and establishing centers for observing the quality of air and the sources of pollution. The Agency monitors operations of solid waste disposal, determines standards, and oversees implementation.

Like many Jordanian laws, the EP Law is too general, if not deficient in articulating specific measures for ensuring effective implementation. Actually, it is difficult to measure definite results or achievements during the Agency's brief independent existence. Thus, accountability and responsibility are even harder to establish or apply. After a discussion with the director of the Agency,[9] I could not determine the dimensions of any future plan of activities nor could I discern the existence of a dependable system of priorities directing current operations.

National Environmental Strategy

Jordan is one of the original group of 30 countries to declare support for the World Conservation Strategy (WCS). An early task of the first administrative unit on the environment, created in the Ministry of Municipal and Rural Affairs in 1980, was to initiate planning for a national environmental strategy. In 1982, the National Environment Commission was founded, and in 1985 the Prime Minister and the Council of Ministers created a committee to begin action for the development of a national strategy. Through agreement with the International Union for the Conservation of Nature and Natural Resources (IUCN), and with funding from the U.S. Agency for International Development (AID), the Jordanian government finally approved and published, in 1991, its strategy for the environment, within the framework of WCS.[10]

Certainly, setting up a comprehensive environmental policy is an important condition for effective laws. "If ecologically-oriented policies, economies, laws and administration are not closely cooperating and are supporting each other, there is little chance for a successful implementation of environmental legislation" (Rudel, 1994: 10).

The pronounced strategy for Jordan (1991), therefore, employs concepts and terms that are gaining universal designations. Sustainability implies indefinite maintenance; sustainable use is employed for utilizing renewable resources. Sustainable development increasingly refers to activities that meet human needs but without depleting energy or preventing the underlying ecosystem from continuously functioning and renewing itself. Jordan's national strategy is fairly comprehensive and "contains over 400 specific recommendations and suggested actions in the field of environmental protection and conservation."[11] Recommendations also include the creation of a legal framework for environmental management, "institutional strengthening," expanding protected areas, public knowledge and awareness, and "stemming population growth."

The vision, definition of goals, and the setting of operational standards in the national strategy were articulated by a group of Jordanians, helped by advisors and foreign consultants, particularly from IUCN in Switzerland. In no small measure, the enactment of the EP Law of 1995 was due to a momentum generated by the promulgation of this national strategy. To what extent the Agency is committed to or even capable of delivering the lofty promises in the national strategy is currently uncertain at best.

Certainly, the National Environment Strategy for Jordan was successful in assessing critical issues affecting the quality of the environment, identifying causes of depletion or damage, and suggesting recommendations for action. Such issues include land and agriculture, surface and groundwater, wildlife and habitat, coastal and marine, energy and mineral resources, population, housing, environmental health, atmosphere and air quality, antiquities and cultural resources. Proposed actions often were sufficiently general to allow a wide range of alternative actions such as the adoption of "educational and training policies that take characteristics of local communities and environmental requirements into account" (National Strategy, 1991: 181).

Citizens Awareness and Participation

Public concern for the environment is a function of awareness, knowledge, and opportunity to participate. Involvement of Jordanian citizens in environmental policy is more noticeable than in any other public policy area. Non-governmental organizations are gradually taking part in an educational process of many dimensions. Perhaps the most widely known organization of this genre is the Jordan Environment Society (JES). It was established to protect and improve elements of the environment (water, air and soil), and to reduce all forms of pollution.[12] The methods used by JES to reach its goals encompass these activities: (1) inviting specialists and interested people to get together to discuss and define critical environmental concerns; (2) use of the mass media to create public awareness of environmental pollutants and the need for protection; (3) organizing seminars and lectures on the subject; (4) influencing national policies and legislation for more proactive and greater environment-friendly initiatives.[13] The JES relies on income mainly from member fees, donations, grants and government aid and has representative groups in various parts of the country. The organization claims 5000 members throughout the country.

Environmental problems are largely the results of human behavior and action, which are highly stimulated by knowledge and awareness. Thus, education and information dissemination are essential for changing human behavior to be more positive and supportive of environmental considerations. Based on this premise, a research project by a graduate students, at the University of Jordan examines some relevant questions.

For the requirements of a Master's thesis, the student (Tubasy, 1996) examined the role of mass media in changing behavior toward the environment. The information was based on content analysis of one-year coverage (1995) in two daily newspapers as well as in radio and television programs. In addition, a targeted sample of 200 persons (88 students, 20 teachers, 30 mass-media personnel, and 60 others—all interested in the environment) were asked to rate the content of mass-media coverage in terms of enlightening citizens about the environment. The results are:

(1) Mass-media efforts to educate the public are rated high by 6% of the respondents, medium by 60%, and poor by 34%.

(2) In one year, the main two newspapers in Jordan (*Ad-Dustour* and *Al-Rai'a*) published 643 "news-items," 51 articles, and 108 reports about environmental issues.

(3) Based on the sample, most Jordanians (70%) rate their knowledge about the environment as average, 16.5% high, and 13.5% low.

(4) Most revealing is the survey finding that the best source of information on the environment is individual reading, followed by television and college education. Less important as a source of information is seminars, public lecturers, radio, or even membership in environmental associations (Tubasy, 1996).

Despite some serious initial efforts for citizen involvement, the development of mechanisms for Jordanian individuals or organizations to participate meaningfully in environmental debates, often encounters profound difficulties. In addition to inadequate "scientific" information, the overall political process is unpredictable and highly personal. Change in political leadership at the cabinet level often results in changes to the process and content of policy. Public involvement in government plans and decisions affecting lives and work is generally hampered by lack of access and poor information. Moreover, leaders of citizen groups are usually distracted by other occupations and responsibilities. The leaders are not on a full-time basis nor do they hold more than amateur grassroots organizational skills or experiences. Still, people wish to be involved in implementing plans and many of their reactions and complaints could be dealt with locally, to bring about changes that effectively suit and serve local communities.

The Royal Society for Environment Protection is also in the business of raising citizens' consciousness through education. It seeks a new understanding and a broader interest in the issues through educational means. The Society, according to its Deputy Director, attempts to tie environmental awareness with educational programs for Jordanian youth.[14] Ultimately, it seems that hopes for behavioral changes are contingent on various future developments. Behavioral-attitudinal changes are expected to result from improvements in information quality and quantity as well as from a gradual softening of the highly-centralized political process to permit more effective citizen participation in public decision making.

The Capacity to Implement

Jordan made significant progress in raising consciousness, establishing standards, and promulgating guidelines and regulations for protecting its environment. The test of success, however, is in the implementation and in ensuring that actions agree with policies and uphold principles and standards. Transforming policy into practice involves numerous conditions and competencies that are not readily available in the country, or in many other developing countries. More than in most other units of public service, institutional capacity for environmental management relies on the operational support and analytical skills of the central department of environment protection.

Another significant constraint on the Agency's operational effectiveness is its reliance on units of government outside its domain for achieving its mission. Namely, the Agency is assigned various functions but the law stipulates implementation in coordination with already existing functional organizations such as the Ministry of Health, the Ministry of Water and Natural Resources, the Traffic Department, and the Ministry of Agriculture. Consequently, the success of the Agency in doing its job is largely dependent on the goodwill and cooperation of others because the Agency has very little implementation capabilities of its own. This is the situation, despite the significant prosecutorial powers the Agency currently has that allow it to impose heavy financial penalties through court action against violators of its rules.

Then there is the familiar weakness of inadequate professional managerial capacity to implement public policies. Often, laws and policies are articulated from the vantage point of "what ought to be done" rather than "what can be done." When published in the *Official Gazette*, laws seem to have been written meticulously, with obvious devotion to legal purity, symmetry of syntax, rationality of structure and functions, and comprehensiveness of coverage of relevant issues. As to implementation, it is dealt with as something else altogether: either assumed or mostly ignored. For politicians as well as bureaucrats, when the matter is discussed within the law it is as if it were being acted upon. Even in interviews, public managers often sprinkle their responses with legal references of "yes, we do this, see article such and such of the law." One has to repeatedly counter with "I know what is in the law but I am interested in what, in fact, you are doing at the present."

As constituted, the Agency is also hindered by fast societal changes which are intensifying internal pressures for action. Particular conditions in Jordan seem to exacerbate environmental problems and impede their solutions. Among these conditions are:

(1) **Congestion**: Jordan has one of the highest population growth rates in the world (over 4% annually). A complicating factor is that 55% of the people live in one metropolitan area, Amman.

(2) **Water Shortage**: Jordan currently produces only about 50% of its water needs. At the same time, demographic forecasts of Jordan's population indicate 100% increase in less than twenty-five years. What measures are being taken by officials to alleviate anticipated economic and political risks of continuing, or indeed increasing, the water shortage to intolerable levels?

Perhaps the answer is found in this public exchange between a top official and a reporter for a local tabloid newspaper:

Sheehan (the newspaper): Jordan is currently enduring a suffocating water crisis. Do you have a clear plan for remedying this shortage?

Minister of Water and Irrigation (Samir Khiwar): With immoderate frankness, we have no comprehensive planning, for the short-run or for the long-run, to deal with citizens' needs (and the needs of other sectors) in a reliably studied way. And we should not deal with the problem of water as a policy of "Faza'a"— a loose community or tribal response to a call of distress. What is needed is intensive and thorough studies that underline negative and positive consequences. Whatever the bitter fact may be ... such studies need funding and appropriate capacities which regretfully my ministry does not have.[15]

(3) **Automobiles**: a major source of air pollution in Jordan is the automobile. The number increased over 200% between 1970 and 1985 (Tell and Sarah, 1987: 51), followed by another 100% increase in the decade after 1985. Over 85% of these vehicles operate in Amman and its surrounding areas, and almost all use leaded gasoline. (Jordanian oil refineries produced a small quantity of non-leaded gasoline only in 1995, but it is still not available in most fueling stations and when available it is at a much higher price.) These factors necessarily make public policy responses to growing citizen needs and demands for clean and safe air limited in scope and in effectiveness.

(4) **Past Policies:** an appraisal of the current difficulties of implementation under-scores the results of bad policies adopted in the past. To illustrate the conse-quences of previous ill-advised decisions, consider the case of the *Fuhais Cement Factory*, constructed in the 1950s by a German contractor to meet a growing need for cement. The first unfortunate decision was the choice of location in the midst of what was once one of the best agricultural and residential areas of the country, within a few kilometers of the capital, and on the edge of several flourishing rural communities. The area produced grapes and raisins for local consumption, and some for export to neighboring countries. Farmers raised wheat, barley, and tobacco crops. Above all, the area was scenic, natural, and hilly. Today, the area consists of craters and carved mountains, and is covered with dust that retards vegetation and plant growth for miles. The quality of the environment is further degraded by huge, noisy trucks and trailers carrying dusty products on narrow winding roads crossing populated areas.

To make things worse, the Ministry of Health conducted a "study" in 1995 which declared that "cement dust is a good (Hameed) dust that has no injurious effect on the human breathing system." The research presumably was conducted by physicians on a sample from the Fuhais population, compared to a control group from another city (less than six miles away), using lung capacity tests and chest X-rays. The published report, titled "The Effect of Cement Dust on the Respiratory System of Al-Fuhais Population" by Ministry of Health, Jordan, 1995, has no individual names on it. There is no mention of other possible effects on the environment and the well-being of the community from the noise, traffic congestion, damage to adjacent farms, or destruction of the beauty of thousands of acres of inhabited farm lands. This report, in fact, served to rationalize existing conditions and to justify a "no action policy" by the government after protests by affected citizens.

Above and beyond Jordan's previously mentioned problems, there is the familiar problem of implementation, which troubles all developing societies. A newly-created agency staffed by employees lacking administrative experience cannot be expected to outshine in specialized environmental work. Moreover, management in the country suffers from the typical ailments that afflict employment in the public sector in general. Decision making in the Jordanian bureaucracy, for example, is not conducive to developing professional managerial capacities. Nepotism and favoritism are powerful influences on decision making, particularly in farming out important positions in government. Citizens cannot predict the outcome of a policy or decision because it often depends on the influence of friends, family members, superiors, or associates who happen to favor one side or the other, on the official making the decision (Jreisat, 1989: 99). Not surprising, when in conflict, personal interests supersede all others (Cunningham and Sarayrah, 1993: 10).

Consequently, as Mintzberg (1979) calls it, the "strategic apex," which consists of those at the top of the hierarchy, together with their own personal aides, is where the organization suffers its greatest weakness. The "strategic apex" of the Agency normally includes the director, minister, and board of directors. Typically, prime bases of power are financial resources, technical skills, and a body of knowledge and expertise supported by a history of successful practice at the operational levels. These qualifications are absent not only in this Agency but in most other public institutions of the country.

Jordan's bureaucracy operates within an excessively centralized system of authority. The cluttered desk of the Director, in contrast to empty desks everywhere else in the offices of the Agency for Environment Protection is symptomatic of this malady. Yet, the Director himself is hampered by the not so infrequent intrusions of his superior, the Minister of Municipal and Rural Affairs. In fact, the Minister appoints the Director and chairs the Board of Directors that sets the general policy for the Agency. On this point, more than one employee from the Ministry of Municipal and Rural Affairs admitted to this author that the current Director was promoted from an assistant position when the former director was terminated by the Minister in a personal vendetta. They describe the former director as "expert" on environmental policy in Jordan. He was instrumental in developing the operative "National Strategy."

The absence of regular, systematic, and reliable feedback on performance perpetuates inaction and incompetence. "In institutions that have basic developmental and pioneering roles, institutional as well as employee evaluations are vital for identifying obstacles to performance as well as proposing corrective and curative measures" (Jreisat, 1990: 419). After more than a year in operation, the Agency has no annual report nor any documentation of accomplishments that are credited to its own performance.

No doubt, enforcement of environmental laws is problematic everywhere, in industrialized as well as in developing countries. Jordan is no exception. Its most common constraints on performance, however, are insufficient funds and shortage of trained personnel. Implementation mainly is opportunistic, largely dictated by donations, grants, or loans rather than based on assessment of critical environmental problems followed by official, sustained commitments to their solutions. Add to this difficulty the inadequate coordination between public agencies and the corporate sector in setting standards and observing them. The rationalization most frequently mentioned by management to explain inaction is lack of budgetary allocations or because the Agency is new.[16] In brief, the statutory powers granted to the Agency are not matched with institutional capacities to enforce them.

The National Environment Strategy of Jordan (1991) identifies general issues that have significant impact on implementation. One issue is that decision-making is unduly influenced by social relations at the expense of technical evaluations or analysis (National Strategy, 1991: 179). While funding is always a hurdle, lack of accurate, clear policies to deal with the environment is also an impediment to enforcement. Moreover, the National Strategy notes that absence of "workable mechanisms" supported by legislation and carried out by trained persons in scientific supervision and evaluation renders agencies with environmental responsibilities incapable of enforcement, following up on problems, or establishing specifications. In fact, since the National Strategy was published, the EP Law of 1995 was enacted. The law created a legislative framework but did not solve other problems such as establishing clear regulations and guidelines, and updating them as required by changing conditions.

In a country with scarce resources such as Jordan, funding for any new program is difficult. Equally compelling are the limitations emanating from weak scientific studies, lack of reliable data, and shortage of specialists to produce these needed studies and to generate essential data. The techno-scientific gap and the absence of tools to measure, verify and resolve conflicting findings, as the *Fuhais Cement Factory* case illustrates, create a shadow of doubt and a hesitancy in enforcement of actions lacking clear and confident scientific support. These problems have the net effect of stifling managerial creativity and limiting the prospect of new ideas surfacing in organizational context such as the one described above.

Conclusions

The government of Jordan has identified what needs to be done in a fairly articulate statement called the National Environmental Strategy, published in 1991. This was followed by legislation in 1995 that defines the organizational and managerial frameworks for enforcing public policies on the environment. Most interesting about the Jordanian experience is that organized citizen groups have been active in awakening national awareness of environmental problems and promoting public demands for solutions.

But the problem in Jordan remains at the resource levels, both human and financial. Goals and ambitions are not matched by essential institutional capacities for action nor by the financial resources available for attaining set objectives. At the same time, much damage to the environment has been brought about by careless development policies that did not assess the costs of environmental abuse nor considered safer alternatives. Impact assessments and reliable evaluations could have helped prevent the adoption of bad policy choices or unjustified decisions.

In Jordan, and in the entire Arab world, environmental institutions lack important capacities for the professional implementation of decisions. Building such institutional capacities is a prerequisite for partaking in the design and implementation of developmental projects. In this regard, productive projects that reduce poverty and safeguard healthy standards of living are determinants of sound, environment-friendly socioeconomic development.

NOTES

1   R.D. Hershey, Jr., *The New York Times*. 19 December, 1995, p. C4.
2   Published annually by Arab Monetary Fund, the League of Arab States, the Arab Fund, and the Organization of Arab Petroleum Exporting Countries.
3   Rami G. Khouri, "The Arab Nation: trends, assets, and directions." *Jordan Times*, 2 April 1996, op-ed page.
4   Ahmad Obeidat, in an address to a meeting on "Environmental Law," Amman, Jordan, 1994.
5   The author interviewed the Director General in his legal counselor and chief financial officer in Amman, 15 July, 1996.
6   The Director General has a Ph.D. in Agriculture from a university in Turkey. The second in command, with the embellished title of "Legal Counselor and Director of Finance and Management," also has a doctorate from a university in the former Soviet Union.
7   A statement by the Minister from Geneva, Switzerland, published in *Al-Rai'a*, 18 July 1996.
8   Statement by Minister of Municipal, Rural, and Environmental Affairs, *Al-Rai'a*, 7 July 1996.
9   Interview in Amman, July 1996.
10 Jordan's Ministry of Municipal and Rural Affairs, Department of Environment, *National Environment Strategy for Jordan*, 1991, p. x (technical advice by IUCN, Gland, Switzerland).
11 Jordan's *Environment Strategy*, p. xi.
12 By-Laws, Jordan Environment Society, Amman, Jordan, p. 2.
13 By-Laws of JES.
14 Leila Sharaf, Deputy President of the Royal Society, *Al-Rai'a*, 22 July 1996.
15 Interview, *Sheehan* (Arabic, weekly), 20 July 1996, p. 8.
16 While interviewing for this article, a senior manager (second in command of the Agency), stated that information on activities and budgets of the Agency should be "discussed only after an official

request is submitted for approval through the channels." The Director General conveniently avoided the embarrassing ruling from his deputy, who is also the legal counselor of the Agency.

REFERENCES

AL-OMARY, Ghaith
   1994 *Environmental Research and Studies: International Environmental Law.* Germany: Jordan Environment Society & Friedrich-Naumann-Stiftung.
AWAD, Adel Rifkhi
   1996 *Management of Industrial Pollution.* (In Arabic, *Edarat al-Talawuth al-Senae'e*). Amman, Jordan: Dar al-Shurouk.
CUNNINGHAM, Robert B. and Y. K. SARAYRAH
   1993 *Wasta: The Hidden Force in Middle Eastern Society.* Westport, Conn: Praeger Publishers.
JREISAT, Jamil E.
   1989 "Bureaucracy and Development in Jordan." *Journal of Asian and African Studies.* Vol. XXIV, Nos. 1-2 (January/April).
   1990 "Administrative Change and the Arab Manager." *Public Administration and Development.* Vol. 10, No. 4 (October/December).
MINTZBERG, Henry
   1979 *The Structure of Organizations.* Englewood-Cliffs, NJ: Prentice-Hall.
RICH, Bruce
   1994 *Mortgaging the Earth: The World Bank, Environmental Impoverishment, and the Crisis of Development.* Boston: Beacon Press.
RUDEL, Walter
   1995 *Environmental Research and Studies: Transfer of Environmentally-Sound Technologies.* Germany: Jordan Environment Society & Friedrich-Naumann-Stiftung.
   1994 *Environmental Research and Studies: International Environmental Law.* Germany: Jordan Environment Society & Friedrich-Naumann-Stiftung.
TELL, Sufian and Yaser SARAH
   1987 *The Condition of the Environment of Jordan.* (A study sponsored by the Department of the Environment of the Ministry of Municipal and Rural Affairs, Jordan, in Arabic).
TUBASY, Adnan
   1996 "Role of Mass Media in Changing Human Behavior Toward the Environment in Jordan," (unpublished Master's Thesis in Educational Psychology, University of Jordan).
Government of Jordan
   1991 *National Environment Strategy for Jordan.* (A document prepared by Ministry of Municipal and Rural Affairs. Department of the Environment, and IUCN-The World Conservation Union.)

Emerging Environmental Concerns
A Perspective from the Sultanate of Oman

JOSEPH A. KECHICHIAN

ABSTRACT

This paper analyses, very carefully, the Sultanate of Oman's determination to promote economic development and growth in order to provide its citizens with high living standards. At the same time, and at the initiative of its ruler, Sultan Qaboos, Oman assumed full responsibility for the protection of its environment from the impact of its major push for economic growth. The Omani government carefully provided for the protection of the quality of its air, fresh water resources, coastal waters, land resources, and the conservation of biological diversity. In its drive for economic growth and industrialization, Oman relied on four governmental units to respond to its environmental needs: the Council for the Conservation of the Environment and Prevention of Pollution, the Ministry of Regional Municipalities and Environment, the Office of Advisor for Conservation of the Environment, and the Planning Committee for the Development and Environment in the Southern Region (Dhuffar).

Introduction

ALTHOUGH OIL fueled the developmental engine of the Sultanate of Oman, Muscat has painstakingly learned that its meager petroleum resources would not be sufficient to propel it into the 21st century. Omani leaders understood that without a massive infusion of fresh financial and industrial resources, the country could not succeed in creating the long-term economic prosperity that it craved.

To be sure, Muscat pushed for a rapid economic growth but, unlike dozens of newly emerging countries around the world, it assumed full responsibility for industrialization's impact on the Omani environment. Given the harsh environmental conditions on the Arabian Peninsula, this attention was even more remarkable, in light of the country's massive socio-economic needs. Furthermore, and because Oman lacked natural water resources, attention to the environment was even more pressing. Draconian measures were necessary to protect scarce water resources. To say that bold initiatives were launched to gain the upper hand in water management would be an understatement.

In addition to a water policy, the Sultanate identified several specific areas for further attention over the long-term: air pollution, non-toxic solid waste, liquid and solid toxic waste generated by industry, as well as other hazardous materials. Towards that objective, the Ministry of Regional Municipalities and Environment initiated several programs, to monitor the growth of these pollutants in the environment. It also paid close attention to the sea. Oman's pristine coastal areas received special care and there was special emphasis on the potential extinction of indigenous species, due to impairment of their natural resources.

If Oman was vigilant of its environment, it was, in large part, due to Sultan Qaboos bin Said. A remarkable statesman, Qaboos initiated awareness programs for well over 20 years, and repeatedly addressed the need to preserve the environment, calling on the population to assume full responsibilities for its quality of life. Since 1970, Muscat issued several decrees, establishing key infrastructure to preserve the environment. In fact, Oman has been a regional leader in environmental issues and through its membership in the Gulf Cooperation Council (GCC) as well as the Regional Organization for the Protection of the Marine Environment (ROPME),[1] led decision-makers to assume their fair share of responsibilities in the Gulf region (Peterson, 1988).

Background

In many ways the modern history of Oman is particularly rich. Indeed, the Sultanate experienced the powerful influence of Islam when different tribes were unified into a new political, legislative and social system. Throughout its history, however, the Sultanate occupied a regional position of strength by virtue of its geographical setting. When, in 1649, Omani forces successfully routed the occupying Portuguese from Muscat and East Africa, a new chapter was opened. The Muscati Empire quickly spread to Africa and, to support this "colony," Oman developed a strong maritime presence. For a time, the Omani naval power in the Indian Ocean was unrivaled, paying regular visits to major ports throughout the world. The result was a vast empire that stretched from Africa to Balouchistan in modern Pakistan/India. A hundred years after these conquests, the Al Bu Said dynasty came into power when Ahmed Bin Said, arguably Oman's greatest leader, acceded to the throne in 1749. The Empire did not last because it clashed with another, more formidable foe—the United Kingdom—that defeated Muscat and, in time, came to influence the Sultanate's internal and foreign policies. Parallel to this great loss, Muscati naval trade was dealt a fatal blow after the opening of the Suez Canal in Egypt. European and Asian ships abandoned the long, circuitous, Cape of Good Hope route in favor of Suez and, more important, preferred to carry whatever goods they needed, in their own ships.

Oman - Roads and Mountain Ranges

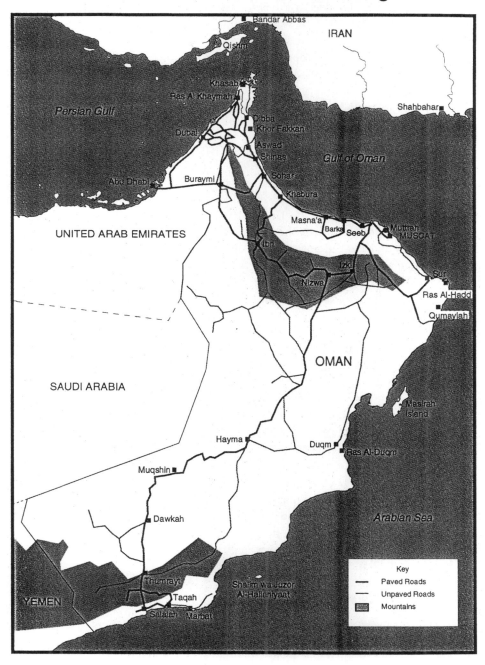

A new era unfolded in 1964, when oil was first discovered in the Sultanate. Exploration was difficult—due to a lack of basic infrastructure—and exports were kept to a minimum after 1967. It was not until 1970, when Qaboos Bin Said came to power, that the Omani "renaissance" started. To his immense credit, Qaboos tapped every rival he could muster for development projects, although the Dhuffar Rebellion in the south drained substantial resources to the war effort. This much was certain: Oman lacked everything and could not pass for a functioning state in 1970. It needed to tackle difficult issues fast and it needed large sums of money to achieve its stated objectives (Kechichian, 1995: 1-13 and 239-247).

Geographical Features

Oman lies on the south-eastern corner of the Arabian Peninsula, occupying close to 300,000 km^2—making it the second largest country on the Peninsula—and is slightly smaller in size than the United Kingdom. Its coastline extends to 1700 km from the Straits of Hormuz in the north to the borders of the Republic of Yemen. Three seas surround the Sultanate: The Arabian/Persian Gulf, the Gulf of Oman, and the Arabian Sea. On land, Oman shares borders with the United Arab Emirates, Saudi Arabia and Yemen.

The Greater Muscat area sits on the northern Batinah Coast but Oman consists of mountains and wadis, as well as plains. In fact, the Batinah occupies an area of 9,000 km^2 (3% of total land), whereas mountain ranges consist of 45,000 km^2 (15%). The remaining area is mainly sand and desert that includes part of the Rub al-Khali (the Great Empty Quarter) that is shared with Saudi Arabia.

Given this vast geographical spread, the climate is varied. While it is hot and humid in the coastal areas—especially in the Summer—it is usually hot and dry in the interior, except in the high mountain ranges where it is cooler throughout the year. Southern Oman enjoys heavy and regular monsoon rain falls between June and October (Sultanate of Oman, 1995).

In 1993, the Sultanate conducted its first ever census, tallying a total of 1.5 million citizens and 300,000 expatriate workers. The estimated average annual population growth rate stood at a dizzying 3.5%. At this rate of growth, the Omani population was poised to double in less than a decade. Although the population was mostly engaged in agriculture, fisheries, traditional industries and handicrafts, an increasing number of Omanis—especially those living in the Greater Muscat area—were involved in trade (Sultanate of Oman, 1993).

Development Policies and Trends

To be sure, raw economic considerations motivated Omani leaders to adopt decisions that, in turn, affected the environment. What were Oman's current development objectives and how did they adversely affect the environment?

First, there was little controversy over the fact that the 1970 Omani renaissance aimed to encourage rapid economic growth—to make up for lost time—even if several policies were haphazardly started. Oman was consistent in both its internal and foreign policies but, and this must be acknowledged, there was plenty of confusion. Often, decisions were reached at the spur of the moment, without any consideration for the long-term environmental impacts. The result was a "helter-skelter" approach to the country's development efforts.

Second, after senior government officials became wary of the rapid growth patterns, Muscat opted to draft five-year plans that, for better or worse, proved to be quite useful. Whether successive five-year plans were ever harmonized may be debatable but, and this much was certain, a minimum commonality has emerged since 1970.

Common Objectives

To date, all six of Oman's development plans shared objectives that have withstood the test of time. Because of Qaboos bin Said's foresight, the Sultanate of Oman aimed:

1. to develop new sources of national income to augment and, in time, replace oil revenues;
2. to increase the ratio of national investments directed to income-generating projects, particularly in manufacturing, mining, agriculture and fisheries;
3. to distribute national investments among geographical regions with a view of spreading prosperity and progress to all regions of the Sultanate;
4. to support the maintenance of existing population centers and communities, to safeguard those communities from potential emigration to densely-populated urban centers, and to protect the environment;
5. to attach high priority to the development of natural water resources;
6. to attach high priority to the development of human resources, and to improve their capacity to contribute to the national economy;
7. to meet infrastructure requirements;
8. to support commercial activities by removing market deficiencies, particularly in the areas of transport, communications and storage, and other obstacles to competitive trading, with a view to enhancing the emergence of a competitive market;
9. to provide for the creation of a national economy based on private enterprise and free from monopolistic practices; and
10. to enhance the efficiency of the Government's administrative machinery (Sultanate of Oman, 1992: 6).

Of course, these objectives were not "finalized" in 1970 when Qaboos acceded to the throne. Rather, an attempt was made to draft broad outlines that would promote development, introduce sorely needed infrastructure and, equally important, allow the average Omani citizen from participating in the Sultanate's renaissance. That Muscat fared better than most Gulf states (with the possible exception of Dubai in the UAE), is testament to this foresight, acknowledged shortcomings notwithstanding.

Development Stages

Arguably, the first five-year plan was the most difficult effort undertaken by the Sultanate's fledgling government, since it aimed to create—literally out of scratch— an entire infrastructure for Oman. In 1970, Oman boasted ten kilometers of paved roads, three primary schools for boys, and a single twelve-bed American missionary clinic (Sultanate of Oman, 1980: 5).

The first five-year plan (1976-1980) was a strategic effort that aimed to harness the benefits of the oil and natural gas booms of the post-1967 period. In a matter of a few short years, a basic infrastructure was laid out, to encourage the private sector to invest in the country. In as much as many Omanis were willing to assume such responsibilities—after decades of neglect—the period between 1976 and 1980 saw the public sector grow by leaps and bounds. Still, for many Omanis, a coveted position was one with the government, not necessarily out of the government. To some extent this was a psychological phenomenon. Every Omani wanted to be close to his ruler who, given Qaboos' predisposition to get involved in all aspects of Omani life, was understandable. What the process did, however, was to allow for a non-competitive process to emerge. This was an important departure from what Qaboos and his cabinet hoped for but, given what Omanis had been through—closed environment and a civil war—entirely logical (Miller, 1991: 25-32).

The second five-year plan (1981-1985) was based on a sharp increase in oil income. Muscat learned from its earlier mistakes and, consequently, initiated the first corrective moves on its development policies. It was during this period, for example, that attention turned to the Sultanate's water resources. Oman invested significant financial resources to harvest the country's meager water potential and, in a second stage, to create desalination plants. Muscat was brave enough to understand that the Sultanate had—and would continue to have—a serious water problem and that there was an urgent need to encourage both conservation and education (Miller, 1991: 33-42).

The third five-year plan (1986-1990) aimed to test the economic foundation on which earlier efforts were based. Like other oil-producing countries, Oman saw a drop in its income when oil prices fell dramatically. Yet, and despite unfavorable conditions, the government decreased expenditures by introducing a unique austerity program. As oil prices rose, Muscat treaded cautiously, avoiding wild economic gyrations. The result was relative stability (Miller, 1991: 42-53).

The fourth five-year plan (1991-1995) focused on developing a new strategy for the balance of the century and beyond. Unlike earlier plans, the fourth expanded the Omani economic base, assessed the impact of development, and placed the Omani economy within its proper regional environment. Towards that end, Muscat aimed to further decrease its dependence on oil income, by encouraging the private sector to become productive in its own right and equip the population with the entrepreneurial wherewithal. The percentage of Omani GDP income from oil and gas sectors dropped from 67% in 1975 to 45% in 1989 and an estimated 42% in 1995 (Miller, 1991: 63-73). Equally important, Oman aimed to halt its reliance on expatriate workers, by calling on citizens from all walks of life to perform a variety of jobs. These economic changes were necessary, senior Omani officials argued, because the entire world economy was changing, demanding rapid adaptation on the part of smaller powers.[2]

Main Economic Features

Oman's GDP, at 1992 market prices, increased from US $30m in 1970 to $1b in 1990 (Sultanate of Oman, 1990: 14). Of course, the oil and gas sectors—representing an average 45% of GDP—were responsible for this astronomical growth rate. The non-oil sector's contribution to the GDP were considerably smaller between 1970 and the mid-1980s. In recent years, however, steady growth in the agricultural, fisheries and industrial sectors, have significantly altered the percentages. Agriculture and fisheries, for example, contributed $5.5m to the national GDP in 1976. The figure jumped to $36m in 1990. The GDP of the industrial sector increased from $1.5m in 1976 to $45m in 1990 (Sultanate of Oman, 1990: 14-16).

Naturally, these limited contributions meant that oil income was vastly superior to everything else. Oil production jumped from 300,000 barrels per day (bpd) in the period 1971-1975 to 393,000 bpd in the period 1981-1985, and 614,000 bpd in the period 1986-1990. It topped the 700,000 bpd mark in 1992 and, since then, the Sultanate has been producing close to 800,000 bpd. Parallel to these production increases, and as a result of considerable investments in oil exploration, known reserves of oil increased from 1.3 billion barrels (bb) in 1975 to 4.5 bb in 1995 (Sultanate of Oman, 1995: 12-13).

To cope with the rapid economic growth of the Sultanate, government expenditures increased as well. Average annual non-military expenditures between 1971 and 1975 were close to $50m. Average yearly non-military expenditures reached $550m between 1981 and 1985, and close to $800m between 1986-1990. Whereas 1,750 persons were employed in the Omani civil service in 1970, an estimated 51,204 had joined in by 1989, and 77,269 by 1992 (Miller, 1991: 119). Although these increases were sudden, given the political reality of Oman—as well as the huge need to equip the country with basic manpower necessities—Muscat invested over $1.5b

in recurrent expenditures between 1970 and 1990. This sum was above and beyond
its investment in infrastructure as well as the modest efforts to boost private sector
initiatives (soft and guaranteed loans to initiate and operate businesses). The civil
service thus reached satisfactory levels in terms of its personnel although additional
training was sought to improve productivity. There remained a psychological factor
to overcome: that the average Omani expected guaranteed employment after grad-
uation from high-school or university. Still, and because of the austerity programs
in place since 1990, fewer and fewer educated Omanis were looking to Muscat
for employment. Rather, most were keen to embark on the free-enterprise band-
wagon, seeking the government's assistance only to lift legal restrictions towards
investments.

Parallel to its manpower policy, Muscat established the State General Reserve
Fund in 1980, earmarking 15% of annual oil revenues to it (Miller, 1991: 33). One of
the main objectives behind the establishment of the State General Reserve Fund was
to balance resources and Government expenditure, as well as to form cash reserves
that could be used to fund budget deficits whenever required. The fund actually
achieved the objective for which it was established as $680m was withdrawn to
cover budget deficits between 1981 and 1985. Despite these withdrawals, $325m
remained in the fund at the end of 1985. Given the significant drop in oil revenues
during the late 1980s, borrowing from the fund was indeed necessary to initiate or
simply maintain critical on-going projects. Additional budget deficits were covered
through commercial borrowings although the preference was for austerity measures
whenever possible.

Government debt reached $190m at the end of 1985 and $250m at the end of
1995 (10% of total available revenues). Keeping the rate low in the mid-1990s
was indeed an important improvement over the 1980s. Under the third plan (1986-
1990), for example, the deficit amounted to $460m, that was equivalent to 23%
of total revenues. The fourth five-year plan aimed to finance deficits through the
withdrawal of $130m from a newly established "Contingency Fund" and by issuing
long and medium-term Government Development bonds to the value of $130m. Debt
servicing, including repayment installments and interest, were estimated to account
for less than 15% of the total value of exports in 1995. Initial demand for bonds
was strong although official preferences were to reduce the government's role in the
economy. In fact, a senior Omani official expressed a desire to see the private sector
step in with vigor, as early as 1992.[3]

Major Environmental Concerns

With rapid industrialization, Oman experienced serious problems with air pollution, the scarcity of water resources, and a lack of coastal, land, and animal management policies. When daunting tasks emerged in the mid-1980s, Omani officials
rose to the challenge.

Protection of Air

To be sure, industry, transportation, oil and gas production and the increased power station outputs have all added to the level of air pollution, especially those of the Suspended Particulate Matter (SPM) variety. As suspected, SPM arose from both natural and artificial sources, including combustion, as well as industrial and agricultural practices. Sulfur dioxide (SO_2) also arose from both natural and man-made activities, including fossil fuel combustion and industrial activities. Likewise, carbon monoxide (CO) was formed both naturally and from industrial processes including the complete combustion of fossil and other carbon-bearing fuels.

Without exception, all of these pollutants flourished in the Sultanate, although emissions from motor vehicles were the most important sources. This was especially true in the urban environment of the capital area where air pollution was most visible. To address this growing problem, Muscat issued specific regulations aimed at the protection of public health, animal and agricultural resources as well as to minimize potential future environmental risks (Sultanate of Oman, 1992: 9-17).

Fresh Water Resources

Because Oman received limited amounts of rain water (that fluctuated widely from year to year), agriculture—on which a majority of the population depended for its livelihood—could not rely exclusively on direct rainfall irrigation. Rather, the reliance was on underground water. For this reason, the falaj systems (man-made canalization) were developed hundreds of years ago. More recently, and often with disastrous consequences, hundreds of farmers have had recourse to artesian wells with pump abstraction (Sultan, 1992: 9). To say that Omanis have over-pumped ground water would be an understatement.

Parallel to this development, and as a result of the country's rapid development and the dramatic improvement in the standard of living, a substantial increase in water consumption has also been recorded. The consumption of water in the Muscat area, for example, increased from 63 million gallons in 1971 to 9 billion gallons in 1989. This increase in consumption rate necessitated the construction of a large desalination plant in the late 1980s (Sultanate of Oman, 1994: 124-131). When UNICEF recently examined the impact of water issues on the Sultanate, it reported that:

> access to drinking water and sanitation facilities has improved considerably throughout the country in the past decade, though major disparities continue to have a negative impact on the health of children and entire families. It is clearly documented, for instance, that the peak of diarrhea attacks against children occurs in the rainy season, when runoff water increases the contamination of drinking and household water sources. National water availability and quality issues are being assessed by the Ministry of Water Resources which was established in January 1990 as a sign of the government's concern about water issues (UNICEF, 1990: 30).[4]

In 1995, close to 58% of the entire population had access to safe drinking water, with 90% access in urban areas and 49% in rural areas. Sanitation facilities were available to 39% of the population, with 75% access in urban areas and 8% in rural areas. The bulk of water resources used in urban areas came from desalination plants or wells, delivered through water-pipe networks or tankers, drawing from private or Government wells. Since new laws required that all homes be equipped with bathrooms and septic tanks, the need for more water will increase over time, adding growing pressures on existing wells.

In an interesting survey conducted by the Ministry of Health in 1989, 26.3% of all Omani households had piped water, 28.4% tankard water, 28% wells and 11.4% drew their needs from springs and/or the falaj—the traditional water conveyance systems that drew water from wells or seasonal wadis (riverbeds). About 42% of all households had water inside their homes and, compared with the pre-1970 period, that was a significant achievement. In about 20% of the remaining households, the water source was more than a 15-minute walk away, and in 18% it was less than 15 minutes. Reportedly, in many rural areas the falaj systems, were in need of repair and control of pollution. The survey, known as "The 1988/89 Child Health Survey," concluded that the availability of clean water, based on quality, quantity, ease of access or reliability of water sources was a problem in some villages. Moreover, it asserted that since most private wells in rural areas were open wells that were susceptible to pollution, there was little doubt that pollution of wells and falaj, especially in rural Oman, was a major problem. Human and animal feces were routinely washed into the water sources and one solution being tested in 1995 was the use of household water-seal latrines or ventilated improved latrines (that did not require water). In as much as public authorities were aware of the problems and, more important, were favorably disposed to address them, all was not lost.

Oceans and Coastal Waters

Through the Ministry of Commerce and Industry, Muscat established the Oman Coastal Zone Management (OCZM), that drew specific plans to deal with environmental issues related to coastal zone management in the Sultanate. The OCZM was mandated:

1. to develop a legal framework to use and protect coastal resources;
2. to establish a nature conservation plan and to enforce laws towards the proper management of the coast;
3. to determine whether rapid urbanization was damaging the coast;
4. to manage the recreation resources of the state as well as the proliferation of private clubs that were taxing the coastal infrastructure; to better manage the rapid growth of water sports activities that were bringing motor boating and water-skiing into conflict with swimming, snorkeling, diving, and wind surfing;

to limit the number of vehicles on beaches that interfered with the peace and safety of other users;

5. to address the role that algae and juvenile fishes may have on the fisheries industry;
6. to protect all coastal archaeological sites from development;
7. to preserve the aesthetic value of coastal areas from rapid development;
8. to protect animal life that thrived on the Sultanate's coasts, including turtles, terns, sooty falcons, herons, ospreys and their nesting habitats; and
9. finally, to manage special issues.

The latter comprised a variety of issues, including the protection of khawrs and mangroves—that were important to fisheries, recreation, and wildlife—as well as sand dunes, coral reefs and the rocky coasts. In the case of the Khawrs and mangroves, a consensus emerged among Omani environmentalists that these were primarily threatened with encroachment by urban development and upstream canalization of wadis, and by dumping of domestic wastes. Furthermore, it was feared that the depletion of freshwater resources for domestic and agricultural purposes could adversely affect mangroves and lowland vegetation through salt water intrusion that, in addition to damaging agricultural land and fresh water wells, would affect wildlife dependent on mangroves and shrubs.

With respect to Oman's rich sand dunes, the consensus was that these were potentially threatened by urban development as well, including the building boom of hotels, housing, roads, and mining facilities. Moreover, sand dunes were routinely disturbed by recreational vehicles, destroying vegetation and hence promoting erosion.

Littering, and the careless fishing practices throughout the Sultanate, were among the main factors that caused damage to corals and reduced the aesthetic quality of reefs for recreation in some places, through entanglement of nets, ropes, anchors, traps, plastic bags, and fabrics, and accumulation of tin cans, tires, and other rubbish.

Finally, Oman's rocky coastal environment was valuable for hard and for soft corals, food and shelter for fish, lobsters, and other marine life. Unquestionably, these were immensely valuable to fisheries and, despite this understanding, the rocky coast was threatened by potential harbor expansions and other marine proposals.

Protection and Management of Land Resources

To be sure, the Sultanate's development plans could not be achieved without careful attention to the environment and, towards that end a variety of concerns needed to be confronted in earnest. Among these were Oman's adjustment of national land-use policies, pricing mechanisms and incentives, integrated plant nutrient and pest management systems, agro-forestry conservation and sustainable use of forests and savannas, halting and reversing land degradation and desertification, promotion of sustainable land-use practices and monitoring and assessment of soil and vegetation. Additional areas of attention were constantly under evaluation both at the Ministry of Commerce and Industry as well as the Ministry of Regional Municipalities and Environment.

There were, nevertheless, a few intangibles. First, Oman had limited arable land and, in 1995, only 0.15% of the total land area was cropped with additional rangeland, mostly in the Dhuffar, being grazed. Coastal soils of the Batinah and Salalah plains were fertile, easily worked, relatively permeable and amenable to mechanization and good management. These soils, however, were being depleted of nutrients partly through cropping and partly by excessive irrigation leaching out fertilizer. Interior wadi and jebel soils were heavier, erodible on the slopes and often interlaced with gravel and rock deposits, making cultivation difficult.

These limitations notwithstanding, the gravest shortfall was that of water: simply stated-lack of water was the major limiting natural resource of the Sultanate. Moreover, and if Oman's wasteful usage was replaced by a more balanced use, a deficit would still remain. According to Omani official sources, and under modern production techniques, current supplies were adequate for perhaps a 40 to 60% increase in cropped area in the medium-term and probably 100% over the long-term. This was largely optimistic since such an expansion would require a shift from flood to modern irrigation, modernization of the falaj system and the cessation of over-pumping near the Batinah coast. Water quality was generally satisfactory except where salinity remained high or was growing at an alarming rate. Since agriculture, fisheries and trade were the backbone of the Omani economy before and since the discovery of oil, close to half of the population lived in agricultural communities and relied on agriculture as its principal source of income. Clearly, the implications of this reality for Muscat were self-evident: The Sultanate's priority—that would drive both domestic and foreign policies—necessitated attention to the agricultural sector.

In view of existing water resource constraints, all land reclamation projects currently contemplated in the Sultanate will, by necessity, be severely curtailed given insufficient water supplies. Still, a number of innovative methods, were under consideration. Omani officials believed that agricultural land productivity could be doubled during the next decade. Clearly, this was overtly optimistic despite a gargantuan effort to provide various services to farmers. A number of agricultural centers were established throughout the country since 1985 to provide improved seeds, tractor services, insecticides, fertilizers, water pumps and other equipment. Some of these services were offered free of charge and others, such as fertilizers and water-pumps, made available at subsidized prices. The Ministry of Education also established agricultural technical schools and more than 20 agricultural cooperative societies were operating in Oman in 1995.

Conservation of Biological Diversity

Omani officials responsible for environmental questions realized that the conservation of natural ecosystems, as well as the maintenance of biological diversity, constituted pressing issues throughout the world. These concerns were, however, primarily understood by "environmentalists," less by decision-makers, or the public at large. Much like in the rest of the world, the effective management of plants and animals in Oman depended upon the maintenance of fragile habitats. To its credit, the Sultanate embarked upon nature conservation several years ago and, since the early 1990s, became a leader in this field in the Middle East.[5]

To their credit, Omani officials adopted several critical policies and plans in the early 1970s, that have withstood the test of time. By Gulf standards, several stand out, and deserve special attention.

In 1974, Sultan Qaboos appointed an environmental advisor, at a time when Oman was mired in the Dhuffar war, and when far more pressing concerns preoccupied him. The advisor was mandated to acquire knowledge about Oman's flora and fauna and, secondly, to ensure that wildlife and other natural resources would be protected and managed in harmony with other forms of development. Towards that end, the Wadi Serin Tahr Reserve was established in 1975, covering an area of about 240 km^2. Although the reserve has never acquired legal status, it has been effectively patrolled and managed by a ranger force and, since 1975, the patrol coverage was extended to about 800 km^2.

Likewise, turtle monitoring programs on Masirah Island and in the Ras al-Hadd areas on the mainland, were institutionalized. During the 1970s, two royal decrees were issued, that aimed at conserving selected species of wild animals as well.

A Natural History Museum was created at the Ministry of National Heritage and Culture, mandated to play an important role in the study of Oman's wildlife. The Museum building was completed in 1980 and since then, specimens, photographs and natural history data have been collected, and a scientific library established on the premises. Reference collections were assembled, particularly of insects, mollusks and snakes.

Equally significant was the 1980 White Oryx Project that aimed to reintroduce the recently extinct Arabian oryx to its former known range on the central plains of the Jiddat al Harasis. The first 10 captive-bred oryxes were received from the United States in 1980 and released in the wild in 1982. Much progress was accomplished in this field. In fact, the lucky visitor to the mountain range can indeed spot an oryx, from time to time.

Finally, specially designated areas were created in the 1980s, including one near Muscat, to protect tidal inlets and mangroves. Building on this precedent, in 1984, Muscat put the Daymaniyat Islands, that lie off the Batinah Coast, under protection as well. A Ministry of Environment was also created by royal decree the same year. This ministry was charged with enforcing and implementing a national plan for conserving the environment. Since then, the Ministry has adopted an ambitious agenda and, more important, pursued carefully managed outreach programs targeted at school-age children.[6] Oman aimed to heighten its population's consciousness on environmental questions.

Environmental Policies

Omanis realized that the wide use of chemicals in industry, commerce and in the home, as well as the generation of wastes of all types, were important features of economic development. They also realized that these had, potentially, tremendous capabilities to harm the environment and the health of the population. Towards that end, Muscat paid attention to hazardous and chemical wastes, but existing regulations and guidelines were still inadequate. It nevertheless embarked on an aggressive plan to equip the country with the institutions that would monitor, assess, and respond to all of its development policies.

Policies

During the past few years, Sultan Qaboos repeatedly expressed his concerns for the environment, arguing for vigilance and conservation. In one of his more recent pronouncements, the ruler declared:

> As a result of our great concern for the protection of the natural environment, and our achievements in this respect, Oman has gained a respectable position among nations concerned with environmental protection; yet, we still have to exert more effort and consider the special conditions relevant to this issue, when we come to plan and implement development projects. We must proceed to develop contacts with regional and international organizations concerned. It is a duty which must be undertaken by each citizen, to guarantee the protection of our natural resources and public health against any harmful effects, and protect the beautiful and distinguished nature which God Almighty granted to our beloved Oman (Sultanate of Oman, 1995).

Similar pronouncements reflected the ruler's keen interest in tackling this question head-on. In addition to his public statements, Qaboos streamlined his environmental policies in 1982, when he issued Royal Decree No. 10 that identified the Sultanate's objectives as follows:

> To provide to the greatest degree possible health and social welfare for the nation and citizens, protect its natural wealth and economic resources, preserve its historical and cultural heritage, and avoid any immediate or long-term damage or side effects which may appear as a result of industrial, agricultural or building programs, or other developments, and cultural programs which aim to improve standards of living and diversify the sources of natural income. The ultimate aim is to protect, develop and use the country's natural resources in the best and most intelligent manner without any damage occurring to the various types of life on the land of the Sultanate and in its

economic quarters, particularly damage resulting from pollution of the basic eco-systems such as air, water, soil and marine, animal and plant wealth (Royal Decree, 10/1982).

The Sultan's Government, more recently, has required "Certificates of No Environmental Objection" for all private and Government projects requiring licenses. The purpose of the certificates was to limit the negative effects of development on land use without necessarily discouraging construction.

Within ROPME, and starting in 1978, Muscat championed the adoption of a variety of programs. It supported the "Kuwait Action Plan"—that aimed to enhance the environmental capabilities of member states—and the "Protocol Concerning Regional Co-operation in Combating Pollution by Oil and other Harmful Substances in Cases of Emergency" (ROPME, 1990). The Sultanate was also instrumental in initiating a number of environmental action policies within the GCC and the League of Arab States.

Legislation

Starting in 1979, special legislations were drafted in three specific areas: (1) wildlife and nature conservation, (2) pollution control and (3) marine protection.

The first decree, 26/1979, provided the authority to establish national parks and nature reserves. Several areas were to be identified as animal reserves. Unfortunately, the legislation was never implemented—the Sultanate lacked the resources to identify specific areas of Oman that would qualify for such reserves. Many changes since the late 1970s altered the country's priorities and it remained to be determined whether a renewed effort would be initiated to resume this stated objective.

A more successful legislation was the 1982 "Law on Conservation of the Environment and Prevention of Pollution" (Royal Decree, No. 10/1982) that was quite comprehensive. It included general provisions on objectives, duties of individuals, Ministries, and organizations to dispose of pollutants in a manner so as to minimize environmental harm. It also included enforcement rules as well as penalties for convicted parties (Sultanate of Oman, 1986). The legislation was further strengthened in 1985 when a number of amendments were enacted (Royal Decree, No. 63/1985) focusing on licensee applications and the conditions that may be imposed on industrial facilities. Not only were violators obliged to clean-up and repair whatever damages may have resulted from these violations, but Muscat diligently pursued a fine policy and, at times, withdrew operating licenses. In late 1996, Omani officials were drafting additional guidelines to tackle the difficult questions associated with solid, non-hazardous waste management.

Since 1979, Oman has also been active in supporting legislation on marine conservation. Royal Decree No. 68/1979 created the Council for the Conservation of the Environment and Prevention of Pollution (CCEPP). A new and updated Marine Pollution Control Law was drafted in 1983 and circulated to interested parties for review. It complied with Omani obligations under the International Maritime Organization (IMO) Conventions and was expected to be completed by the end of 1996. Over the years, a number of other decrees were issued to regulate fishing and recreational uses of the coast.

Conclusions

The Sultanate of Oman relied on four governmental units to deal with its environmental needs.

First, there was the Council for the Conservation of the Environment and Prevention of Pollution (CCEPP) that was created in 1979, to oversee the control of marine pollution pursuant to Muscat's treaty obligations to ROPME. In 1984, these responsibilities were expanded to cover protection of the environment and prevention of pollution in general (Royal Decree, No. 46/1984). Second, the Ministry of Regional Municipalities and Environment (Royal Decree, No. 117/1991)—created in 1984 as the Ministry of Environment—was mandated to assume full governmental responsibilities. Third, the "Office of Advisor for Conservation of the Environment," was created in 1974 within the Diwan of Royal Court Affairs. This office concentrated on matters related to and affecting the conservation of nature and wildlife resources. Fourth, the "Planning Committee for the Development and Environment in the Southern Region (Dhuffar)," was established in May, 1984. As the name suggested, the Committee's primary task was to overlook environmental issues in southern Oman.

All four of these institutions were led by individuals who were keenly aware of the Sultanate's needs to remain vigilant and protect the environment. This overall realization was in force even if development priorities were in full effect. To be sure, development was a recent phenomenon in Oman—starting from scratch in 1970 when the country came under Sultan Qaboos' rule—yet attention to the environment was never neglected. There was much more to do but the visitor to any region of Oman in late 1996 quickly recognized that the Omani people were sensitive to preserving their environment. In some ways, Oman was perhaps lucky to have started late and, more important, to have had a visionary leader at its helm.

NOTES

1   In addition to the GCC member-states (Bahrain, Kuwait, Oman, Qatar, Saudi Arabia, and the United Arab Emirates), ROPME included Iran and Iraq, and was headquatered in Kuwait.
2   Interview with Amir bin Shuwayn Al-Hosni, Minister for Regional Municipalities and Environment, Muscat, 20 October 1992. This significant realization was confirmed by the late Qais bin 'Abdul

Munim Al-Zawawi, Deputy Prime Minister for Financial and Economic Affairs, during a Muscat interview on 27 September 1993.

3 This point was repeatedly emphasized by Ahmed bin 'And Al-Nabi Macki, the Deputy Prime Minister for Economic Affairs. Interviews in Muscat with Minister Macki on 17 October 1992, 27 January and 21 September 1993 and 21 March 1995.

4 It must be emphasized here that Omani officials have adopted novel approach to educating the population about the environment. In fact, special emphasis is placed on women and children, and their roles in achieving environmental objectives. See, for example, Sultanate of Oman, *Al-Nadwat al-Wataniyat li-dawr al-Mar'at fi Himayat al-Bi'at* [National Conference on the Role of Women to Protect the Environment], Muscat: Ministry of Regional Municipalities and Environment, 19-21 December 1994, p. 49-57; see also Sultanate of Oman, *Al-Nadwat al-Wataniyat li-dawr al Shabab fi Himayat al-Bi'at* [National Conference on the Role of Youth to Protect the Environment], Muscat: Ministry of Regional Municipalities and Environment, 12-14 September 1993.

5 Interview with Amir bin Shuwayn Al-Hosni, Minister for Regional Municipalities and Environment, Muscat, 10 October 1992.

6 The Ministry organizes regular contests open to children of all ages. In June 1996, the author attended a reception for the winners of a Musat-Muttrah competition, that brought dozens of youngsters in close contact with senior officials. Prizes were awarded to best paintings offering tips on how to protect the environment. In some ways, it was remarkable that the renewed awareness espoused by senior officials were the results of Omani children's specific suggestions. In response, special publications, primarily aimed at children, were widely available in both Arabic and English to schoolchildren. See, for example, Anna Hywel-Davies, *Lamahat 'An Asmak 'Uman* [A First Look at Fishes of Oman], Muscat: Ministry of Regional Municipalities and Environment, n.d.; and Alec Dawson Shepherd, *Lanata 'raf 'ala al-Shawatiq* [Understanding Beaches], Muscat: Ministry of Regional Municipalities and Environment, n.d.; and Carolyn Glascodine, *Fifty Simple Things You Can Do To Save Oman's Environment,* Muscat: Ministry of Regional Municipalities and Environment, n.d.

REFERENCES

GLASCODINE, Carolyn
    1996 *Fifty Simple Things You Can Do To Save Oman's Environment.* Muscat: Ministry of Regional Municipalities and Environment, n.d.

KECHICHIAN, Joseph A.
    1995 *Oman and the World: The Emergence of an Independent Foreign Policy.* Santa Monica, California: Rand.

MILLER, Duncan R.
    1991 *Economic Development Planning in The Sultanate of Oman.* Ruwi, Sultanate of Oman: United Media Services.

PETERSON, Erik R.
    1988 *The Gulf Cooperation Council: Search for Unity in a Dynamic Region.* Boulder and London: Westview Press.

ROPME
    1990 *ROPME Achievements Within a Decade (1979-1989).* Kuwait: ROPME.

Royal Decree 10/1982.

SULTAN, Kamal Abdulredha
    1992 "Oman Needs Thorough Farm Strategy." *Oman Daily Observer,* 5 December.

Sultanate of Oman, Development Council, General Secretariat, Directorate General of National Statistics.
 1995 *Statistical Yearbook Twenty-Third Issue.* Muscat.
Sultanate of Oman, Development Council, General Secretariat
 1993 *Preliminary Results of the General Census of Population, Housing and Establishments.* Muscat.
Sultanate of Oman
 1992 *The Sultanate of Oman National Report to the United Nations Conference on Environment and Development.* Rio de Janeiro, Brazil. Muscat: Ministry of Regional Municipalities and Environment.
 1980 *Oman '80.* Muscat: Ministry of Information and Youth Affairs.
 1990 *Facts and Figures.* Muscat: Development Council.
 1995 *Annual Report for 1995 to His Majesty Sultan Qaboos bin Said, Sultan of Oman.* Muscat: Petroleum Development Oman.
 1992 *Final Report and Main Conclusions and Recommendations of International Symposium on the National Conservation Strategy of Oman.* Muscat: Ministry of Regional Municipalities and Environment.
 1994 *Oman '94.* Muscat: Ministry of Information.
 1995 *Speech by His Majesty Sultan Qaboos bin Said Al Said.* Muscat: Ministry of Information.
 1986 *The World Conservation Union (IUCN) Proposals for A System of Nature Conservation Areas.* Muscat: Diwan of the Royal Court.
UNICEF
 1990 *Situation Analysis of Women and Children in the Sultanate of Oman, 1990.* Unpublished Draft Report (PRO/004/095). New York: UNICEF.

The State of the Environment in Iran

SEID M. ZEKAVAT*

ABSTRACT

In the last two decades, Iran has experienced the most dramatic and probably the greatest political and economic changes in its history. These changes are evident in the country's demographic, environmental, developmental and political trends. The quest for economic development has made Iran one of the main contributors to global environmental deterioration. This study examines the impact of the political regimes of the Monarchy and the Islamic Republic on Iran's environment. It also examines the causes of environmental deterioration and evaluates Iran's policies and practices in protecting its environment. The findings of the study show that while Iran has adopted environmental protection measures and is cooperating with international agencies, the implementation of these measures has been hampered by budgetary demands in areas other than the environment. The government's inability to implement economic control mechanisms to slow population growth and inflation, and to raise public awareness to the economic realities, have resulted in a decreased quality of life for the majority of Iranians. Present consumption levels have put Iran's future economic stability in jeopardy. In order to reverse this trend, Iran must (1) stabilize its population growth at a zero rate; (2) make environmental protection a budgetary priority; (3) promote a blanket campaign for public awareness of the consequences of environmental deterioration; and (4) bring natural resources and the environment into the domain of the markets.

Introduction

AFTER OBSERVING THE PLANET earth from space in 1983, Commander Paul Weitz of the space shuttle Challenger remarked: "Unfortunately, this world is becoming a gray planet. . . . Our environment apparently is going downhill. . . . We are fouling our own nest" (Southwick, 1985). Air and water pollution, loss of fields and forests to urban and suburban development to accommodate the rapidly growing population, soil erosion, coastal pollution and damage to green forests by acid rain can no longer be considered local environmental issues. The accumulation of local and regional environmental events have already assumed global importance.

---

*   Loyola Marymount University, Los Angeles, CA 90045-8316, U.S.A.

© Koninklijke Brill, Leiden, 1997   *Journal of Developing Societies*, Vol. XIII, 1

It is estimated that by the year 2025, Third World countries will contribute fifty percent of the world's CO_2 emission (Goodstein, 1995). Iran's high population growth, increased per capita energy use, and urban and suburban development have led to unsustainable development as oil revenues are used for the importation of basic foodstuffs.

This study focuses on the following questions: How much has Iran's pollution impacted the local and global environment? What corrective environmental policies and practices have been adopted by the Shah and the Islamic Republic to address this problem? How effective have these policies been under each of the two systems of government? To what extent has Iran been cooperating with the World Health Organization in promoting a healthy global environment? Can sustainable development and improved quality of life be achieved?

Inevitable Trend Towards Local and Global Environmental Degradation

In 1953, Dr. Mohamed Mossaddegh, then Prime Minister of Iran, nationalized the Iranian Petroleum Industry. Soon, Iran exercised its right to set its petroleum price in line with the level set by other oil-producing nations. With increased oil revenue, Iran launched a series of ambitious development programs which changed the country from a nearly agrarian state to an industrial-based economy in a couple of decades.

The accelerated industrialization, coupled with rapid population growth, brought about increased urbanization, a higher standard of living, and expansion of modern technology. Economic development and environmental deterioration replaced the once spacious, serene, clean and healthy environment. Cement plants, oil refineries, sulfuric acid plants, plaster works, brick baking incinerators, foundries, steel plants, fossil fuel power plants, textile plants, chemical fiber plants, phosphate fertilizer plants, ammonia plants, pulp mills, copper and aluminum smelters, soft-drink plants and slaughtering houses, to name a few, now dotted the landscape. Rivers became polluted with industrial waste, flowing into the Persian Gulf in the south and the Caspian Sea in the north. Major streams and lakes became receptacles for chemical waste disposal.

Industrial progress lured peasants to the cities in search of employment and other economic opportunities. This movement was intensified by the transition from traditional agrarian farming to large-scale, market-oriented agriculture. With OPEC oil selling at $35 to $39 a barrel, and increased wages and employment opportunities, a new middle and upper class emerged. Many Iranians were now experiencing economic mobility and new purchasing power, resulting in a greater demand for privately owned automobiles. Highways became congested with automobiles, and the emissions from unburned hydrocarbons, nitrogen oxides and carbon monoxide spread over Tehran, Esfahan, Shiraz, Tabriz, other major western and northern cities, and into the countryside.

The synthesis of plastics generated a variety of toxic pollutants and introduced non-recyclable and non-biodegradable waste into the environment. Marine life, in particular, sea turtles, fish, and shrimp, are now threatened with extinction from accidental oil spills, tanker flush-outs, and oil platform wastes discharged into the Persian Gulf. New environmental burdens were introduced to the farmlands as Iran rapidly expanded its use of nitrogenous fertilizers and pesticides such as DDT, leaving nitrates in groundwater, and residues from insecticides and herbicides in the soil. Desertification of agricultural land continued, due to loss of organic matter, soil erosion, salinization, waterlogging, and overgrazing. Deforestation gradually advanced to the main northern forests because of agricultural expansion, housing development, and use of trees for firewood.

Although no study has yet been done on the possibility of air pollution and acid rain damage in Iran's forests, one can assume with a high degree of certainty that the pines in the northern region have not been immune to the pollutants.

By the late 1970s, Iran had all the physical manifestations of the environmental degradation of a nation that had advanced from a developing to a developed one. Iran's new place on the world stage was summed up in the Shah's famous televised remark: "... Iran is entering 'The Dawn of a New Civilization'." Iran's "Dawn" was short lived as the country was soon plunged into darkness by executions and destructive wars, resulting in an exodus of valuable human resources to Europe and the United States, and regression and decline in economic advancement.

The 1990 Gulf War further complicated Iran's environmental dilemma when Iraq's Saddam Hussein deliberately set fire to the Kuwait oil wells and thick clouds of smoke blanketed some 500,000 square kilometers of Iran's territory. Acid rain fell as far as the north-east of the country. According to the Iranian National Report, *Desert Storm* or *the Gulf War* caused health problems for some 12,500,000 Iranians, destroyed 5,000,000 hectares of agricultural land, 8,000,000 hectares of forests, 8,500,000 hectares of pastures, and uncounted numbers of species and their habitats (National Report, 1992).

Environmental Policy and Regulation Under the Shah

In early 1970, Iran began to show serious concern for the maintenance of a sound environment. It was not expected, however, that Iran would sacrifice economic growth in favor of the environment. Nor was it wise for Iranian officials to ignore the compounding environmental problems. A program of pollution control and environmental protection was integrated with the current development plans to ensure that environmental problems were not isolated from national development activities (Zerbonia and Soraya, 1978).

1. Policy and Legislation

In 1974, the Iranian Parliament enacted the Environmental Protection and Enhancement Act. The Act governed Iran's environmental policy until the Islamic Revolution of 1979. It authorized the establishment of the Department of Environment. Its objectives included the restoration or enhancement of the quality of the ambient air (Zerbonia and Soraya, 1978).

A year later, the National Clean Air Regulations were passed as an addendum to the Environmental Protection Act. They called for: (1) the advancement of a uniform approach to air pollution control across the country; (2) the effective implementation of air pollution control measures; and (3) delineation of the Department's leadership role in such areas as establishment of national air quality standards, control of the composition of fuel, compilation of source emission data, and establishment of national industrial and motor vehicle standards.

2. Stationary and Mobile Air Pollution Control Strategies

The two most serious sources of air pollution in all major cities are industries and automobiles. The following control strategies were adopted to alleviate pollution problems.

a. Industrial Pollution Control

The approach used by the Department of Environment was to contain pollution at the source. In support of containment at the source, certain industrial emission standards were adopted. These standards reflected the degree of emission limitation achievable through the application of the best available system of emission reduction or "the best practicable technology available." It seems this approach was intended to establish a balance between the extent of pollution control and ongoing economic development (Zerbonia and Soraya, 1978).

b. Mobile Source Control

During the period 1970 to 1975, the number of cars in major cities increased 2.5 times. The concentration of carbon monoxide, hydrocarbons, and nitrogen oxides reached an alarmingly high level and threatened public health. According to a report by the Department of Environment, concentration of these pollutants exceeded the primary ambient air quality standards of the United States. The Department of Environment predicted that by the early 1990s, the number of cars would increase by a factor of 5 (Zerbonia and Soraya, 1978).

In an effort to control mobile emission sources of air pollution, the Department of Environment adopted a number of air pollution control strategies. They included: (a) the installation of a catalytic oxidization system in some cars and minor changes in the design and adjustment of the engine in others; (b) periodic emission inspection for all used private cars, livery vehicles, taxis, trucks, and buses; (c) conversion of gasoline and diesel fuel livery vehicles to LPG and CNG gaseous fuels; and (d) improvement of traffic management with an increase of roads, highways and public transportation.

3. Implementation Problems

Early in 1977, the Department of Environment started an air pollution surveillance network with fully automatic air monitoring stations in Tehran, Esfahan, and Shiraz, each with several stations installed at the industrial sites. When the operation began, standardization of monitoring techniques in the surveillance network system became a serious problem. There was no coordination among the various agencies operating the systems, which led to a lack of comparability in data from different air monitoring stations. Therefore, there were no uniform data collections and interpretations to ensure maintenance of uniform air quality.

By 1978, three years after the adoption of the environmental control strategies, only a handful of regulations had been enforced. There were a number of major factors inhibiting implementation. The first was budget limitations. Substantial funds were needed for the installation and maintenance of equipment, and salaries for management and personnel. Another problem with industrial air pollution control was the limited resources made available to environmental control programs. At the time when Iran began to pay serious attention to the degradation of its environment, there were two other very important programs in progress, namely, industrial development and military preparedness. The newly-initiated environmental program had very little chance of claiming a fair share of the nation's resources. One could not expect that economic growth, and the updating of military hardware to existing state-of-the-art hardware, would be sacrificed in favor of the environment. The problem was compounded by the shortage of skilled professionals in the environmental field and the fact that it would take several years to complete in-country training. Therefore the Department, faced with limited funds and personnel resources, had to choose a program of selective environmental control strategies. Due to the lack of general public awareness, coupled with the updating of warfare technology and expanding economic development, the relative merits of air pollution control were overlooked. In 1979, the Islamic Revolution disrupted all the environmental programs for a period of five years as the Iraq-Iran War escalated.

Environmental Policy and Regulations Under the Islamic Republic

Article 50 of the Constitution of the Islamic Republic of Iran reads:

It is the duty of every individual in the Islamic Republic, to protect the environment so that present and future generations would be able to realize their potential growth. Therefore, any economic or other activities which cause environmental pollution or deterioration are prohibited. (Environmental Laws and Regulations, 1993: 1.)

1. Regulations on Water Pollution

In 1984, the Council of Ministers passed a resolution prohibiting the pollution of Iranian waters, including surface waters, rivers, underground water, lakes, sea, and the Caspian and Persian Gulf shores. It specified water pollutants such as human or animal waste, soil of any kind, ashes, animal corpses, city or industrial refuse, chemical and biological waste, sewer water, and hospital waste. Waterfront parks, campgrounds, tourist attractions, and lakeside picnic areas were also included under the water pollution control resolution (Environmental Laws and Regulations, 1993).

The 1984 Resolution defined the water pollution standard at a specified allowable level determined in accordance with the principle of maintenance and enhancement of the environment.

Safe water pollution standards were specified for industries which produced essential goods or services for daily consumption, with a provision to employ the best available technology to minimize water pollution. It clearly defined environmental violations and penalties.

2. Regulations on Air Pollution

With the exception of changes in administrative personnel and enforcement mechanisms, the 1974-1975 air pollution regulations remained as the standing air pollution laws of the nation under the Islamic Republic. Minor clarifications of the various sources of air pollution and penalties for violators have been added to the existing laws.

In addition to mobile sources of pollution, heavy industries such as petroleum refineries, cement, copper, aluminum, and steel smelters, and a number of chemical and petrochemical plants, contribute to the deterioration in the quality of the environment. Since Iranian houses are constructed with steel beams and bricks instead of lumber, there are thousands of brick-making incinerators in operation on the outskirts of the major cities. The majority of these brick-making plants use crude refinery by-products which produce heavy black smoke and release black particles into the air.

One would expect that the enforcement of the National Clean Air Regulations of 1975 would alleviate air pollution. However, air quality continued to deteriorate and automobiles and factories continued to be the major sources. This can readily be detected from Iran's environmental protection goals presented at the Rio Earth Summit, which convey an impression of being just a start in the air pollution battle.

Iran's Environmental Goals Presented at the 1992 Rio Earth Summit

The main purpose of the Earth Summit was two-fold: First, to control CO_2 emissions in accordance with emission reduction rates, in order to slow the global warming trend. Second, to protect biodiversity, or simply to protect endangered species. It is worth noting that third world countries, including Iran, were hopeful that developed countries would finance the implementation of the poorer countries' environmental protection projects (Goodstein, 1995).

Iran presented a comprehensive national environmental report at the Summit. The report was composed of: (1) the status of Iran's land, water and human resources and the sources of environmental pollution; (2) a number of projects designed to improve the quality of the environment; and (3) Iran's cooperation with the world environmental protection agencies. The proposed environmental projects fall into four categories (National Report, 1993):

1. Public Awareness Projects

In an effort to increase public awareness of environmental issues, the Iranian Government declared its intention to engage in the following projects:

  a. build new, and expand existing, libraries as environmental information banks;
  b. print and distribute environmental publications and conference proceedings;
  c. purchase and produce film and video tapes related to environmental updates;
  d. establish short- and long-term environmental learning classes and training centers.

The proposed budget is estimated at 550 million Rials.

2. Research Projects

Environmental research was emphasized as the essential means of learning how to control pollution growth. With the aid of related departments in major universities and skilled professionals, the following research projects were to be conducted:

  a. measuring and recording surface and ground water pollution;
  b. solid waste management in populated cities;
  c. reduction of industrial and mobile air pollutants in the four most populated provinces;
  d. recycling industrial waste water in five provinces;
  e. reduction of air and sound pollution in Tehran;
  f. survey of physical, biological and chemical characteristics of the Iranian sea shores;
  g. environmental impact of economic development on future generations;
  h. establishment of environmental research facilities; and
  i. restoration and expansion of natural recreation parks and wild habitats.

The environmental research projects were estimated to cost 3,522 million Rials.

3. Pollution Control and Surveillance Projects

The report recognized that it was the prime responsibility of the Iranian government to put in place the mechanisms for enforcing the environmental laws of the country. To ensure full compliance, enforcement activities were to have an adequate budget, a mechanism for inspection procedures and detection, and punishment of violators.

Specifically, these projects were intended to use the environmental enforcement laws to prevent the establishment of any damaging industry or workshop, and any potential damage to the ecosystem and wildlife. The costs of these projects were estimated at 100 million Rials.

4. Environmental Protection Projects

The aim of these projects was to expand and enhance Tehran's Natural Park into a "nature's paradise." The park was portrayed as a "man-made" paradise with natural landscaping, an aquarium, an attractive botanic garden, a wild-life park, and a natural science center for studying and exchanging scientific information. The park would also have (1) a control and monitoring center for environmental pollutants; (2) a museum of natural history; and (3) toxicity workshops. These projects would cost 1,500 million Rials.

Evaluation of Iran's Environmental Policy and Implementation

1. Air Pollution

At the present time, there are no subways or rapid transit systems in Iran. The main means of transportation is by private automobiles. Overcrowded city buses are used by those who cannot afford to own cars. There is serious traffic congestion on the major cities' highways and streets, due to the increasing numbers of automobiles and inadequate roads and highways. This causes excessive air pollution in large cities. Forty percent of all automobiles in Iran are driven in Tehran.

The 1974 air pollution laws, and added amendments, cover every type and source of air pollution. The penalties for air pollution in excess of the standards set by law are clear and specific. Implementation of these laws, however, is handicapped by lagging clean air technology, budgetary problems, and general noncompliance.

The present environmental deterioration in Iran, as indicated by recent studies, reveals that none of the above projects presented in Rio has been implemented, although it is evident that Iran has faced the challenges of environmental issues and has adopted a comprehensive environmental protection program. The implementation of these programs has been carried out only to the extent of available resources, expertise, the state of technology, and compliance. In fact, the last few pages of the

1992 Economic Report of the Islamic Republic of Iran, gives only a brief account of the protection of biodiversity. The section ends with this statement: "Needless to say the Environmental Protection Organization is faced with financial difficulties due to rising prices and the employment of expertise" (Annual Economic Report, 1991: 596). There is no mention of any fund to be allocated to the program. Nor is there any indication of implementing the detailed projects presented at the Earth Summit.

Just how successful has Iran been in its environmental protection programs? One way to measure the extent of its success is to review recent studies on environmental problems and issues, as reported by Iranian environmental specialists and scholars, and reliable eyewitness accounts.

2. Use of Poisons in Iranian Agriculture

Iran is largely dependent on the use of pesticides for the control of agricultural pests (Saha, 1993). The annual use of pesticides and herbicides has been successful in reducing crop loss and increasing strategic agricultural products, geared towards agricultural self-sufficiency. It has also been reported that 30% of Iran's agricultural production is lost due to various pests and weeds (National Report, 1992). A recent study on sustainable agricultural development and policy in Iran reports that in 1992 alone, 605,000 kilograms of poisons were used for weed elimination and three groups of pest control in Fars Province (E. Karami, 1992). In addition, the amount of chemical poisons used in the preceding years and in the years 1993 to the present leaves no doubt as to their seepage into the ground water supply and nearby surfaces. The same study indicates that there has been a seasonal appearance of a large number of dead fish on the surface of the rivers which receive agricultural irrigation run-off. Poisons used in Iranian agriculture are chlorites (known as DDT, DDE, DDD, and their family derivatives), insecticides (phosphate poisons), and herbicides (2,4-d and 2,4,S-D).

Chlorites (pesticides) are the most dangerous agricultural poisons known to the environment. These poisons remain in the environment for as long as fifteen years. When poisons are absorbed by animal and human fat tissues, they are very difficult to eliminate, and often do not break down or deteriorate easily. Rather, poisons accumulate in living tissues and enter the food chain cycle. This process is called Biological Magnification. Another problem with this group of pesticides is that after a few applications, most pests develop an immunity to the poison and the evolving species become more difficult to eradicate (B. Karimi, 1994). A study of the effects of DDT on red scales which grow on citrus fruits indicates that after a few DDT spray applications, red scales increased from 36 to 463 times (B. Karimi, 1994).

Phosphate poisons (insecticides) are the most popular poisons against insects in Iran. The effects of these poisons last from one to twelve weeks. In some cases, the effects may last several years. In animals and humans the effects are more serious and long lasting.

Weed killers (herbicides) are also one of the most widely used poisons. The effects lasts from a few days to several weeks. The effects of herbicides on humans are less severe than the two previously mentioned poisons.

Major problems arising from the increasing and indiscriminate use of pesticides in crop production have been the residue of these contaminants in plant and plant products. Further problems are due to deleterious effects on the pests' natural enemies, pest resistance to pesticides, an outbreak of secondary pests, and the adverse effects on health and the environment (E. Karami, 1992). The majority of Iranian farmers are ignorant of the hazards associated with the indiscriminate use of pesticides. Excessive use and dosage of pesticides for immediate results while not observing an adequate time interval before harvest—especially with short duration crops such as vegetables and fruits—are common. This is mainly due to lack of education and proper training in the safe and efficient use of pesticides (E. Karami, 1992).

Researchers recommend that Iran should follow the Integrated Pest Management (IPM) program of FAO. Accordingly, Iran should: a) make farmers aware of the undesirable effects of pesticides, including the development of pest species resistant to pesticides, upsurge of primary and secondary pests, human health hazards, and contamination of the environment; b) develop an effective system of pest control training workshops and communication of pest control strategies to farmers; c) conduct research on developing crop varieties that have durable resistance to various crop pests (B. Karimi, 1994); d) organize nationwide surveillance and forecasting systems for timely and effective pest control; and e) develop and supplement relevant biological and physical pest control practices (Saha, 1993).

3. Application of Chemical Fertilizer

The decline in Iranian agricultural productivity and heavy reliance on food imports are to a large extent caused by the use of modern fertilizer, which has scorched the thin Iranian soil (Iran, 1989). In 1949, the first fertilizer production factory began operation in Northern Tehran. It produced between 4 to 5 tons of chemical fertilizer a year. Five years later, Iran began to import fertilizer containing 100 tons of nitrate ammonium, 100 tons of sulfate ammonium, and 50 tons of sulphur phosphate. By 1987, the imports of these three chemicals increased to 32,000, 42,000, and 2,000 tons, respectively. In addition, there were 747,000 tons of Urea, and 908,000 tons of diammonium phosphate (Karimian, 1992: 435-436). These figures show that the use of chemical fertilizer increased from 5,000 tons to 1,700,000 tons in a 50-year span, while there was no significant aggregate increase in Iran's agricultural land in that same period.

A study on the trend of tree farming population and the land under cultivation from 1960 to 1988 shows that the number of farmers declined from 15,994,000 to 13,389,000 and the land under cultivation fell from 16,000,000 to 15,660,000 hectares (Raesdana, 1993).

The increase in the application of chemical fertilizer has resulted not only in the decline of agricultural production but also in a change in the balance of the nutritious ingredients of the soil. The adverse impact of applying excessive phosphate chemical fertilizer has not been limited to the quality and quantity of agricultural production. Chemical fertilizer has been one of the major elements responsible for the contamination of the ground water sources in Iran.

4. Pollution of Water and Land Resources by Industries

In the last two decades Iran has witnessed an impressive growth of 100% in the nation's industries. Although this increase has resulted in economic growth and employment, it has also contributed to the deterioration of the environment. There are five major cities with 600 active industrial units. According to the National Report of 1992, 23 new industrial cities have been established.

Major sources of land and water pollution are industrial wastes discharged into rivers, streams and lakes. There are two major problems associated with river pollution. First, the wetlands at the river terminals that serve as habitats for many different land and water species are contaminated. Second, the ground water along the river, used for drinking and domestic use by settlers who live along the riverbanks, poses potential health risks due to contamination.

In 1995, comprehensive studies were conducted by specialists on the environmental impact of industrial and agricultural pollutants on water resources. The purpose was to determine whether the pollution of Iranian waters by hazardous liquids and solid wastes has surpassed the limits set by regulatory standards. The areas of investigation were Lake Maharloo and the Korr River in the southern province, and the Black River in the northern province of Iran. It should be noted that there are other lakes, rivers, and water streams which have been polluted as a result of population growth and urban and industrial expansion. These water resources were chosen because of their uniqueness and also because they have been subjected to human and industrial abuse for many years.

The Maharloo Salt Lake

In the southwest of Shiraz, a major city in the Southern Iranian Province, there is a salt lake tributary called Lake Maharloo with a surface area of 31 by 11 kilometers. The age of the lake is estimated at over 20,000 years and the beginning of salt accumulation dates back to 1,000 years ago. For centuries it has been providing salt for human consumption and industrial use. Accumulated salt in the lake is estimated at 50 million tons. In 1984 the quantity of salt taken from the lake for industrial use was 150,000 tons, and for human consumption 30,000 tons (Koochmeshkian, 1994).

Since the surrounding agricultural land, villages, and cities are on higher ground level, household, sewer and industrial waste water find their way into the lake. In addition, the lake is a terminal point for canals which carry rain, flood water and agricultural run-off from the nearby cities and farmland.

Several seasonal rivers terminate at the lake. The largest containing harmful pollutants is the Shiraz Dry River, which carries raw sewer water from Shiraz and other cities to the lake. Before discharging into the lake, much of the sewer water is used to irrigate nearby farms. During winter and spring the flood water carries all the accumulated refuse, solid and liquid wastes, and polluted run-off from the surrounding cities to the lake.

In 1991, a study was conducted on the absorption of hazardous elements by vegetables produced along the river. Of 920 hectares of farmland, 282 hectares were irrigated with the well water near the river and 170 hectares with the raw sewer water directly from the river. The study found that, despite government sanctions against the use of raw sewer water for farming, most farmers irrigate their land with raw sewage to avoid the cost of fertilizer and electric power to pump ground water. The study also found that in each liter of raw sewer water there were 100 milligrams of BOD and 200 milligrams of COD. In addition there was a considerable amount of heavy metal, such as cadmium, cobalt, nickel, lead, and copper. These elements which had accumulated in the land for years were eventually absorbed by the vegetables slated for human consumption (Koochmeshkian, 1994).

No study has yet been done to determine the exact level of arsenic in the sewer water entering the Shiraz Dry River. Traditional toiletries, most especially Iranian-made hair removing creams used in public and private baths, contain high levels of arsenic. The arsenic content of the sewer run-off has been reported in environmental studies.

Another major polluter of the Shiraz Dry River is the Namazi Hospital, one of the largest health-care facilities in the Fars Province. In the summer of 1993, the author observed that the hospital refuse and solid wastes were being dumped in the river. In June 1996, two designated independent eye-witnesses reported that the hospital no longer dumps the solid wastes but continues to discharge the raw liquid wastes into the river. The results have been ground water contamination and absorption of radioactive material by farm vegetables and by the salt lake. Again, eyewitness reports indicated that despite repeated government warnings through the media on the hazardous elements in the Maharloo Salt Lake, some bakeries and restaurants purchase their salt in large quantities from this source at a much cheaper price than salt peddlers.

Polluted waters entering the lake have been contaminating it for many years. The recent concerns for environmental safety as exhibited by both local and international environmentalists have prompted researchers to conduct studies on the contents of the lake. In 1995, similar studies were conducted by the Environmental Organization, Petrochemical Department, College of Science, University of Shiraz, the Department of Standards, and the Department of Health and Remedy. The elements found in the lake include iron, copper, lead, and arsenic. In addition there were chromium, cadmium, nickel, mercury, cobalt, molybdenum, magnesium, nitrogen, and phosphorus. The lake water has a distinct odor of household and public bath sewer water, with floating algae forming near the shore. The salt is formed in the shallow areas of the lake during the summer as water evaporates. It has a yellowish-brown color.

Findings of these studies are comparable, each showing the amount of harmful elements in the salty water and in the extracted salts. Based on the Codex International Standards, consumption of the salt extracted from Maharloo Salt Lake is hazardous to human health (Koochmeshkian, 1994).

The Korr River

This river is one of the major rivers of the Fars Province. It originates from the Zagros Mountain Range and terminates in Bakhtegan Lake. The length of the river is 280 kilometers. It is considered the lifeline of Fars' and is essential for urban development, industrial expansion and the quantity and quality of agricultural products. The river water is used for agriculture, household consumption, drinking, industrial activities, recreation, transportation and generation of electricity. It supports 204 agricultural units with a population of 241,338, and irrigates 40,000 acres. The main products are grains, beans. alfalfa, potato, rice, and sugar beets. The total annual water used for irrigation is 415,716,380 cubic meters. Upstream, settlers along the riverbank use 30,000,000 cubic meters of the river's water for domestic and drinking purposes. The estimate on the industrial use ranges between 13 to 15 million cubic meters (B. Karimi, 1994).

Pollution of the river stems from human, industrial, agricultural, and animal sources. Since the ground water level is high, the traditional septic well, designed to absorb solid waste and sewer water, is not practical. Therefore, cities and communities around the river have dug canals of different widths to carry the sewer and waste water down to agricultural farm land. For houses with septic wells, commercial tanker trucks pump out the waste and carry it away. The tankers discharge the waste further down in the river. Furthermore, rain and floodwater wash down city refuse, motor oil on roads, contaminated substances, and exhaust residuals on pavements and structures to the river. The settlers along the river use it for bathing, washing household items and clothes, animals, and cars. They also use the river as a garbage dump.

The polluting industries along the river include a petrochemical plant, a slaughtering and meat packing complex, a food processing facility and cannery, a leather factory, plastic and sheet metal manufacturing units, a biscuit factory, a sugar factory, and a flour mill. The human and industrial sewer water from these factories goes through biological filtration systems and out to the canals which carry the filtered sewer water to the farmland. During the rainy season when there is no need for irrigation, the sewer water enters the river through these canals.

a) Pollution of water by organic matter. Animal parts that are discarded after the animals are slaughtered are not fully filtered and the waste water from these establishments does not meet environmental standards. Most of the discarded animal parts are carried away by tanker trucks to a dumpsite. This system of disposal poses a threat to human health and constitutes a hazard to the environment. The slaughtering houses should install a system to grind, dust, and treat the discarded animal remains for safe disposal.

b) Petrochemical pollutants. The petrochemical plant has 3,100 employees and is the first chemical fertilizer manufacturing complex in Iran. The complex uses natural gas, calcium rocks, table salt, phosphoric acid, sodium sulfate and other chemical elements as raw materials. It produces liquid and solid ammonia, urea, nitric acid, ammonium nitrate, sodium phosphate, sodium carbonate, sodium bicarbonate, agricultural and explosive ammonium nitrate, liquid chlorine, and hydrochloric acid. The waste water from the petrochemical complex contains hazardous elements. The water goes through a biological filtration system before eventually discharging into the river. Its high ammonium content, however, destroys animal life, reduces the oxygen in the water and causes the growth of algae detrimental to animal reproduction on the river bottom. The most harmful element to the environment, however, is the mercury in the sewer water. The petrochemical complex has not made any effort to devise a method of extracting the mercury element. As a result, this poisonous element has been entering the farmland and agricultural food by way of the Korr River (B. Karimi, 1994).

c) The leather manufacturing plants. Next to the slaughtering houses are several plants that manufacture leather from sheepskin and cowhide. The plants use chemical substances to process the hides. In addition, animal hairs, wool, skin trims, fat, salt, and excess chemicals enter the sewer water. In each liter of the sewer water discharged by the plants there are eight milligrams of these elements. The hazardous pollutants are chrome and organic elements from animal skins.

d) Pollution of the river by large appliance manufacturing units. These plants use 17 different chemicals to produce water pumps, electric motors, freezers, refrigerators, portable coolers, washer and dryers. The waste water is stored in underground septic tanks and periodically pumped out by tanker trucks. It is believed that the tanker trucks discharge the content into the Korr River downstream.

e) Heavy metals in the Korr River. Metals with a density equal to or greater than iron are known as heavy metals. Although cadmium and arsenic are lighter than iron, because of their poisonous nature and their hazardous potential to the environment, they are also classified as heavy metals. Heavy metals possess certain unique characteristics. When ingested by humans or animals, they remain in the fat, bones or other tissues of the host. When introduced into water, the poisonous capability of heavy metals expands. Mixed with other heavy metals, the collective effects are far greater than the sum of the individual effects. The main sources of heavy metal pollution in the Korr River are the petrochemical complex, leather manufacturing plants, and heavy home appliance factories.

Mercury from the petrochemical plant's waste discharge has been deposited in the bottom of septic tanks for years. The company intends to devise a method of collecting the deposits in the form of solid cakes by 1996 and burying them so that the mercury will have no chance of entering the river.

Analysis of the sewer water from the leather factories and heavy appliance manufacturing plants has not been encouraging. The chromium in each liter of waste water was found to be about 6.34, an amount far above the allowable standard. Further, since the sewer water is used for agriculture, heavy metal residues are absorbed by the agricultural products (B. Karimi, 1994).

The Black River

In 1995 the Black River was the subject of intensive research by a group of Iranian scientists and environmental specialists. This river has been a convenient site for the factories and plants to dump and discharge their solid and liquid wastes for years. Ironically, this river once was referred to as the White River. It originates from the Alborz Range in the north and terminates in the Caspian Sea. The water from the Black River is used solely for agricultural purposes. The pollutants are sewer water from residences and industrial plants, and run-off from agricultural irrigation which is polluted with chemical fertilizer, pesticides and insecticides. The river has become a dumping site for all sorts of hazardous wastes (Karbassi et al., 1995).

A survey of the river water was done in 1985 to determine the impact of the water pollution on the ecology of the surrounding area. Since the river enters the Caspian Sea, biological and ecological changes in the region were of primary concern. It was concluded that in due time the pollution would have distinct adverse effects on the species that inhabit the water.

The 1995 research was conducted to determine the levels of heavy metals such as manganese, zinc, chromium, copper, lead, calcium, and iron, deposited in the Black River bed and compare these with tests done in similar environmental conditions in Japan, England, and Scotland. Chemical analysis of fourteen samples from the riverbed showed that at the delta, heavy metal and poisonous elements were far above allowable standards and the marine life in the Caspian Sea was threatened

(Karbassi et al., 1995). The possibility of other dangers include, but are not limited to, contamination of agricultural products and ground water in the vicinity of the Black River. The researchers strongly recommended the installation of a filtering station and the burying of the heavy metal and other poisonous substances in a suitable site.

4. Health-Care Waste Management

The term health-care waste refers to all infectious and hazardous wastes produced in health-care facilities. In addition to domestic-type wastes, hospitals across the country produce problematic wastes that cause environmental pollution and carry the risk of transmission of infectious diseases.

There are as many as 80,300 hospital beds in Iran, 27,200 of which are in Tehran. In addition, there are 3,000 health-care centers in that city. According to Baghaii (1991), each bed produces an average of 3.14 kilograms, or an aggregate of 505 tons, of waste each day.

In 1993, the Institute of Environmental Studies at the University of Tehran, under the direction of M.A. Abduli, engaged in a study on hospital waste management in Tehran. A field investigation of 133 hospitals with a total of 26,682 beds was conducted involving a survey of all steps taken in waste management inside and outside hospitals. The Institute found that:

a. the interim and the central waste storage areas are not designed and constructed for proper waste management;

b. in almost all of the hospitals, wastes are separated illegally and in an unsanitary manner, and some disposable items such as gloves are separated and sold elsewhere;

c. radioactive wastes are found in the domestic-type wastes;

d. no special attention is paid to the possible transmission of infectious disease and rapid deterioration of hospital wastes;

e. in the summer and winter seasons, the frequency of waste collection is once a day and in a large percentage of cases, pests, rodents and other disease-carrying animals infest the waste; and

f. no distinction is made between pathological and domestic-type wastes, and no hygienic and legal recycling program exists in the hospitals (Abduli, 1994).

The Institute's recommendations called for: (1) enactment and enforcement of laws and regulations concerning all functional elements of hospital waste management; (2) development of organizational structure within the hospitals for a proper system of solid waste management; and (3) continual training programs for hospital custodians and their supervisors regarding quality, quantity, composition, and proper classification and disposal of hospital waste (Abduli, 1994).

All the hospital wastes in Tehran, with the exception of a small percentage which is incinerated, are transported to the Kahrizak landfill, 35 km south of Tehran. In other cities hospital wastes are handled in a more dangerous manner than in Tehran.

5. Exposure to Lead

Lead has been known to cause birth defects and developmental problems in children, and heart disease and stroke in adults. Lead, a component of gasoline, is emitted into the air when the fuel is burned in automobile engines.

Due to high tariffs on new automobiles and the high price of domestically produced automobiles, the majority of cars are old and use leaded gasoline. In order to determine whether those exposed to lead particles in the air are at risk, research was conducted in 1982 by Farsam, Sallari, and Nadeem, under the guidance of the Institute of Public Health Research, University of Tehran. The study sampled 228 police officers who control traffic in the streets and 68 officers who have desk duties in the precincts.

The average amount of lead found in the blood of the traffic officers was significantly higher than that of the other officers. Since no correlation was found between other variables and the blood lead content of the traffic officers, the study concluded that lead emissions from motor vehicles were the sole cause of high lead concentration in the blood of the traffic officers (Farsam et al., 1982).

6. Soil Erosion

Spurred by both population growth and the rising standard of living, Iran's demand for food increases each year. The increasing demand has resulted in increased cultivation of Iran's already limited agricultural land, thus accelerating the rate of soil erosion. To achieve agricultural self-sufficiency, farmers have been pushed into steeply sloping, already erosive land which is rapidly losing its topsoil. Due to the lack of sufficient irrigation water, 66% of the grains are produced by dry farming on hillsides with an average slope of 20%. This has contributed to a substantial loss in natural nutrients.

The Iranian National Report on land erosion indicates that soil erosion has been increasing. The report attributes loss of topsoil to desertification, deforestation, overgrazing, removal of natural land vegetation cover, hillside dry farming, abuse of agricultural land, and poor land management by the Iranian officials.

Another report indicates that 125 million hectares of Iranian land are under threat of land erosion and 1.5 billion tons of topsoil are moved to other locations each year (Monnavari, 1994). It is estimated that the annual siltation of Iranian reservoirs is 100,000,000 cm, the loss of cropland topsoil is 1,500,000,000 cm, and the average annual loss of soil nutrients is 117 kilograms (National Report, 1992).

7. Desertification

In Iran there are 90 million hectares of pasture land, of which only 14,000 hectares are good grazing land. The grazing quality of the remainder of the land ranges from poor to fair. On the other hand, there are some 99 million head of livestock of which 60 million depend solely on grazing land for food. The entire grazing land can support 15 million head of livestock. In other words, Iran's pastures are grazed four times more heavily than they should be. This situation accelerates the deterioration of Iran's grazing land into desert (National Report, 1994).

Sustainable Development and the Quality of Life

When one looks at the often overwhelming and interrelated problems of environmental degradation, unemployment, poverty, and population growth, Iran's hopes for a brighter future seem dim. Population explosion, ecological degradation, and depletion of the country's natural resources have been undermining sustainability at the cost of future generations.

The term sustainable development gained widespread recognition in 1987 with the publication of a book by the United Nations entitled *Our Common Future*, also known as the Bruntland Commission (Goodstein, 1995). Since then the concept of sustainability has been defined and redefined. Considering intergenerational justice, sustainable development must benefit both current and future generations. In the words of Theodore Panayotou:

> "Sustainable development must benefit both current and future generations. Sustainability requires alleviation of poverty, a decline in fertility, the substitution of human capital for natural resources, effective demand for environmental quality and the responsive supply". (Panayotou, 1993: 141.)

Using the Panayolou definition of sustainability and the outline of the Bruntland Commission report as a measuring tool, it is apparent that Iran has not been able to meet the criteria of sustainability.

1. Population and Human Resources

In 1995 Iran's population reached 67 million with a growth rate of 3.6 percent. It is estimated that Iran's population will reach over 100 million by the year 2000 (National Trade Data Bank, 1994). It is not difficult to see that the country is already experiencing serious problems in maintaining its current infrastructure, housing, food, and educational facilities. Millions of people apply to the institutions of higher learning, but because of the limited number of institutions, only a fraction of applicants is accepted. Therefore entrance examinations are designed to be especially difficult in the hope that a large number of people become discouraged and do not apply to the institutions. This is especially hard on the female population who are motivated by their aspirations to advance themselves to socially respectable positions and enjoy financial independence. Instead, women surrender to arranged marriages and live a subordinate life. The lower the level of education in Iranian social groups, the higher is the supremacy of men over women and the more frequent is the practice of polygyny. The quality of life for the woman and consequently for the children in such households is bound to be poor and full of hardships.

To accommodate for its rapidly growing population, Iran must increase investment in infrastructure, food production, housing, and educational facilities by about 33 percent by the year 2000. Alternatively, Iran could reduce its rate of population growth to zero thus allowing the economy to grow at a sustainable rate.

2. Food Security

For nearly two decades, Iran has been struggling to restore agricultural self-sufficiency. Up to 1970 Iran was self-sufficient in food supply and exported its surplus to neighboring countries. Today, not only does the prospect of achieving food self-sufficiency look dim, but there is also convincing evidence that Iran will be permanently dependent upon imports of foodstuffs (McLachlin, 1988).

Proponents of the law of comparative advantage argue that Iran has an absolute advantage in the production of mineral resources such as oil. It is also argued that since Iran has abundant oil resources, its food shortages can be resolved simply by trading food for oil. Natural gas, copper, lead, and internationally marketable items such as Persian rugs and pistachio nuts can finance the import of equipment needed for development.

This argument, though seemingly valid at face value, has its shortcomings. First, it does not consider the long-term implications of mineral resources-for-food trade. Irreplaceable underground resources will eventually be depleted. These resources should be used to promote economic growth and long-term investments. There is a growing need to preserve much of Iran's natural/capital resources for the benefit of future generations. Second, Iran is already trading natural resources for food imports, and the demand for food continues to exceed the supply, resulting in a widening gap between available food items and food consumption (Zekavat, 1996).

3. Lack of Clean Technology

If population growth continues at the present rate, Iranian children will age in a country whose population has doubled. It is inconceivable to imagine Iran in the future having twice as many automobiles, coal and oil-fired power plants, hazardous liquid and solid wastes, and air pollution. Today, the major cities have reached an intolerable level of air and water pollution, and the amount of land devoted to housing and agriculture is increasing.

The development of clean energy and manufacturing technologies in Iran is a prerequisite for a sustainable future. Currently, the average age of automobiles driven on the Iranian highways and streets is between 15 to 20 years. The Islamic Republic has made it nearly impossible to import new automobiles by imposing very high tariffs. Iranian-made automobiles use foreign-made engines and the parts to these engines are equally hard and expensive to get. A car appreciates in value as it gets older due to the high rate of inflation.

Iran has a long and difficult road ahead. It has to stabilize its population growth, raise income levels, and develop new and clean technologies and make them available to the people.

4. Declining Net National Welfare

A recent method of measuring the overall welfare or good quality of life is called net national welfare (NNW). This method incorporates changes in the consumption of goods and services and environmental quality, measured on a per capita basis. Therefore, as an indirect way to determine whether the natural resources of the country are being conserved, one can use the sustainable development criterion by showing that NNW for the great majority of the Iranian population has not and will not fall over time. The variables used in the computation of NNW include gross domestic product and non-market output minus such items as depreciation of both natural and created capital, pollution abatement, environmental health and clean-up, and externality costs (Goodstein, 1995).

The question arises: Has Iran's NNW per capita risen during the last 15 years? Although the precise measurement of NNW is not possible due to a lack of relevant data for the variables mentioned above, the evidence indicates that it has not.

There are several major problems in measuring NNW in Iran. First, there is no quantitative account of the depreciation of natural capital. Second, there are no studies showing the link between certain health problems and environmental degradation. Third, the value placed on life is very low in Iran. Iranians hold a fatalistic view of life. That is, whatever happens to a person is his or her fate; this life is not meant to be happy. For the religiously virtuous, a happy life begins after death. Fourth, a realistic estimation of pollution abatement, environmentally related health problems, and clean-up costs is relevant only if serious steps are taken to control environmental pollution. Just how bad the quality of life has been for Iranians due to environmental degradation is difficult to determine through the net national welfare formula.

In Iranian culture, quality of life is synonymous with a good standard of living. It involves an adequate quantity and quality of food and employment. The chances of attaining these values necessary for a good standard of living are being increasingly and seriously diminished by a high rate of population growth and runaway inflation at 30 to 50 percent. Once population growth is halted and inflation is controlled, prudent use of natural resources should ultimately result in the enhancement of the overall welfare of the average Iranian across all generations.

Participation in International Environmental Protection Conventions

Iran has participated in international conventions and protocols and has signed agreements on a number of global environmental issues. The main conventions and protocols include the Montreal Protocol on the problem of ozone layer reduction in 1987; Protection of the ozone layer in Vienna, 1985; the Kuwait Protocols on sea water pollution by oil due to off-shore drilling and pumping in 1978 and 1989; prohibition of international transaction of plants and animal species which are on the verge of extinction, held in Washington, 1973; Paris Convention on the preservation of the world's cultural and natural inheritance, 1972; International Convention to prevent production, spread and use of chemical and biological warfare, 1972; Paris Protocol on protection of the water-bird habitats, 1982; and the Earth Summit in Rio De Janeiro, 1992 (National Report, 1992).

At the 1992 Earth Summit, Iran issued a statement of full cooperation with international environmental organizations and signed an agreement on a list of environmental protection issues. The list included the development and use of biological pest control, reduction of chemical pollutants such as pesticides and chemical fertilizers in agriculture to a safe level, and preventing the discharge of pollutants into the Caspian Sea (National Report, 1992). The report further stated that Iran has been a member of 140 United Nations organizations with good standing, and full cooperation and participation in global environmental problems. According to the same statement, Iran has sponsored a number of seminars and conferences on global environmental issues. The country designated nine regions for wild life preservation.

Iran, like other developing countries, expects monetary assistance and aid from rich nations for a simple reason: The earth has been polluted for years by developed countries while they were experiencing economic development and industrialization. It is now Iran's turn to pursue its economic development. The accomplished nations are expected to shoulder part, if not all, of the costs for global environmental protection.

Conclusion and Recommendation

Based on the evidence presented in this study, Iran has been facing local and global environmental challenges created by its developmental activities. Since early 1970, Iranian officials have been aware of the environmental problems and have enacted detailed environmental policies and regulations with implementing organizations. The actual prevention and enforcement measures, however, have been lacking.

The inability of Iranian officials to control the environment is due to (1) poor enforcement programs; (2) lack of public awareness and noncompliance of firms and individuals with policies and regulations; and (3) budget appropriation priorities in areas other than the environment. The paper further confirms that the NNW and hence the quality of life in Iran has been on the decline and will continue to worsen for years to come.

In promoting environmental protection, the role of the Iranian Government, both under the monarchy and the Islamic Republic regimes, has been one of direct command-and-control rather than one of fostering competition, efficiency, and conservation through market mechanisms. The Iranian landscape, water, air, and atmosphere, which are essential elements of the quality of life, have been considered public goods or everybody's property and kept outside the domain of the markets. The consequence has been waste, inefficiency, resource depletion and environmental degradation. Iran can break the link between its industrial growth and environmental degradation by promoting a consistent structure of market-based economic incentives and disincentives rather than bureaucratic command-and-control regulations; in other words, polluters of the environment or beneficiaries of natural resources would pay the social and development costs of their wealth.

Rapid population growth at a rate of 3.6% has undercut Iran's sustainable developmental efforts. It has also deprived Iran of the benefits of economic growth and a better quality of life. At the same time it has been burdening the nation with resource depletion, environmental degradation, and ecological disturbance. Sustainable growth with desired quality of life can be achieved if Iran reduces its population growth to a zero rate and adopts and enforces corrective environmental protection policies.

Environmental degradation and the failure to achieve sustainable growth stem from the value judgments of the two regimes in their budgetary prioritization. The Shah was preoccupied with westernization and attainment of military supremacy in the Middle East, and the Islamic Republic has been obsessed with spreading and exporting the Islamic revolution to other Islamic countries, and providing financial support to such causes.

In any political system where the chain of command is dictatorial rather than democratic, a demand for environmental protection can only be expressed through government action. The key issue under the present system of government has two sides: Do Iranians show serious concern for environmental degradation and demand protection? And, does the Islamic Republic respond effectively to this kind of demand and provide protection? Affirmative answers to these two questions are the necessary ingredients for a successful environmental policy. We do not yet have the answers.

Acknowledgments

The author thanks Professor Emeritus Yahya Zekavat of the University of Shiraz, Iran for his assistance in gathering and sending data and research references pertinent to this study, and Margaret Edwards for her assistance in copy editing.

REFERENCES

ABDULI, M.A.
　　1994 "Hospital Waste Management in Tehran." *Environmental Science and Health* A29 (3): 477-492.
BAGHAII, M.D.
　　1991 "Survey on the Collection and Disposal of Hospital Waste in Tehran." Medical University of Iran, Tehran, Technical Report (Farsi).
FARSAM, H., G. SALARI and A. NADIM
　　1982 "Absorption of Lead in Tehran Traffic Policemen." *American Industrial Hygiene Association Journal* 43 (5): 373-376.
GOODSTEIN, Eban S.
　　1995 *Economics and the Environment.* Englewood Cliffs, New Jersey: Prentice-Hall.
　　1989 *Iran: A Country Study.* Washington, D.C.: United States Government Printing Office (prepared by Foreign Area Studies, American University, under the auspices of the United States Department of Defense).
Islamic Republic of Iran, Environmental Protection Agency
　　1992 *National Report.* Tehran (Farsi).
Islamic Republic of Iran, Environmental Protection Agency
　　1993 *Environmental Laws and Regulations.* Tehran (Farsi).
Islamic Republic of Iran, Plan and Budget Organization
　　1991 *Annual Economic Report.* Tehran (Farsi).
KARAMI, E.
　　1992 "Sustainable Development and Agricultural Policy." Symposium on Economic Development and Agricultural Policy, University of Shiraz (Farsi; unpublished).
KARAMI, Yahya
　　1994 "An Investigation of Water Quality in the Korr and Sivant Rivers." First Annual Report, University of Shiraz, Environmental Management of Land and Water Resources (Farsi).
KARBASSI, A., M. ABDULI and N. MOEMENI
　　1995 "Concentration and Origin of Heavy Metal Deposits in the Black River Bed." *Scientific Journal of the Environment* 7 (2): 35-40 (Farsi).
KARIMI, B.M.
　　1994 "The Extent of the Use of Agricultural Poisons and Their Effect on the Environment." *Scientific Journal of the Environment* 7 (1): 76-80 (Farsi).
KARIMIAN, N.
　　1992 "Consideration of Land Nutrients in Applying Chemical Fertilizer." Symposium on Economic Development and Agricultural Policy, University of Shiraz (Farsi; unpublished).
KOOCHMESHKIAN, M.
　　1994 "A Study of the Quality of Salt from the Maharloo Lake." University of Shiraz, Environmental Evaluation of Water and Land Resources. First Year Report of the Investigation of the Status of the Maharloo Salt Lake (Farsi; funded by the Islamic Republic of Iran).

MCLACHLIN, Keith
    1988 *The Neglected Garden: The Politics and Ecology of Agriculture in Iran.* London: I.B. Tauris
        & Co., Ltd.
MONNAVARI, S.M.
    1994 "The Importance of Environmental Policies in the Nation's Development Program." *Scientific
        Journal of the Environment* 7 (2): 72-75 (Farsi).
PANAYOTOU, Theodore
    1993 *Green Markets: The Economics of Sustainable Development.* Co-published by the Interna-
        tional Center for Economic Growth and the Harvard Institute for International Development.
        San Francisco: Institute for Contemporary Studies Press.
RAESDANA, Farivars
    1993 "A Systematic Approach to Agricultural Development in Iran." Symposium on Economic
        Development and Agricultural Policy, University of Shiraz (Farsi; unpublished).
SAHA, P.K.
    1993 "Overview of Pest Control in Asia." Conference on Pest Control in Asia and the Pacific.
        Asian Productivity Organization, Tokyo, Japan.
SOUTHWICK, Charles H.
    1985 "The Biosphere." In: Charles H. Southwick (Ed.), *Global Ecology.* Sunderland, Mas-
        sachusetts: Sinauer Associates, Inc.: 1-4.
United States, Department of Commerce, Economics and Statistics Administration, Office of Business
        Analysis
    1997 The National Trade Data Bank (computer laser optical disks). Washington, D.C.
ZEKAVAT, S.M.
    1996 "An Economic Analysis of Agricultural Self-Sufficiency in Iran." Forthcoming in the *Atlantic
        Economic Journal.*
ZORBONIA, R., and SORAYA, B.
    1978 "Air Pollution Control in Iran." *Journal of the Air Pollution Control Association* 28 (4):
        334-337 (published in Iran in English).

Environmental Challenges in Lebanon

RANIA MASRI*

ABSTRACT

Lebanon is facing a multitude of environmental challenges. Symptoms of the environmental mismanagement in Lebanon include: dramatic soil erosion; a vulnerable, threatened agriculture; forests
that serve more as relics than as the needed economic, environmental and cultural contributions; a col-
lapsing fisheries industry; and an inadequate solid waste and wastewater treatment infrastructure. In
addition, almost all the waters in Lebanon are polluted, posing serious human health risks, and the air
quality in the congested, urban areas has reached detrimental levels. In response to these problems,
government involvement, non-governmental environmental organizations, and environmental awareness
are increasing, although they are still far from sufficient.

I. The Setting

THIS DOCUMENT aims to present the critical, imposing environmental
challenges facing Lebanon today. In so doing, a primarily negative portrayal of
Lebanon's environment is given. However, despite the ravages of war, occupation,
and centuries of environmental degradation, Lebanon remains embraced in its inherent, remarkable beauty: a tribute to the wonder of nature.

Lebanon, one of the smallest countries in the world, has been blessed with exceptional climatic and ecological diversity. The mountains and the Mediterranean
Sea tightly enclose the country, producing this diversity of micro-climates and land-
scapes. The mountains, overlooking the Mediterranean to the west and the Beka'a
valley to the east, run parallel to the 225 km coast and rise up to more than 3,000
meters. The Beka'a valley separates the Lebanon Mountains from the parallel Anti-
Lebanon range to the east, and serves as the source of two rivers, the Aasi (Orontes)
and the Litani, which flow north and south respectively.

The first official census in Lebanon since 1932 published 15 October, 1996
estimated the population of Lebanon at 3.11 million, exluding the 350,000 Palestinian refugees and the hundreds of thousands of non-Lebanese inhabitants (FTV,

* North Carolina State University, Raleigh, NC 27695, U.S.A.

15 October 1996; UPI, 15 October 1996). The annual population growth rate is approximately 2.2% (METAP, 1995). According to the latest UNDP survey, one million Lebanese (32%) are poor, including 250,000 living below the poverty line (UPI, 17 October 1996). Lebanon's poor are concentrated mainly in urban areas, and lack proper housing, health care and education. The Lebanese civil ware was cited among the primary reasons behind the impoverishment of the Lebanese population (UPI, 17 October, 1996).

During the past 20 years, the urban population has increased to more than 85% of the total population (Ayad, 1993), and is expected to reach almost 95% by the year 2025 (World Resources Institute, 1996). More than 50% of the population lives along the coastal zone, primarily Beirut and Tripoli, at a population density of 1,610 persons/km^2. Tripoli alone has a population density of 12,000 persons/km^2. The population density of Beirut, which houses approximately 30% of the population in the Greater Beirut Area, reaches 40,000 persons/km^2 in its inner circle. Outside the key urban areas, the population density is still high at 390 persons/km^2 (METAP, 1995). When compared with other countries, Lebanon's population density becomes apparent: Belgium at 330; India at 300; Sri Lanka at 277 (World Resources Institute, 1996).

These high population densities have evolved as a result of unplanned, uncontrolled development—partly a consequence of the war and ensuing deterioration of authority, and partly due to the high economic activity in the coastal urban centers. The rapid urbanization will increasingly concentrate both population and economic growth in the coastal cities, thus intensifying the problems of the urban environment and threatening the coastal ecosystems. Urbanization is expected to increase further, especially as tourism and private real-estate are encouraged.

The growth of the tourism sector,[1] concentrated primarily around the coast, will further degrade the environment. Currently, the coast is being transformed into a chaotic assortment of hotels and resorts. The urbanization trends towards unconfined sprawl and privatization of beaches, and the resulting increased demand on water supply (especially high during the peak tourism seasons) will damage the environment, and add pressure on an already inadequate infrastructure. Tourism is an industry strongly dependent on the aesthetics and health of the environment. Thus, in the long run, the consequential environmental damage, brought on by unregulated tourism industries, will harm tourism's own interests and cause a decline in the industry.

Historical Factors

Lebanon has been exposed to a succession of occupying forces throughout its history. Lebanon was under Ottoman rule for 400 years until 1917, when the French mandate was imposed until 1943. The creation of Israel on the land of Palestine in 1948 triggered an influx of Palestinian refugees into Lebanon, and resulted in the Israeli occupation of several southern Lebanese villages, changing Lebanon's land area from 10,800 km^2 to 10,452 km. The Lebanese civil war erupted in 1975. Israel invaded in 1978, and again in 1982.[2] Along with the killing of several thousand civilians and the displacement of hundreds of thousands from their homes, the 1982 Israeli invasion caused the dislocation of the Lebanese governmental structure. In 1991, the Taef agreement brought a semblance of peace to Lebanon, and the reconstruction and rehabilitation process began.

Each of the occupying forces throughout Lebanon's history have regarded Lebanon as an appendage to its mother colony, and Lebanon's environment prime for exploitation. The timber of the vast, ancient forests was the original resource of this exploitation. The Cedar of Lebanon (*Cedrus libani*), one of the most significant tree species in world history, was the key Lebanese species utilized by both the occupying forces and the local people. The cedar had been used for the construction of temples, palaces, and boats. The export of cedar wood to Egypt was an important factor in the growth of the native Phoenician prosperity, and provided capital to launch international trading, navigation, and arts and crafts. The Assyrians, the Romans, King David, King of Babylonia, Herod the Great, and the Turks in the Ottoman Empire also utilized the cedars. During World War I, most of the remaining stands were further exploited and destroyed for railroad fuel (Chaney and Basbous, 1978). As a consequence, today only scattered remnants of the once extensive forests of cedar, fir, pine and juniper remain, and most of the oak forests have either disappeared or have been reduced to scrub and spiny shrubs (Thirgood, 1981; Hughes, 1982; Mikesell, 1969).

The massive deforestation in Lebanon (and in the Fertile Crescent as a whole) resulted not only in a loss of timber resources, but also contributed to wildlife extinction and endangerment, caused dramatic soil erosion and consequential loss of agricultural potential, negatively impacted water quality, and altered the microclimate[3] (Brown, 1969).

Effects of the Recent Wars in Lebanon (1975-1990) on the Environment

In addition to the deaths of approximately 250,000 people and the displacement of 800,000 others from their homes, the wars in Lebanon significantly affected the economy and the environment. Prior to the recent period of wars and civil unrest (1975-1990), the Lebanese economy was one of the most dynamic and stable in the Middle East. Lebanon had a combination of a stable macro-economic environment and laissez-faire economics, and served as a regional intermediary between the developed economies of Europe and the developing economies of the Middle East (Eken et al., 1995). The Lebanese economy has not suffered solely from the destruction of infrastructure and industrial facilities, and the ensuing flight of professional and entrepreneurial skills, but also from the already present and consequential environmental degradation, worsened by the wars and chaos. The environment has been affected through physical damage and destruction, decreased investment in necessary infrastructure, and lack of regulation due to the disintegration of the civil authority.

The physical effects of the wars in Lebanon include: an increase in forest fires due to armed conflicts and neglect; degradation of fishing grounds and fish habitat; damage to the physical infrastructure in the water sector,[4] untreated solid waste; destruction of agricultural fields and equipment, amounting to a direct loss of approximately US$300 million,[5] and the loss of farm labor; destruction of 15 industrial factories, and the closure of 200 plants; and damage to the two refineries and the transportation network (METAP, 1995). Another consequence of the war has been the severely inadequate investment in the necessary infrastructure. The ensuing breakdown in civil authority further led to: unregulated, chaotic urbanization, most clearly witnessed by the encroachment of the coastline and coastal access roads with architectural eye-sores; a dramatic increase in private wells; and an excessive use of agricultural chemicals. The governmental failure in implementing land use planning has resulted in direct discharges of human and industrial effluents and solid waste, and high levels of air pollution, particularly around urban centers.

Attitudes of Government Officials and Citizens

The environment is commonly regarded as something to be dealt with *after* development. This outlook is held most strongly by the government (as it is by most governments in the world), whose main objective now is the commercial development and rehabilitation of Lebanon.

Socioeconomic factors and historical elements are crucial in further understanding people's attitude towards the environment. Villages which depend upon the environment economically (agricultural communities, for example), have relatively equal land tenure, and have not experienced significant migration, tend to have communal solidarity and active involvement in local environmental protection, such as in the maintenance of soil terraces. On the other hand, villages with significant land abandonment (either through migration, or from no longer working directly with the land), with unevenly distributed land among the community, and whose inhabitants have little control over their own resources, tend towards weak communal solidarity. Such a community will lack a feeling of land stewardship and may adopt a fatalistic regard to the environment as a whole; consequently, environmental protection becomes disregarded (Zurayk, 1994b).

II. Biodiversity

The wars in Lebanon and the ensuing breakdown in authority, although not the instigators, have contributed to further loss of biodiversity. Numerous mammals, fish, birds, and wild plants are threatened with local extinction. Two main factors affect the disappearance and endangerment of both the flora and the fauna (in order of importance): loss of habitat and hunting.

Threats to Fauna and/or Flora

1. Loss of Habitat

Wetlands, plains and coastal areas have been altered to make room for agriculture or urban development at the direct expense of the habitat's native inhabitants. The majority of Lebanese inland and coastal plains have been turned into agricultural lands. Wetlands have been particularly affected. The central part of the Beka'a Valley was once occupied by lakes and swamps (Mikesell, 1969). Today, most of the area is cultivated, leaving only Ammiq Swamp, a 280-hectare wetland—the largest remaining freshwater wetland in Lebanon. Ammiq Swamp has already been reduced to one tenth of its former area. This wetland plays a vital role in the cycle of bird migration through Lebanon, as it is a major resting and watering spot for migratory birds. However, draining, well digging and canal digging are continuing and Ammiq is projected to disappear completely in the next few years if no action is taken to preserve it.

The coastal strip, extending 225 km from extreme north to extreme south, and home to several species of wildlife, is also under threat of further degradation. The strip has been disappearing over the past 150 years as a result of uncontrolled building, sand stripping, and dumping into the sea. The coastal strip is also faced with a greater demand for urban development in the wake of Lebanon's construction boom. The embankments, industrial establishments and other buildings, most of which are illegal, disfigure the natural geomorphology and environment. Resident breeding population of passerines have already been reduced to approximately ten species (Zurayk, 1995a).

The loss of natural habitat and consequent land alteration have changed the ecological balance. Many species denied their natural habitat have decreased in population, some to the point of extinction, while rodents and other species that quickly adapted, have flourished in the absence of their natural predators. Some of these rodents have since become significant agricultural pests.

2. Over Hunting

The National Board of Hunting is responsible for regulating hunting practices. In the last few years, its enforcement authority has almost completely deteriorated. More than 500,000 people hunt in Lebanon, most of whom do not have a license (METAP, 1995). Shooting is conducted indiscriminately, and without regard to environmental consequences. More than ten million birds were, until recently, shot in Lebanon every year. A large number of these birds are considered inedible and were left in the fields. Under pressure from environmental organizations, a ban on all hunting on Lebanese land for two years was recently implemented, beginning on 1 January 1996 and extending to 31 December 1997 (Masri, R., 1996a).

3. Other Factors

Additional factors that directly contribute to the degradation of natural habitat and threaten the native species with extinction include the misuse of pesticides, the use of explosives, and overall pollution in the country. The excessive use of pesticides and the utilization of banned, toxic agricultural chemicals, regularly kill thousands of birds. In addition, fish are endangered by the continued use of explosives for fishing and the significant levels of water pollution in their habitat.

Table 1

Current Known Wildlife Status in Lebanon

	Locally Extinct	Endangered or Threatened
Birds	Rough-legged Buzzard, Peregrine, Shelduck, Black Francolin, Great Bustard, Houbara Bustard, Corn Crake, Stone-curlew, Cream-colored Courser, Pratincole, Black-bellied Sandgrouse, Rock Dove, Short-eared Owl, Syrian woodpecker, Dipper, Blue tit	Imperial Eagle, Syrian Serin, Lesser Kestrel, Audouin's Gull, Chukar Partridge, Great Snipe, Ferruginous Duck, Great Bittern, Saker, Lesser spotted Eagle, Greater spotted Eagle, Pallid Harrier, Dalmatian Pelican, Yellow-legged Gull, European Honey Buzzard, Eurasian Griffon vulture, Levant Sparrowhawk, *Cinereous bunting*
Carnivores	Asiatic Lion, Cheetah, Leopard, Asiatic Jackal, Wolf, Syrian Bear, Egyptian Mongoose, Beech Martey, Marbled Polecat, Weasel, Common Otter, Wild Cat, Caracal Lynx	Striped Hyena, Badger, Mediterranean Monk Seal
Ungulates	Asiatic Wild Ass, Nubian Ibex, Wild Goat, Mountain Gazelle, Fallow Deer, Roe Deer	Palestinian Mountain Gazelle, *Capra aegagrus*
Bats		*Rhinolophus ferrumeqainum, Rhinolophus hipposideros,* Long-fingered Bat, Greater Mouse-eared Bat
Insects		Rosalia Longhorn, *Archon apollianaris*
Lagomorphs		Hyrax, Syrian Hare
Rodents		Persian Squirrel, Indian Crested Porcupine, Grey Hamster, *Eliomys melanourus,* Snow Vole
Reptiles		*Vipera bornmuelleri,* Spur-thighed Tortoise

Sources: Evans, 1994; Tohmé, 1986; Tohmé, 1985a; Tohmé, 1985b; World Conservation Monitoring Centre, 1993.

Current Situation

Flora

In Lebanon's small territory, nearly 2,600 plant species grow in a spontaneous state (Nehmeh, 1978; Tohmé, 1985a). This richness of flora is due to the country's general climatic conditions, specifically the multiplicity of micro-climates which favored the formations of numerous endemic species. A great number of flowers were botanically described in Lebanon and many bear its name. Rapid urbanization, excessive use of agro-chemicals and the consequential soil pollution, and general environmental degradation are leading to the disappearance of a number of reputed flowers.

Fauna

Numerous native animals have been driven to extinction in Lebanon and this process is continuing (see Table 1). While carnivore and herbivore species are threatened with extinction, rodents are on the increase, flourishing in the absence of their predators. Many more species, such as the bats which prey on rodents and insects, could likely be endangered due to the degradation of their habitats. However, due to inadequate research, the population status of many species is unknown.

Lebanon is a key area for migratory birds, being rich in both number and variety. Over 300 different species of birds can be found, 50 of which breed there. Millions of soaring birds, especially birds of prey, storks and pelicans, pass through the skies, especially during the autumn migration to Africa. Millions of larks migrate through the northern Beka'a valley each year, where they had been prey to hunting. Of the fifteen known endangered bird species in Lebanon, five are globally threatened species[6] (Evans, 1994).

III. Natural Resource Management

Deforestation, land abandonment and agricultural mismanagement have led to the intensification of water-caused soil erosion, as witnessed by the considerable amounts of alluvions[7] carried by the rivers, and by the deep gullying in the sandy soils of the mountains. The heaviest landscape degradation is where ancient deforestation has been carried out and followed by grazing, generally above 1000 meters in the Beka'a and the Anti-Lebanon mountains (Zurayk, 1995a).

The land damage is principally the result of three factors: tree cutting that began at least 4,000 years ago; continuous, uncontrolled grazing by sheep and goats; and abandoned agricultural cultivation (Mikesell, 1969; Ryan, 1983). Soil erosion was instigated primarily by the massive deforestation in Lebanon thousands of years ago (Dregne, 1982; Mikesell, 1969), and encouraged by the consequential livestock grazing on the mountain slopes. As the forests disappeared, agricultural cultivation also expanded further along the slopes of the mountain chains. Mountain agriculture required the construction of stone-walled bench terraces, some of which were built more than 2,500 years ago (Zurayk, 1994a). These essential soil conservation structures demand intense maintenance and communal effort. Land abandonment, encouraged primarily by rural migration (both voluntary, and forced as a result of the war), has resulted in significant damage to these soil terraces. Today, agricultural production on the neglected terraced lands is at a near standstill. Planned soil conservation efforts are crucial for preserving agricultural productivity.

Twenty percent of the permanent soil productivity in Lebanon's hilly lands was estimated to be lost[8] in 1982 (Dregne, 1982). The soil erosion rates are believed to be especially high in Mount Lebanon, occurring mainly on the extensive areas of abandoned, dilapidated terraces and overgrazed marginal land. The sediment load[9] of the principal littoral rivers is 2 million m^3/year, equivalent to the degradation of 500 hectares of agricultural land. This value could be halved with an increase in forest cover to 25-30% on the western slopes of Mount Lebanon (Zurayk, 1995a).

Forests

The majority of Lebanon's forests have been removed over the past 2,000 years. Most of present-day Lebanon was covered with lush, coniferous forest; only the north-eastern Beka'a, the central channel between the Lebanon and Anti-Lebanon Ranges, has grassland as its climax vegetation. Except for this outlier of the Syrian steppe, no substantial part of Lebanon is too dry to support trees (Mikesell, 1969). However, several millennia of deforestation, over-grazing and ensuing soil erosion have dramatically altered the landscape and prevented the regeneration of the forest. Furthermore, the region's micro-climate probably has been affected by the severe decrease in forest cover. Based upon historical data and scientific estimates, the perennial springs of higher Lebanon today were much fuller and more constant, and the lower slopes green and moist. There may even have been greater annual rainfall through the recirculation of water on the western slopes of Mount Lebanon by the transpiration of the forest (Brown, 1969).[10]

Much of the mountain terrain is now devoid of topsoil, and what soil remains is shallow, sustaining only a sparse vegetative cover. Current estimates put forest cover at only 7% (Ryan, 1983; Zurayk, 1994a), a meager sum especially when considering that mountains cover 73% of Lebanon's territory. On mountain slopes, forests are critically needed to protect the soil from erosion, especially now that the agricultural soil terraces have been disregarded and ill-maintained.

The war in Lebanon prevented the development, and seriously hampered the control and conservation, of forest resources. Reforestation is practically non-existent. The meager reforestation undertaken is done so primarily by local non-governmental organizations and, to a small extent, by the Ministry of the Environment. (Although the Ministry of the Environment (1991) cites reforestation "at a 5% rate," this number is practically meaningless since the Ministry undertakes almost no monitoring or even simple assessment.) At times, seedlings are planted at inappropriate seasons, such as during the summer due to the increased availability of volunteers (Scout Troops and students) and the pleasant weather. Overall monitoring and maintenance of the reforestation projects are slight and inadequate. Reforestation is further impeded by the continued, persistent presence of goat herds, and lack of community support.

Present Forest Status

Current information on forests in Lebanon depends primarily on 1966 studies by the Green Plan[11] and the United Nations FAO. This data forms the foundation of research on the integrated landscape management of Lebanon. Based upon their mapping study, it is deduced that approximately 66,000 hectares (7% of Lebanon's land area) support forest stands of 10% density crown closure or more. An additional 66,000 hectares have a density of less than 10% crown closure (METAP, 1995). Most of the woods are either of poor quality, degraded, or offer little economic incentives for management. The main species are oak (40,000 ha), pine (15,000 ha), juniper (8,000 ha), and cedar (2,000 ha) (METAP, 1995; MoE, 1991). The known endangered tree species are the *Abies cilica* (Cicilian Fir), the *Quercus cerris* (Turkey Oak), and the *Ceratonia silica* (True Locust Bean). In addition, due to its low germination rate in nurseries and small total area, the *Juniperus excelsa* (Grecian Juniper) could likely be threatened.

The oaks and pines extend along the coast to elevations of 1,200 to 1,600 meters on the western slopes of Mount Lebanon. The oak forests of the oak-pine level have almost completely disappeared, primarily due to logging and fires. From 1,200 to 2,000 meters, where firs, junipers and cedars were once the dominant species, the current vegetation now consists only of sparsely distributed oak and juniper stands (Zurayk, 1995a). The cedars and junipers can only be found as relics.

On the eastern slopes of Mount Lebanon, and on the Anti-Lebanon mountains, trees are scattered and rare, if present at all. These are fragile ecosystems, which are grazed extensively in the spring and fall. To the south, on the eastern slopes of Jabal el-Sheikh, more vegetation and a greater forest area are present due to the increased precipitation. In general, the steep slopes, long dry season, intense rainfall, and extensive calcareous soils in Lebanon are not favorable to vegetation preservation in the mountains (Zurayk, 1995a). Human activities, inducing accelerated erosion, further exacerbate these problematic factors.

State of the Cedrus libani in Lebanon: Examination of Two Key Areas

The cedar is now limited to twelve separate stands, and is often located within dominant stands of fir, juniper, and oak. Many of these stands are degraded by goats and soil erosion and compaction. The Bcharre cedars, the most famous stand of cedars in Lebanon, comprise only 7 hectares. (Mistakenly, the cedars of Bcharre are commonly referred to as the very last remnant of cedar forest in Lebanon.) This stand contains the oldest and largest specimens of *Cedrus libani*, reported to be over 2000 years old, and has been nominated as a World Heritage area by the Society for the Protection of Nature in Lebanon (SPNL). However, the stand faces numerous problems, including scant cedar reproduction, age stress, drought, macro and micro nutrient deficiency, and soil erosion and compaction. In addition, due to the almost complete absence of accompanying flora and all kinds of beneficial birds, the cedars have been subjected to increased insect and pathogen attacks.

Jabal el-Barouk, the largest naturally regenerating cedar forest in Lebanon, has a fascinating, important history with regards to the management and current situation of the cedars. This relatively well-protected forest, covering a total of only 216 hectares, comprises three adjacent but separate stands of cedars: Maasser el-Chouf, Ain Zhalta, and Arz el-Barouk. Jabal el-Barouk had been grazed extensively from the months of May to October by an estimated 2,000 goats. In addition, about every twenty years, the oak forests had been cut for commercial purposes (Dean, 1994a). The logging stopped in 1960, when the Forest Department and the FAO began re-forestation efforts, known as the Green Plan. Terraces were created throughout the forests of Jabal el-Barouk, and cedars were planted at relatively close, regular inter-vals. Fifty-two hectares in Ain Zhalta were reforested. In 1975, reforestation efforts ended with the start of the war. Jabal el-Barouk was closed off to civilians and grazing in the forest was prohibited. In 1982, the Israeli army occupied Ain Zhalta. The Israeli occupation of Arz Ain Zhalta resulted in, among many other things, the spread of the war to the cedar forest resulting in shrapnel damage and mortality to some cedars. More significantly, the Israeli army caused almost permanent destruc-tion of close to 5% of the cedar forest due to the intense soil compaction by its heavy machinery and road construction. The closure of the forest, and the prohi-bition of grazing, resulted in a change in the under-story vegetation (from pioneer species to later successional species) and, most likely, significantly contributed in the protection and maintenance of the forest (Masri, R., 1995). The forest is now under governmental protection, and access is limited.

Current Causes of Deforestation

The need for firewood and the occurrence of uncontrolled fire events are the primary causes of current forest cover reduction in Lebanon. Firewood consumption was estimated at 377 million cubic meters in 1963, all produced locally by logging oak coppices (METAP, 1995). In 1988, the figure dropped to 482,000 cubic meters, and in 1991 to 300,000 cubic meters (MoE, 1991). This tremendous decrease in firewood consumption, by a factor of more than 1,000 in less than 30 years, is not surprising due to the increased availability of other combustibles.[12] However, logging for firewood is still undertaken without any harvest or regeneration plan; trees are simply logged when and where it is appropriate for the logger.

Uncontrolled fire events have further destroyed vast expanses of land, often irreversibly due to the ensuing grazing which prevents regeneration. The Lebanese forestry service estimates a loss of 1,000 to 1,200 hectares each year (Zuryak, 1994c). The scant resources of the fire fighting agencies cannot cope with the seasonal concentration of fire events, which are usually clustered in the first weeks of October and November (Zurayk, 1995a).

Stone Pine (Pinus pinea)

In 1982, Lebanon's exports in forest products was worth more than US$9.5 million. Of the tree species grown, Italian Stone Pine (*Pinus pinea*) serves as the main benefit to the economy through the production and sale of its edible pine nuts. Italian Stone Pine is of economic, touristic, and environmental value in Lebanon.

Currently, Stone Pine is estimated to encompass between 7-11,000 hectares. Most of the pine is regenerated with direct human intervention, through planting, pruning, and protection from competitive species during the first two years of growth. Based upon estimates by the Ministry of Agriculture, 591 tons of the edible pine seed were sold in 1994; this number is considered a conservative figure that is much lower than the pine farmers' estimations. The pine seed is sold at an average of $20/kg., thus the average annual pine seed production, based on the government's conservative figures, is US$1.2 million (Masri, T., 1996).

The pine forests have been decreasing, and are further threatened by the aggression of the sand and cement quarries, increase of construction and development of roads, fires caused by excess litter in the forest, and by a recent epidemic instigated by a drought. These reasons, however, are the consequences of the shift in utilization of the pine.

Pinus pinea has been utilized for multiple purposes, in addition to the well-known use of its edible seed. Its wood was used for the production of boxes to store fruits, and its branches were used to stabilize the grapevines and serve as fuel to heat the homes. In addition, use of the forest was not limited strictly to the utilization of the pine trees, but encompassed the understory vegetation (including the gorse, wormwood, and thistle). These plants were gathered and utilized in the production of silk and the fermentation of grapes. The weeds were gathered to feed the goats. This all-encompassing utilization protected the forest from fires by removing debris and litter, and integrated it into the economic sustainability of the villages (Masri, T., 1996).

Fire protection and pine reforestation will only be successful with community support. An effective method of integrating the community is to provide added economic incentives; the sale and utilization of the understory vegetation in the Stone Pine ecosystem is one practical alternative. If wiser management of the Stone Pine is not re-integrated into the pine production, and urban extension not carefully allocated, then this valuable tree could be lost, or become merely another relic.

Agriculture

Approximately 365,000 hectares (35% of Lebanon's land area) is cultivable for agriculture (METAP, 1995; Doueiri, 1996),[13] of which roughly 285,000 ha is cultivated and only 67,000 ha are irrigated. Nearly half of the cultivated lands are on mountain slopes (MoE, 1991; METAP, 1995), where terracing is necessary to decrease erosion.

The agricultural sector constitutes 11% of the country's gross domestic product (Doueiri, 1996). Despite the difficulties of the war and the ensuing lack of significant investment in infrastructure, the Ministry of the Environment contends that Lebanese agricultural production[14] has increased albeit feebly (MoE, 1991). However, at present Lebanon relies on food imports for a larger portion of its consumption (Doueiri, 1996). Traditionally, Lebanon has been a fruit and vegetable exporter to Arab countries. Now, it has become more of a net importer of food. High food prices drain up to 70% of consumers' personal incomes.

The loss of soil productivity from erosion, pesticide residues and salination has a serious negative impact on the future of agricultural production. However, it is not the only reason behind the current, vulnerable state of agriculture in Lebanon. The factors affecting agriculture include the marketing channels and regional competition, dilemma of importing subsidized food, political economy of the water question, increasing price and fragmentation of farm property, and loss of agricultural land.

Among the most serious damages caused to the agricultural sector is the occupation of southern Lebanon. The South traditionally contributed 40% of the agricultural production of the country (75% of tobacco, 90% of banana, and 70% of citrus production). The Israeli occupation of south Lebanon, since 1978, has put considerable pressure on the farmer to quit cultivating the land and migrate.[15]

Still, the most devastating and long-lasting effect to arable land in Lebanon has been the extension of urbanization, encouraged by the high prices offered by developers. For agricultural land around major cities, landlords are offered US$3 million for property they lease to farmers for only US$4,000 a year (Doueiri, 1996). In the past 20 years alone, urbanization around cities and highways has taken about 20,000 ha (or 7%) of all cultivated land, and a higher proportion (15%) of irrigated land (METAP, 1995). A large part of these agricultural lands is situated near the bases of urban extensions in the suburbs of Tripoli, Jounieh, Beirut, Sidon, Tyre (Sour), and Zahlé. This land loss has affected agriculture by more than simply transforming potential agricultural land into urban growth. The disappearance of primary predators, encouraged by the loss of habitat, has resulted in an increased population of field mice and rats. These rodents have ravaged agricultural fields and caused several billion Lebanese Lira in losses every year (Doueiri, 1996). Carefully planned land-zoning systems are needed—allocating primarily *non-arable* land to urban development needs. In the words of the Ministry of the Environment, "if strict measures are not taken and applied by the authorities, the agricultural sector would be under the threat of disappearance in Lebanon" (MoE, 1991). The Ministry of the Environment, itself one of those authorities, has yet to undertake any of these "strict measures," namely enforcing land use planning.

In addition to the availability of cultivable land, agriculture is highly dependent on water availability. Water in Lebanon is poorly managed. Yet, the question of water policy is not strictly internal, but is deeply influenced by external forces, namely Israel. Israel's theft of the Litani waters and acquisition of other groundwater sources is a violation of Lebanon's territorial sovereignty, and a direct threat to the future of agriculture. Doueiri (1996) argues that "if Lebanon cannot manage its water resources, as has been the case for the past 50 years due to internal and external factors, it will remain a marginal food producer... its rural economy will be destroyed; its agricultural output on a per hectare basis will remain low; its national economy will suffer; its fallow cultivable land will never be used; and its disappearing forest will not be rejuvenated."

Through comprehensive planning, considerable investment,[16] a multitude of conservation measures, and the effective development of water projects in Lebanon, the agricultural sector has the potential to be reinvigorated and to substantially contribute to the country's economic and social well-being, especially after the South is freed from Israel's occupation and aggressions. Further, as Doueiri (1996) eloquently states, "developing the agricultural sector... requires a unified approach where integrated pest management is as important to consider as integrated rural development, and where comprehensive economic measures for improving agricultural production should meet the national objectives of food policy."

Key Environmental Impacts

The overuse of agricultural chemicals, the misuse of water, and the over-grazing of livestock, as well as the abandonment of soil terraces in mountain agriculture, pose serious long-term effects on the environment and ecosystems. These issues need to be solved through education, farmer support programs and extension services, and investments in and rehabilitation of terraces.

1. Over-use of Agricultural Chemicals

A lack of guidance, education, control and enforcement has resulted in an almost chaotic application of pesticides, and an overall dangerous situation. Utilizing incorrect equipment, farmers usually apply pesticides in much greater quantities than needed. Although the overall use of fertilizer has declined, the application rates on horticultural and fruit crops has increased, especially in areas of dense population and agricultural activity, particularly in the coastal zone. In addition, and of significant danger to the health of farmers and consumers, farmers rarely conform to the minimum waiting period before harvesting the crops from the fields and greenhouses.

This mis-practice becomes compounded by the utilization of banned pesticides. Although Law 11-1978 prohibits the importation of any pesticide into Lebanon that is banned for use in its country of origin, pesticides such as DDT, Aldrin, carbofuran and parathion are widely available (Doueiri, 1996; METAP, 1995). The expiration data, commercial and scientific names, and application instructions are commonly concealed by the pesticide salesmen (METAP, 1995).

The excessive use of these agrochemicals damages the soil, and pollutes water supplies with nitrates. The build-up of these chemicals in crops and soils is leached to underground waters in the form of aquifers or underground streams which can eventually reach the sea (Atallah, 1992). In addition, the misuse of these toxic chemicals harms wildlife. Hundreds of dead birds and animals are found in various areas of Lebanon during the first week after pesticide spraying (Zurayk, 1995a). Furthermore, since they leach into the groundwater supply, these chemicals pose a serious risk to human health.

Extension services, distribution of vital agricultural information, and enforcement of regulations are critically needed. The Lebanese Government has responded by formulating decrees and setting up a Pesticide Committee to control the use of pesticides (METAP, 1995).

2. Misuse of Water

Approximately 24% of agricultural land is irrigated (Doueiri, 1996; METAP, 1995). In most areas, irrigation is inefficient (40% losses arising from damaged networks). In addition, more water is applied than is necessary. The majority of the irrigation systems are based on basin flooding, while the remaining significant portion utilizes wells. Re-use of untreated wastewater for irrigation is common practice where no other irrigation schemes are available (METAP, 1995). Furthermore, due to lack of government-sponsored projects, farmers have relied heavily on private wells for irrigation (Doueiri, 1996). Thus, the number of wells has increased, resulting in salination of underground aquifers from the sea.

3. Over-grazing of Livestock Production

Natural vegetation provides 80% of livestock diet (METAP, 1995). The majority of range lands, especially in Mount Lebanon and Anti-Lebanon, have been overgrazed beyond their carrying capacity, resulting in deterioration of plant species, increased soil erosion, and impediment of natural forest regeneration. In addition, livestock overloading has resulted in increased soil compaction, a significant problem that further hinders regeneration.

Fisheries

The fisheries industry is closely associated with the development of the coastal zone. It is not being developed, but rather is looked upon as serving primarily cultural significance. The industry currently employs only 4,000 people, whose average income from fishing is roughly US$800/year. Fish catches declined 70% from 1974 to 1994, although the total number of working fishing boats did not significantly decline[17] during this time—thus the catch per vessel must have fallen sharply, a direct consequence of the over-exploitation of fish resources (METAP, 1995; Doueiri, 1996).

In an effort to increase their meager income of $2/day, fishermen have been utilizing dynamite, and injecting poisonous chemicals into the water to absorb the oxygen and suffocate the fish. Both of these methods result in the indiscriminate killing of aquatic life, including small and large fish and their eggs (Doueiri, 1996). This problem has been compounded by oil leaks, garbage disposal, and pollution, especially from the shores of Tripoli. In addition, south Lebanon's fishermen, faced with successive blockades by the Israeli government,[18] are forced to over-fish a limited area, and thus further contribute to localized over-exploitation of the resource.

Although facing numerous problems ranging from internal environmental mis-management to external foreign pressure, it is argued that, if managed properly, the Lebanese fishing industry can transform Lebanon from a net importer to a net ex-porter of seafood (Doueiri, 1996). Lebanon currently imports 10,000 to 11,000 met-ric tons of fresh fish, mainly from neighboring Greece, Syria and Turkey (who obtain some of their fish from the international waters north of Lebanon), and frozen and canned seafood from several European and Asian countries. The Lebanese waters could serve—not only as resources for seafood—but also as sources of protein, oils, pharmaceutical, and industrial products, such as vitamins, ointments, and sponges (Doueiri, 1996). If well managed, the economic potential could be significant.

Quarries

There are at least 600 quarrying sites in Lebanon, employing 14,000 workers (10% of the industrial workforce). Approximately 85 sites are over 1,000 m^2 in area. Sixty percent excavate rocks, while 40% are sand quarries[19] (Fanar, 1994; METAP, 1995; Khawli, 1994). Quarries, especially rock quarries, are considered a principal natural Lebanese wealth and represent the primary material and foundation in the construction industry (Fanar, 1994). The sand quarry operations are located predominately in the western half, and are concentrated in some of the major sites of certain localities (Metn, Zahlé, and the North).

Quarrying activities are of serious concern due to the geological characteristics of the sites, the seismic potentials of Lebanon, and the urban encroachment. No environmental assessments and considerations are conducted in locating and working the quarries; instead the operations proceed in an abusive, chaotic fashion (Khawli, 1994; Fanar, 1994). The operations are directly and indirectly affecting public safety and health within and far from their locations by impacting humans and natural habitat. The grave consequences include atmospheric pollution caused by dust and nitrous vapors from the detonations of ammonium nitrate, resulting in a hazard to human health. The dust also seriously damages the nearby agricultural crops and trees (Fanar, 1994). In addition, due to the lack of rehabilitation efforts, the quarrying operations permanently alter the landscape and transform the mountains into unsightly caves.

IV. Water Resource Management

Lebanon *could* be considered a water-rich country, especially when compared to others in the Middle East. Approximately 83% of Lebanon's water is from completely internal sources. The remaining 17% includes three international rivers (Doueiri, 1996). However, due to high population density, high demand, inefficient use, uneven distribution, illegal pumping of water to Israel, and an increasing shortage of clean water, Lebanon has become a water-deficient country[20] (Khair et al., 1994; Doueiri, 1996). Statistics point out that Lebanon will have a serious deficit in water resources by the turn of the century. Thus, "Lebanon cannot afford to sell any of its national water nor to give up its fair share of its international water" (Doueiri, 1996).

Drinking Water

Between 1975 and 1992, there was a 60% decrease in the quantity of water available from municipal sources (Kolars, 1992), while the population continued to grow at a rate of 2.2% per annum. Most areas suffer from water shortages caused by major demographic changes which have not been accompanied by the necessary infrastructural improvement (see Table 2). Damage to networks and pumping stations caused by shelling, neglect, lack of maintenance, or looting is also a major cause.

In most of the villages and poor urban zones of Lebanon, water is still obtained from springs, rainwater collection wells, or dry wells tapping the groundwater. Approximately 65% of the drinking water is withdrawn from surface water.

Table 2
Access to Reliable Drinking Water

District (*Caza*)	Villages Lacking Access to Reliable Drinking Water (%)	Villages not Connected to Municipal Network (%)
Baalbek	41	38
Hermel	38	44
Tripoli	35	22
Akkar	6	44

Source: METAP, 1995—taken from UNICEF, 1993.

Unfortunately, between 60 to 70% of the natural water resources, used as sources of potable water, is exposed to bacteriological contamination (Khair et al., 1994; Jurdi, 1992). In a study conducted in 1992, 66% of town water networks and 78% of village networks were found to be microbially contaminated. Of the 352 wells used for drinking water supplies, only 28 were provided with operating chlorinates in 1992. In a few cases, chlorination was performed by dropping chlorine solutions in the wells. Eight of the water authorities supplying 23% of the total population undertook no disinfection of the water (METAP, 1995). In general, most of the wells utilized for potable water supplies undertake no chlorination,[21] or any other disinfection method (METAP, 1995; MoE, 1991).

Water-borne infectious diseases are most frequently associated with inadequate disinfection or equipment failure (Bull, 1992), a significant problem in Lebanon where chlorination rates are very low, and water treatment is practically nonexistent. The areas most affected by water pollution are the Beka'a, the North, and the South (Jurdi, 1992). This situation is particularly severe in the rural areas, where a country-wide survey found evidence of contamination in 78% of the water resources of rural households. This pollution was caused by sewage leakages from poorly maintained systems, and resulted in several major epidemics in the Akkar region of North Lebanon (Al-Khalidi and Zurayk, 1994). The prevalent diseases in Lebanon believed to be transmitted by water are typhoid, hepatitis, and dysentery (MoE, 1991). In 1990 alone, there were four known epidemics transmitted by polluted drinking water, primarily in rural areas.[22] A correlation was found between the number of cases relating to each of these diseases in a given month and the characteristics of the flow-rate of water streams, particularly during periods of vegetable-crop irrigation with polluted waters (MoE, 1991). The Lebanese government's recovery program strives to ensure clean drinking water to most of the urban population. However, it does not propose treatment plants outside the urban concentration of Beirut (METAP, 1995), thus ignoring the most affected regions in Lebanon: the rural areas.

Furthermore, a recent government developmental plan may result in an increase in cancer in local regions. In 1996, the government decided to utilize asbestos-constructed water pipes to provide water for numerous villages in the mountains, especially in the Metn. As this chapter goes to print, protests and controversy surround this decision, and the outcome remains uncertain. However, construction has begun in many villages, such as Ras El-Metn.[23] There is considerable debate in the scientific literature about the harmful effects of asbestos fibers in drinking water, and the extent of health risks from ingestion of fibers (AWWA, 1986). Nonetheless, asbestos may become airborne when released into the air during a shower, and, according to the United States Environmental Protection Agency, there is no safe threshold of exposure for airborne asbestos. Inhalation of asbestos dust could cause asbestosis, lung cancer, and mesothelioma. In addition, although the risk may be small, there may be a direct association between asbestos in drinking water and gastrointestinal cancer (Toft et al., 1984). Since a legitimate risk to human health exists from the utilization of asbestos-constructed water pipes, an alternative should be studied and undertaken.

Water Pollution—Status

Most ground and surface water, springs, wells, numerous rivers, and most drinking water (METAP, 1995; Khair et al., 1994; Jurdi, 1992) are bacterially contaminated. In addition, the Lebanese territorial waters of the Mediterranean faces significant coastal pollution and contamination (Lakkis, 1994; New Scientist, 1995). With the exception of waters at high altitudes where there are, at present, no constructions above their levels, all Lebanese waters are exposed to pollution.

The waters have been badly degraded in the Antelias River, Nahr el-Kalb (Khalaf, 1994), and Bardauni River (Alouf, 1994), all of which are regions of high urban and touristic concentration in which the waters are used for drinking, irrigation, bathing, and sport. The Litani River, one of the three major rivers in Lebanon, was found to be contaminated with fecal coliform in twelve locations beyond the levels acceptable for the irrigation of crops eaten raw (Al-Khalidi and Zurayk, 1994). In addition, the Ibrahim River, characterized by three dams that supply three hydro-electric centers, has been negatively affected by the presence of a nearby enormous quarry that dumps significant quantities of fine sediments into the river (Khalaf, 1994). The Mtein River has also been polluted, due primarily to small-scale fisheries.

In addition to the effect of commercial exploitation and urbanization, the Lebanese coast has been badly damaged from global and localized pollution. Pollution constitutes the second factor of the deterioration of the coastal sites and the coastal waters. The sources of the pollution (urban, organic, industrial, chemical, and petroleum) throw their wastes directly into the sea without any treatment (Lakkis, 1994). Furthermore, the discharge of cooling water from Lebanon's three major coastal power plants can induce a number of damaging impacts on the marine environment. As of late 1996, there had not been an assessment of these discharges.

The main environmental concerns at Lebanese sea ports include the discharge and disposal of ballast waters, the effects of dredging, and accidental spills from petroleum tankers at sea terminals. The movement of oil tankers along the Lebanese coast, as well as their docking, unloading and storage, pose the risk of an oil spill with serious impacts on marine and coastal ecosystems, especially since Lebanon currently has no oil spill response facilities.

Years of global pollution, over-fishing and over-development have left the Mediterranean Sea in crisis. The problem is so severe that parts of the sea are devoid of life altogether. The main problems, especially where large populations discharge wastes into isolated bodies of water, include: 1) eutrophication; 2) changes to nu-trient cycling; 3) loss of biodiversity; 4) accumulation of contaminants in the food chain; and 5) decline in recreational and tourism value (METAP, 1995). The key sources of marine and freshwater pollution include land-based, shipping-related, and international. International sources are quite significant since three-quarters of the pollution in the Mediterranean Sea comes from the industrialized nations of France, Spain, and Italy (New Scientist, 1995).

Water Pollution—Causes

Overall, the lack of a system for the evacuation of solid and liquid residues, the lack of a control and water-protection system against pollution, and, primar-ily, the poor management of water resources have resulted in such extensive, and easily avoidable, pollution. The primary causes of water pollution are the poorly constructed domestic and industrial water-treatment systems, the general release of untreated effluents into the soil or water, and the excessive construction of private wells.

The high population density, coupled with the ensuing increase in water demand and the current poor management of natural water resources, have resulted indirectly in the salination of the groundwater. Faced with an inadequate national infrastructure, individuals have drilled private wells to such an extreme extent that "the number of wells drilled since 1980 have exceeded the number of wells drilled in Lebanon since its existence" (Khair et al., 1994). Most of these wells are located near the sea shore, and almost all are drilled and used incorrectly (Abu Nasr and Zankoul, 1992). This has resulted in an increase of salinity of extracted water from coastal waters by sea water encroachment (METAP, 1995; Khair et al., 1994; Abu Nasr and Zankoul, 1992). In addition, the excessive pumping of groundwater, plus the reduction or fluctuation in precipitation rates, have resulted in the fall of the water-table level; this drop is reflected by the significant decline in the discharge of many springs and rivers (Khair et al., 1994).

Bacterial contamination of the water bodies is caused by three factors: cesspools and leaking sewers, contamination from sewer pipes lying alongside leaking potable water pipes (Khair et al., 1994), and industrial effluents (MOE, 1991). Despite the high risk of water pollution and contamination, cesspools account for 64% of sewage disposal methods, and sewer lines, many of which are leaking and damaged, account for the remaining 36% (Khair et al., 1994). The shelling from the war, coupled with incomplete construction, rendered the five waste-water treatment plants in Lebanon ineffective. Consequently, individuals are utilizing aquifers in many areas as disastrous 'bottomless septic tanks,' and disposing of the sewage directly in cesspools, instead of in correctly-designed septic tanks (Khair et al., 1994).

Table 3
Access to Wastewater Systems

Governorate (*Mohafaza*)	Population Served (%)
Greater Beirut:	
• Ghadir system	50
• North Metn	65
North Lebanon	46 (90 in Tripoli)
Mount Lebanon	54
South Lebanon	21
Nabatiyeh	14
Beka'a	28

Source: METAP, 1995.

Wastewater Management

As with access to reliable (although not necessarily clean) drinking water, a significant portion of the Lebanese population has no access to wastewater services. Direct damage during the war, lack of maintenance, neglect, and incomplete construction have resulted in an undersized and inadequate wastewater infrastructure, creating an urgent need for reconstruction and rehabilitation (see Table 3). While 50% of the population has access to some form of wastewater disposal services, only 8% of the rural population is served by a sewer collection system (Al-Khalidi and Zurayk, 1994). The rest of the population has developed rudimentary individual methods of wastewater disposal. In both cases, whether the community is afforded governmental disposal services or adopts methods of its own, the existing conditions remain unsatisfactory (METAP, 1995).

The primary modes of wastewater disposal in Lebanon are cesspools and sewer lines. Where there are no sewers, disposal is via poorly designed unlined cesspools which increase the risk of water contamination. This problem is especially severe in the rural areas, in which 68% of the people depend on cesspools for wastewater disposal while others dispose of their sewage directly on land, in disused wells or in seasonal streams (see Table 4). This uncontrolled collection and disposal of wastewater is a main cause of groundwater and spring contamination, ultimately affecting populations away from the disposal site (Al-Khalidi, 1994).

Not one of the five wastewater treatment plants in Lebanon is functioning, either due to shelling during the war or due to incomplete construction (AUB, 1994). Approximately 60% of the wastewater collected in the sewer networks is discharged in rivers and in the sea, while the remainder is disposed of on-land, without any technical provisions (Jurdi, 1992). In Beirut, 15 independent systems collect and discharge wastewater in the sea at 15 different locations along the coast (AUB, 1994). Thus, "treatment" becomes simply directly discharging the raw sewage into the sea

Table 4

Access to Sanitation Facilities

District (Caza)	Villages Served by Sewer Network (%)	Villages Served by Open Channels and Cesspools (%)	Villages Lacking Both—Open Air Disposal (%)
Baalbek	2	54	44
Hermel	–	9	91
Tripoli	8	43	49
Akkar	2	31	67

Source: METAP, 1995.

along the coastal strip where the majority of the population resides; discharging it into storm water, culverts or storm sewers; or utilizing the inland rivers, ravines and valleys as dump sites for the untreated wastewater. A total of 65,300 tons of Biological Oxygen Demand (BOD) each year (180 t/day) is discharged into Lebanon's rivers and sea. All these discharges eventually lead to degradation of land, surface water, ground water and sea water, and ultimately pose serious risks to human health (METAP, 1995).

IV. Solid Waste Management

There are numerous laws, some dating back to 1931, relating to solid waste management. Interestingly, there were no laws that specifically mentioned industrial solid wastes until 1988 although the problem was apparent long before then. The Ministry of the Environment (MoE), while promoting laws and regulations to control environmental pollution resulting from solid wastes and other sources, does not have the resources to provide an effective monitoring and policing service, nor does it have adequate technical expertise in solid waste management.

Composition and Generation Rates

Domestic waste amounts for approximately 60% of the waste generated in Lebanon (see Chart). Utilizing population estimates, total current domestic waste for Lebanon is approximated at one million tons each year (Mt/year).[24] Based solely on the projected population increase and assuming no increase in waste generation (an unlikely assumption, and thus a conservative figure), domestic waste is projected to increase to 1.7 Mt/year over 20 years (METAP, 1995). Examination of the domestic waste composition reveals that more than half of the waste is of vegetable and decayable constituent (50-65%). Paper and cardboard, and plastic constituents comprise the remaining large proportions of the waste (METAP, 1995). The high proportion of the waste that is vegetable and putrescible material (much higher than

Total Waste: 1.7 million tons per year (1994)

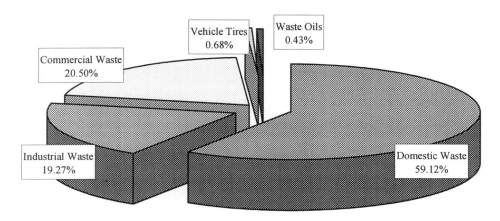

Chart. Primary known sources of solid waste generation (1994). Source: METAP, 1995.

that commonly found in northern Europe or the USA) makes the waste very suitable for composting, turning this waste into humus-like material that can improve the soil's structure and properties.

Total industrial waste generated in Lebanon (1994) is estimated to be approximately 326,000 t/year. The greatest regional share of industrial waste generation (57%) originates from Mount Lebanon, and is clustered in Baabda, Metn, and Kesrouan (METAP, 1995). If industrial output grows as projected (8% growth each year), total industrial waste will increase by almost 60% by the year 2000 (METAP, 1995). Much of the industrial waste comes from small industries, many of which are chaotically distributed amongst residential areas so that their waste is mixed with domestic waste. The composition of the industrial waste ranges from motor oil to animal carcasses, much of which is simply dumped into rivers or onto open ground. Commercial waste, or waste generated from service industries, is estimated at 346,750 t/year, or 760-1,140 t/day (METAP, 1995).

Based upon the life of a tire and the number of cars in Lebanon, the number of vehicle tires discarded is estimated at between 1 to 1.3 million each year, equivalent to 10,000 to 13,000 tons. Used tires are currently dumped or burned, thus giving rise to a range of environmental problems. A more suitable option would be to utilize the tires as fuel in place of coal in cement plants (METAP, 1995).

Comprising less than 0.5% of the waste generation, the power sector generates an estimated 300 t/year of waste oil, and vehicles release 7,000 t/year of used lubricating oil. Waste oil is currently disposed of in sewers, drains, waste land, waterways, municipal dumps, or is burned. In addition, some petrol stations collect and recycle waste oil. Although this reduces the amount of oil refuse, it contributes to air pollution by producing poor quality fuel with high particulate emissions (METAP, 1995).

Although of significant importance, there is very little information on hospital waste generation. No laboratory surveyed by METAP consultants in 1995 had any estimates for their hazardous waste quantities, and few hospitals surveyed had any understanding of the need to separate special or dangerous wastes from the waste stream. Most of the waste generated is simply collected and disposed of by the municipalities, without removing or separating pathogenic wastes, thus creating a serious risk of an epidemic and infection (METAP, 1995). Although the degree of danger from clinical wastes varies by hospital and by the type of waste, all hospital wastes need special management.

Italian Toxic Waste Scandal

Even though the Toxic Waste Scandal resulted from internal corruption and chaos, the problem has moved from one of strictly political amorality to include gross environmental mismanagement. The Lebanese government has yet to clean up the sites, specifically Shannir, the quarry believed to be the main dump for 2,411 tons of toxic waste. In addition, the government has allowed a barn for cows to be built on one site, covered another site with rocks, and, on April 4, 1996, secretly shipped 12 containers of more than 77 tons of toxic waste and contaminated land from Beirut to Marseilles for incineration (UPI, 17 May 1996). In September 1996, the Lebanese government officially closed the toxic waste file, despite the presence of several thousand toxic waste containers.

In 1987, at a time of internal chaos, a shipment of hazardous wastes was imported to the country and never treated or disposed of properly. Fifteen thousand eight hundred barrels of different sizes, 20 containers of highly toxic industrial waste (Greenpeace Mediterranean, 1995), and some 30,000 tons of contaminated and waste tobacco (METAP, 1995) were illegally brought to Lebanon from Italy in exchange for cash payment to a local militia. The waste was dispersed throughout the country, buried in both coastal and inland hilly areas. The toxic waste consisted of: the explosive substance nitrocellulose; outdated and toxic adhesives banned in Europe, organophosphate pesticides, solvents as well as outdated medication, oil residues and highly toxic heavy metals like lead, mercury and cadmium; arsenic; chlorinated substances; PCBs; wastes from chemical weapons and explosive materials (all difficult to dispose of in industrialized Europe), and other very dangerous substances. Hundreds of barrels contained extremely high concentrations of dioxin (Greenpeace Mediterranean, 1995; METAP, 1995).

In 1988, 5,500 barrels were removed from Lebanon due to public pressure, yet approximately 2,500 tons of toxic waste are believed to have been dumped 40 to 50 kilometers east of Famagusta, between Lebanon and Cyprus. More than

10,000 barrels and the contents of several containers remain in Lebanon or have been dumped along its shores. Technical assistance has been requested from the United Nations Development Programme (UNDP) to locate the drums and properly dispose of their contents.

These remaining wastes, believed to be harmless, were used in dangerous fashions: as fertilizer, pesticide, herbicide, or as so-called raw material to produce paints for furniture and polyurethane for the production of foam mattresses. Some of the toxic waste has been dumped into valleys, household landfills, and quarries. Other barrels were emptied and sold as storage for petrol, water or food, or burned in open air, dumped in the sea, or in the Kesrouan mountains east of Beirut (Greenpeace Mediterranean, 1995).

There have been at least 16 reported serious casualties (including two fatalities) as a direct consequence of the toxic wastes. In addition, swimmers in the Mediterranean Sea have suffered from severe skin cauterizations, a possible consequence of the toxins. Further cases of poisoning, due to leakage of substances into groundwater, have been registered in Okkaibeh (in Kesrouan). Forty goats have died in Uyun al-Siman after drinking polluted water (Greenpeace Mediterranean, 1995). There is also an unsubstantiated rumor that 300 sheep in Zahlé have died due to the toxic wastes (METAP, 1995).

Clearly, there is serious and legitimate concern that water supplies may be poisoned in years to come as the toxic contents of the drums leak into ground and surface water, thereby contaminating soils over a wide area and poisoning wildlife and human populations through bioaccumulation.

Waste Collection

In all of Lebanon, only Beirut had, before the war in 1975, a working solid-waste treatment plan. Beirut's treatment facilities had a capacity of 700 tons per day which has now gone down to no more than 100 tons/day. Compost was produced through a combined mechanical and biological treatment (MoE, 1991).

As a result of the war, the daily collection of refuse has been replaced by a community bin system which requires that residents bring their waste to a communal container up to 50 meters from their homes. This is an uncomfortable change to the residents who were accustomed, before the war, to having their garbage collected at their doorstep (METAP, 1995). Only 57% of the population is served by waste collection services (see Table 5). Facilities for solid waste collection, treatment and disposal are highly inadequate throughout, and especially so in the rural areas.

Waste management is the responsibility of the municipalities, which are often small, have inadequate budgets, and are generally restricted to large urban areas with a population of more than 5,000 (MoE, 1991; METAP, 1995). There are approximately one thousand villages which have no municipalities, and therefore

Table 5

Proportion of Population Served by Solid Waste Collection Operations (1994)

Governorate (*Mohafaza*)	Percentage of Population Served
Beirut	100
North Lebanon	45
Mount Lebanon	57
South Lebanon	18
Beka'a	85
Average in Lebanon	57

Source: METAP, 1995.

have no authority responsible for solid wastes (MoE, 1991). In these villages, solid waste disposal becomes the individual's responsibility. Wastes are deposited at street corners, often for several days awaiting collection, and, in the process, creating major health hazards.

Waste Treatment and Disposal

Current Practices

Most, if not all, of the current disposal sites in Lebanon are uncontrolled dumps (METAP, 1995). Only a fraction (10%) of the collected solid waste is disposed of properly (Fawaz, 1994). Waste is usually dumped with no form of treatment (crude-dumping), transferred to uncontrolled discharge sites which pollute the air, sea and waters, spoil the scenery, and represent imminent risks to public health. Hazardous waste from hospitals are mixed in with other waste and are visible on the surface. In major city disposal sites, which are established without any environmental planning assistance, waste is piled up and then compacted with the help of bulldozers before being pushed towards the sea. In rural areas, solid waste is disposed of into stream beds and rivers, in valleys, and often by the side of the road, a few hundred meters outside the locality. These are regularly set on fire, causing fire hazards as well as serious localized air pollution (Zurayk, 1995b). Many of the coastal towns dump their waste on the shoreline, thus avoiding pollution of potable groundwater, but polluting the beaches and degrading marine life instead (METAP, 1995).

Closer Examination of Four Primary Dump Sites

The *East Beirut-Borj Hammoud* dump receives approximately 3,000 truckloads of waste each day, 90% of which is thought to be demolition waste. This site is planned to be replaced by a wastewater treatment plant and possibly an incinerator (under the name of Dora) (METAP, 1995). Approximately 2,000 barrels of toxic waste were dumped in this landfill from 1987 to 1988. They were part of the 15,800 barrels and 20 containers of toxic waste imported illegally from Italy in 1987 (Greenpeace, 1996).

The notorious *West Beirut-Normandy Bay* site, no longer in use, towers 20 meters above its surroundings. From 1975, Beirut's solid wastes have been thrown in the Normandy dump, on the sea shore at close proximity to the port (Zurayk, 1995b). It consists of approximately 70% municipal solid waste, covered with construction debris. Fires and explosions have occurred at times due to methane production from the anaerobic decomposition of the garbage. There are plans to utilize the waste to form a level surface about five meters above sea level after digging up extract ferrous metal for recycling (METAP, 1995).

The *Tripoli dump*, located at the mouth of the river Abou Ali, blocks half of the river, and encroaches about 150 meters into the sea. Fishermen have complained that the seabed is covered in plastic waste and is damaging to the boat engines.

The *Saida dump* is considered better than average, primarily as a result of the efforts of the municipality and the financial support of the business community (METAP, 1995). Nevertheless, the dump deposits its untreated waste onto the sea shore and near the Saytanig river (Zurayk, 1995b).

Other Facilities for Waste Treatment and Disposal

Waste treatment is virtually nonexistent. The only "treatments" that are utilized are one composting plant and two incinerators. The compost plant, located in Karantina (in southern Beirut) was built between 1975 and 1978. The plant never operated successfully, due to wartime disruptions, low quantity and quality of output, and poor product marketing (METAP, 1995).

During the war, a small incinerator was erected in the Choueifat area, rehabilitated in 1993, and is still operational (Zurayk, 1995b). The incinerator in Amroussieh, near Beirut Airport, is a larger incinerator, built in the 1980s, and whose operations resumed in 1993. This incinerator is not operating to designer specifications primarily due to the nature of waste being burned. The high moisture content of the waste causes low combustion temperature, giving rise to corrosive, and potentially carcinogenic, atmospheric emissions. Nearby residents have protested about odors from incoming waste and from flue gases (METAP, 1995). In addition, the toxic ash of the Amroussieh incinerator is being dumped in the Borj Hammoud landfill (Greenpeace Mediterranean, 1996). On the basis of experience to date, incineration has not been shown to be a satisfactory option, neither technically nor environmentally.

Governmental Plans for Treatment and Disposal

In December 1995, the MoE and the Council for Development and Reconstruction (CDR) formulated waste management plans relying primarily on incinerators and landfills to address Lebanon's growing waste problem. The waste management plan, agreed upon without discussion of alternatives to incineration and landfills, failed to mention waste prevention and reduction, or clean production. A policy focusing on source reduction, and reuse and recycling strategies is critically needed; only then can the cycle of waste production, incineration and landfill-creation be managed.

Incinerators & Landfills

Although incinerators have been scientifically proven to be a main source of air, soil and water pollution, four new incinerators have been proposed by the Ministry of the Environment (Dora in Beirut; Tripoli; Zouk; and Saida). In addition, designs for large landfills have been prepared for five priority towns (Zahlé, Chouf, Tyre (Sour), Baalbek, and Saida), and smaller landfills for each district (total of 24 districts, or *cazas*). The landfills are planned to remain in operation for 15-20 years. However, considering that the waste generation rate is now at an average of 0.8 kg/capita/day, the landfill life will be limited to only 10-15 years. Calcareous rocks, much of which are heavily fissured, underlie the majority of Lebanon. Thus, landfills in the mountains and in the Beka'a valley threaten the country's groundwater reservoirs by allowing rapid percolation of leachate into the groundwater. This problem is exasperated in dump sites which are situated on porous sandy soils, for example, in Metn and Jezzine.

Consultants from the Mediterranean Environmental Technical Assistance Program (METAP) recommend a smaller number of larger landfill sites, instead of a landfill in each of the 24 districts. Landfills are particularly harmful in the mountainous areas where the substratum is fissured limestone (METAP, 1995). It would be better still to encourage waste reduction and recovery to reduce the total volume for final disposal.

Industrial, Clinical and Construction Wastes

The Ministry of the Environment has no special plans for industrial, clinical, and construction waste management. The only plans are to reclaim land from the sea at Beirut using construction waste as filler material, a proposal for which no assessment has been undertaken concerning the potential impacts on currents and marine ecology. Clinical and industrial waste management has not been considered. Clinical waste is an urgent and immediate problem, due to the health risks involved in its mismanagement. If the clinical waste is properly separated, the majority could be dealt with alongside municipal waste. Industrial waste, here, poses another difficulty due to its large quantities (326,000 t/year) and the geographical concentration (50% generated in Greater Beirut Area and Mount Lebanon) (METAP, 1995).

Environmental Impacts of Current Waste Management Practices

One of the most urgent issues affecting waste management is the unknown quantity and locations of the Italian toxic waste. These hazardous wastes pose a grave risk of contaminating water supplies, soils, and agricultural products, bioaccumulating in wildlife, and presenting dangerous implications for human health.

The second critical issue is the dumping of waste along the coast in Tripoli, Beirut, Tyre (Sour), and Saida, which seriously impacts the coastal water quality. The absence of adequate solid waste management has taken a tremendous toll on the marine environment, and degraded the coastal marine ecosystem. Partly due to the accumulation of plastic and metallic waste on the sea bed, fish catches have plummeted from 6,000 t/year in the early 1970s to just 2,500 t/year in the early 1990s (Zurayk, 1995b). Marine pollution can also cause direct health hazards to humans through swimming, and through the bioconcentration of certain contaminants (heavy metals and pesticides).

In addition, the current waste management practices present severe health risk to scavengers and to workers at the dumps, particularly from clinical waste intermixed with domestic waste. The disposal routes of industrial wastes pose serious threats to ground and surface water, particularly in Metn, Aley, and Baabda, where the industry is concentrated. A series of forest fires in the Mount Lebanon area have been associated with unmanaged waste dumps. Lastly, the problem of odor and dust from unmanaged dumps needs to be managed (METAP, 1995).

Management of both the existing dumps and clean-up operations remains unresolved by the government. Solid waste management expertise at the government and contractor level is needed; however, there is a shortage of people in Lebanon with the theoretical knowledge and practical experience in waste management. Options for charging industries and communities for waste collection and disposal as an incentive for waste minimization should be researched. Finally, public awareness and participation is key and fundamental to the success of any environmental project. An awareness campaign in Tripoli/El Mina encouraged residents to use plastic bags to store their waste. Fines for improper disposal increased to about US$12, and a special police force was recruited to enforce littering laws. The amount of waste failing to enter the official collection system each day was reduced by half from over 60 tons, with the best response coming from low-income citizens (METAP, 1995).

V. Air Pollution

Air pollution has not been the subject of any regulation with the exception of the prohibition of the importation and use of diesel vehicles[25] and the required conditions for vehicle engines (MoE, 1991). Both of these regulations are not enforced, and are, for all practical purposes, forgotten. There exists no authority in Lebanon which is directly responsible for air quality protection.

Predictions of the current air quality are based on a 1974 global survey of air pollutants in Lebanon conducted by the National Council for Scientific Research (NCSR) since there is no current data on Lebanese air quality. These predictions

Table 6

Approximation of Current Air Pollutants (1994)

Air Pollutant	1974 Estimate (t/yr.)	1994 Estimate (t/yr.)
CO_2	32,400	259,200
SO_3	475	2,850
Particulate matter	125,000	1,500,000
NO	15,700	125,600
CO	15,230	2,103,220
Hydrocarbons	5,500	2,121,000

Source: Khawlie, 1994.

incorporated the increase in the number of cars, private generators, industries, and other air-polluting sources (see Table 6). This data can serve as a trend indicator.

The primary sources of air pollution arise from gases emitted from automobile combustion and private generators, and from industrial emissions (Slim, 1993). High levels of air pollution are congested particularly around urban centers due to the concentration of traffic and industry, and present a potential health hazard (METAP, 1995).

Vehicle Emissions

There are more than 1.5 million cars in Lebanon, one for every 2 to 3 persons. This ratio is approximately ten times higher than the average in the Middle East of 44.6 cars for every 1000 people (World Resources Institute, 1996). (Improving and extending public transportation would significantly lessen the demand for private vehicles.) Most of the cars are old and poorly maintained,[26] thus their environmental impact is increased due to incomplete fuel combustion. Vehicles are responsible for approximately 70% of the total NOx released into the atmosphere. This figure is expected to rise as the demand for vehicles increases. Furthermore, the import and use of low quality, leaded fuel has resulted in higher toxicity emissions.[27] In addition to NOx, the concentration of lead that is emitted from the cars is predicted to be higher than the World Health Organization guidelines for annual ambient lead concentrations (Slim, 1993).

Power Section Emissions

The power sector consists of thermo-electric power houses, a multiplicity of small combustion sources, and generators installed at numerous industrial premises and residences to compensate for power cuts. This sector is the major emitter of sulfur dioxide (75% in 1993 and 1994, of which 71% was emitted by thermal power stations). The total SO_2 emissions in 1993 was approximately 85,000 tons. With the expected rehabilitation of the power sector and the consequent increased power production, the total SO_2 emissions for the year 2010 are expected to be 180,000 tons. High-sulfur content fuel is commonly used in Lebanon, probably because it is 20 to 30% cheaper than the low sulfur fuel (MoE, 1991).

Industry Emissions

The impact of industry is presumed to be limited due to its modest size. However, it is significant enough to cause serious localized pollution (refer to health section on Chekka/Selaata). Cement production accounts for the main source of the industrial pollutants. This industry produces two kinds of emissions: SO_2, CO, NOx and particulates mainly from combustion; and significant particulate emissions associated with the handling of raw materials and final product. Emissions of SO_2, CO, NOx would increase, and a variety of hydrocarbon emissions would arise, if either of the existing refineries were reopened.

Possible Link between Air Pollution and Various Ailments

Given the information available on primary sources of air pollution, a serious potential hazard to human health from air pollution is clear. There are four main potentially damaging gases: lead, NOx, SO_2, and ozone. Due to the scarcity of information available on the other gases, only lead shall be discussed.

The concentration of lead emitted from cars is predicted to be greater than 1.0 $\mu g/m^3$, higher than the World Health Organization guidelines for annual ambient lead concentrations (Slim, 1993). The main source of lead, a multi-level pollutant, is as an anti-knock additive in gasoline (Nadakavokaren, 1986). Between one-third and one-half of inhaled lead reaches the bloodstream (Nadakavokaren, 1986), making the airborne lead contribution of the same order as that of ingested lead in food (Goyer, 1972). As an airborne pollutant, lead has been strongly implicated in the widespread contamination of human diet (Nriago, 1980), and determined to cause damage to human health.

Among the health effects of lead in the atmosphere are anemia, hypertension, gastrointestinal distress, adverse reproductive outcomes, and both peripheral and central nervous system abnormalities (Wegman, 1993; Mahaffey, 1992; Nadakavokaren, 1986; Nriago, 1980). In addition, evidence indicates that chronic low-level exposure to lead can inhibit the normal development of children's intellectual abilities. In 1986, the learning ability and behavior of as many as 18% of all US inner city children were being adversely affected by sub-clinical levels of lead in their systems, due primarily to inhalation of lead particles from automobile exhausts (Nadakavokaren, 1986). Such evidence is of critical importance and relevance to Lebanon, where most of the population resides in high density, traffic-congested urban areas.

Based upon experience, the removal of lead as a gasoline additive will help reduce the population blood lead values (Wegman, 1993). What is critically needed is the replacement of leaded fuel with unleaded fuel, stricter regulations and maintenance of car quality, specifically with regards to exhaust efficiency, and research on and monitoring of the overall health of the population (such as assessing blood lead values).

Problem Area: Chekka/Selaata Region

Living in and around the Chekka/Selaata region has become a health hazard.

The cement, asbestos and chemical industries in Chekka and Selaata in northern Lebanon are a major source of local marine, groundwater, soil and air pollution. Along the northern coast, six factories producing cement, lime, sugar, and paper contribute significantly to air quality degradation. Asbestos is still currently used in spite of an international ban on this carcinogen. Two cement industries discharge their toxic effluents directly into beaches or near beaches where people swim. Solidified industrial waste is also piled outside of the plants, and thus poses a serious danger of contaminating the surrounding ground by attaching to dust particles. Some reports already attribute incidences of asthma and death from cancer in the region due to the high levels of air pollution.

Sample tests carried out in 1996 by the Earth Research Center revealed groundwater contamination by several toxic chemicals, including HCH,[28] an organohalogen compound that causes diarrhea, tremors, convulsions, circulatory collapse and cancer. Chlorinated insecticides were also found. This insecticide accumulates in humans, animals, birds and the general environment. Samples further revealed the presence of a wide range of polcyclic aromatic hydrocarbons (PAH), a persistent toxic chemical that bioaccumulates in fish and invertebrates, thus posing a danger to the human population through ingestion of contaminated seafood products. Furthermore, chronic exposure to the PAHs as vapors or as attachments to dust particles can cause lung and respiratory cancer (Greenpeace Mediterranean, 1996; Lave, 1987).

A large number of children have been affected by silicoses, with a high incidence of acute respiratory diseases. Vegetation in the area also shows clear signs of damage caused by the dust and chemicals (Greenpeace Research Laboratories, 1996). The Sibline cement factory on the southern coast of Lebanon is accused of similar ills, with inhabitants and doctors of the neighboring Barja village reporting a high incidence of asthma (Greenpeace Research Laboratories, 1996).

VI. Response to Environmental Concerns

Government

The Ministry of Environment (MoE) was created in 1993[29] as a response to growing public concern over the environmental degradation in Lebanon. Three years later, the decree creating the MoE has yet to be fully implemented, and thus the MoE is unable to perform the wide range of duties assigned to it. It is afforded minuscule funding; in 1995, its budget was approximately US$5 million (METAP, 1995). It has a weak tax base, and suffers from a significant lack of proper management and qualified technical personnel. All these characteristics render the Ministry unable to enforce its own laws and decrees, or even to conduct preliminary monitoring.

The MoE is not alone in administering environmental management, but shares responsibility[30] for environmental management with eight other ministries[31] and eight key institutions[32] (METAP, 1995). Lack of coordination and lack of a unified vision are rampant between these organizations, and serves to further render enforcement, monitoring, and any kind of environmental management weak and inefficient.

The Lebanese government has been attempting to appease the growing concern for environmental protection, yet its main objective remains short-term, quick development and construction, primarily of Beirut. Its environmental concerns are limited to solving the immediate problems of pollution control, namely those which pose a clear and direct risk to human health and that may impede the government's ambitious plans for the commercial development of the country. In the arena of waste management and pollution control—with the exception of air pollution—the government is making preliminary progress, again mainly limited to Beirut. However, the more complex problems of environmental management, the issues requiring long-term vision and integration of activities, have yet to be faced. Conservation and sustainable use of environmental resources, for example, have not received the necessary attention or been given serious consideration. In addition, although Lebanon is a signatory of several international conventions,[33] it has yet to implement any of the requirements or guidelines.

Programs

Reconstruction Plans

In its plan for reconstruction and development, the Horizon 2000 governmental program assigns priority to primary infrastructure restoration (see Table 7). Unfortunately, no environmental assessment or mitigation is followed, or even required, by the government for any of the programs and projects. Most of the expenditure for transportation is allotted to road construction, thus taking more land into urban development and possibly increasing traffic flow. The net impact on the environment will likely be negative, especially since no environmental assessments are undertaken in road design and construction.

One of the governmental programs with immediate effects on the environment is the introduction and rehabilitation of solid waste management. The immediate effect will be the removal of solid waste from the streets; however, the long-term effect will be negative if, as proposed, this process will be through the utilization of incinerators and numerous, small landfills. Fortunately, included in the governmental plans for the power sector is the construction of new plants to run on either low sulfur oil or natural gas, thereby leading to lower emissions of sulfur dioxide.

Table 7

Expenditures for the Horizon 2000 *Governmental Plan*

Sectors	Percentage of Total Expenditure
Transportation	25
Electricity	17.7
Education	10.8
Housing and Reconstruction	9
Sewers and Septic Tanks	6.5
Telecommunications	5.5
Health	5.4
Agriculture	5.4
Water	4.6
Industry	3.5
Governmental Buildings	2.2
Garbage Collection and Treatment	1.5
Services of the Private Sector	1.5
Oil and Gas	0.7
	Total US$13,000 million

Source: Delphi Consulting International, 1995.

Education

The Ministry of Environment, in cooperation with the Ministry of Education, have vowed to increase environmental programs throughout the public schools. The Lebanese government has also began an awareness campaign for solid waste management as part of the solid waste management program for Beirut.

Legislation and Policy

The past several years have witnessed a proliferation of laws to protect and manage the environment. At first glance, the laws and decrees may seem to be precisely what the environment requires. Upon closer examination, the laws reveal themselves as weak, antiseptic-lacking Band-Aids; they merely attempt to deal with the symptoms, the visible wounds, and usually fail to even heal those wounds adequately. Most laws are not implemented either due to financial constraints, lack of effective institutional capacity, internal corruption and inter-agency strife, shortage of technical expertise in the private and public sector, and/or, occasionally, due to public opposition.

Conservation Measures: Protected Areas

The creation of protected areas in Lebanon is a preliminary step towards the protection of Lebanese natural resources and heritage. Currently, less than 0.5% of Lebanon's total area is protected (Dean, 1994b). Several laws and decrees have been drafted and passed that aim to protect certain endangered, or high-biodiversity habitats. Ehden Forest, the most floristically rich area in Lebanon, and Palm Islands, the three islands of the coast of Tripoli that serve as prime areas for migratory birds, were declared protected areas in 1992. However, only recently (4 years later) are protective measures beginning to be enforced. A 1993 draft law, stressing the need to prevent the destruction of forests and set up protected areas, remains a draft due to financial constraints. In addition, a recent degree (August 1996) by the National Council of Scientific Research declared all cedar forests protected areas. The means through which this decree is to be enforced are unknown.

In 1996, the Lebanese government signed the United Nations proposal for Protected Areas for Sustainable Development in Lebanon, accepted by the UN in May 1995 (Masri, R., 1996b). The project will be funded with US$2.5 million from the United Nations and US$578,000 from the Lebanese government.[34] The project's overall development objectives are to conserve endemic and endangered wildlife and their habitats, incorporate wildlife conservation as an integral part of sustainable human development, and strengthen the institutional capacity of governmental agencies and non-governmental organizations (NGOs). The proposal declares three sites[35] to be nationally protected areas: Ehden Forest, Barouk Mountain, and Palm Islands (Dean, 1994a).

Conservation Measures: Hunting Legislation

The creation of protected areas alone will not suffice to protect wildlife, especially birds. "Most of Lebanon can be considered as a huge 'bottleneck' for migratory raptors and storks, therefore. . . to conserve these species, wide-scale enforcement of the current hunting regulations is necessary" (Evans, 1994). Hunting legislation has been highly subject to public pressure, both from those who are struggling to protect the wildlife and those who enjoy hunting and rely on the hunting industry for their incomes (i.e. those who sell guns, bullets, etc.). A law banning all hunting for three years (from 1995-1997) was passed in January 1995. Despite appeals from environmental organizations and animal rights lobbyists, the law was repealed in September due to greater pressure from the Association of Gun Salesmen (Reuter, 1 September 1996; Reuter, 5 September 1996; Reuter, 13 September 1996). A shorter ban on all hunting on Lebanese soil was then passed, this time limiting the moratorium to two years (1996-1997) (Masri, R., 1996a). Success of this latest ban has not yet been scientifically assessed; however, the number of birds has visibly increased and their singing is once again heard in Lebanon.

Pollution Prevention

The Lebanese government has been increasing its attention on pollution prevention; as of yet, all that has been allotted is 'attention' and little 'action.' In late 1994, the MoE established environmental standards for protection of the environment from pollution, governing both air and water pollution. Although a starting point, the MoE lacks institutional capacity for effective implementation of the standards and there is virtually no capacity within industry for measurement and control of emissions.

Similar problems arise with the enforcement of laws prepared by the Ministry for Industry and Petroleum for regulating storage, transportation and distribution facilities of petroleum products.

Quarries

The only legislation to require environmental impact assessment and restoration remains merely ink on paper. Grassroot pressure led the government to initiate a UNDP-funded project that culminated in the introduction of a new law for regulating quarrying. The law required that sites suitable for quarrying in Lebanon be determined by the MoE, and that a multi-sectoral National Commission for Quarries be formed to evaluate and update the quarries regulations, ensure that sites are rehabilitated, evaluate application for licenses and recommend legal action when needed. In addition, the law required an environmental impact study and land rehabilitation. Work must cease if any historical, natural (fossils) or archaeological items are found (METAP, 1995). This law, altough most definitely a step forward, remains ineffective due to lack of finances and technical expertise.

Non-Governmental Organizations (NGOs)

"The awareness of the need to conserve and protect ecosystems at risk has trickled down from local NGOs to the governmental offices over the past three years" (Zurayk, 1995a). The rise and increasing popularity of environmental NGOs has been the instigator for the governmental actions to protect the environment. Environmental NGOs were first established in Lebanon in the 1970s.[36] Their activities decreased during the war, when environmental concern became viewed as a luxury, and then resurfaced in strength as the war lessened. By the mid 1990s, approximately 120 environmental NGOs had formed (most of which are local), including thirty-two primary institutions and societies (René Moawad Foundation, 1994; METAP, 1995).

The activities of the NGOs focus primarily on local issues, with the exception of a few primary national NGOs,[37] and on increasing awareness. In this regard, they have the potential to play a significant role, and have already demonstrated this potential in certain, localized examples. However, like the governmental agencies, the NGOs suffer from a lack of technical expertise, coordination, and finances.

Public education of environmental issues is generally low, as revealed by confessions of environmentally destructive and dangerous activities in polls taken by METAP consultants. However, the presence of such a relatively high number[38] of active environmental NGOs reflects growing environmental awareness and highlights the inefficiency and inadequacy of governmental activities and support. There is considerable scope, and a definite need, for the involvement of NGOs and the private sector in the environmental management process.

Foreign Governments

The main foreign governments that are assisting Lebanon in environmental management are Japan and France. Japan has recently given Lebanon a US$130 million loan as part of its participation in the reconstruction of the war-damaged country.[39] The 25-year-loan, bearing a 2.5% interest and a 7-year grace period, has been allocated to treat polluted Lebanese shores (UPI, 1 April 1996). France has assisted Lebanon primarily through scientific and technical skills. French researchers have worked considerably with Lebanese scientists on the management and protection of the cedars in Bcharre. In addition, they have designed Beirut's urban park, the first national park in Lebanon.

International Agencies and NGOs

The primary international agencies that have contributed to Lebanon's environmental welfare include the United Nations (through the UNDP and FAO projects), the World Conservation Union and International Council for Bird Preservation (both of whom work with the nationally based NGO-SPNL), BirdLife International, and Greenpeace Mediterranean (working with the Greenline in Lebanon).

The World Bank has assisted through the funding of projects. It recently approved a US$31 million loan to Lebanon to assist in developing land and water resources. The credit is to fund a project aimed at increasing access to isolated rural areas and improving the institutional capacity of the Ministry of Agriculture. The project will include soil terraces, pond construction on hills, and the provision of fruit trees and irrigation equipment (UPI, 16 September 1996).

VIII. Conclusion

Having endured centuries of environmental degradation, Lebanon can no longer continue on this route of commercial development without serious regard to the environment. The very health of Lebanon's residents and its marine and terrestrial ecosystems are threatened. Lebanon's economic integrity also depends upon the health of its environment.

Environmental mismanagement is guided by the present social, economic, and political climate—all of which are affected by internal and external factors. The direct consequences, and the ensuing repercussions, of the wars in Lebanon severely affected the state of the environment. In addition, Israel's occupation of 160 villages in south Lebanon, its continuous terrorization of Lebanese people—especially in the South—and its theft of Lebanese waters from the Litani River are significant obstacles to complete environmental management. Other major factors that contribute to the current environmental hardship include: (1) the change in the socio-economic lifestyle and the lack of environmental awareness; and (2) the government's inefficiency at implementing regulations and its financial constraints.

Recommendations and Horizons for Further Research

The key priority areas for environmental action (that have yet to be sufficiently discussed and implemented) include: (1) the development and implementation of wise land-use planning, with a focus on the coastal zone; (2) water resource management and investment; (3) control of soil erosion; (4) management of hazardous and toxic wastes; (5) waste reduction, and utilization of composting; and (6) control and improvement of urban air quality. To solve these problems, a multi-dimensional approach should be followed, including institutional, economic, and educational reforms. Governmental institutions should coordinate their activities more efficiently, strive towards the enforcement of their laws and regulations, create and extend extension education, and undertake data gathering. Environmental management should not be directed merely through regulations, but should also include the use of economic incentives and various market-based instruments for environmental protection by the private sector. Education and increased environmental awareness are critical to further strengthen and encourage wise environmental management, and to build a wide base of community support and public understanding.

In addition, the establishment and maintenance of a scientific data base is needed, particularly for monitoring human impact on the environment. However, despite the lack of an adequate scientific data base, the more important constraints on environmental management are not scientific but are political, social, and economic. Efforts and plans towards natural resource management and conservation must seek this cross-functional integration. Strategies are required that work with the traditional systems and recognize the economic and social requirements of the users of the land (Stocking, 1981). Agro-forestry or forestry projects, public extension education, community rather than individual action, and long-term investment (Ryan, 1983; Zurayk, 1995a) are vital for soil conservation, agricultural production, and forestry management and regeneration. Environmental sustainability cannot be separated from the socio-economic constraints of the community, nor from the overall political situation in the country.

NOTES

1   In February 1993, the Minister of Tourism announced a plan for the development of the tourism sector. The plan included rehabilitation of hotels, service and management training, rehabilitation of the Ministry of Tourism, the cleaning of beaches, and the building of tourism offices throughout the country. In addition, 1994 was declared the year of the tourist in Lebanon.

2   Israel invaded Lebanon again in 1993, and attacked Lebanon for 17 days in April 1996. In addition, Israel has been occupying approximately 12% of Lebanon's land area since 1978. The April 1996 aggression resulted in the deaths of more than 200 people, destruction of main electrical power plants and of primary water reservoirs, and significant harm to 147 towns and villages in the south (Masri, R., 1996c).

3   Decreased precipitation.

4   Specifically, the war destroyed wastewater treatment plants and sewerage systems. The 1992
     estimate to rehabilitate the physical infrastructure in the water sector alone is US$45 million
     (METAP, 1995).

5   The agricultural losses in 1975-1976 alone were more than US$175 million. In 1989-1990, the
     losses amounted to US$50 million (METAP, 1995). The losses from 1976 until 1989 are unknown.

6   Imperial Eagle, Corn Crake, Syrian Serin, Lesser Kestrel, and Audouin's Gull

7   Material deposited by flood

8   Due to the slow rates of soil formation, this reduction in land productivity is an irreversible process.

9   In addition to its direct ecological costs to agriculture and forestry, soil erosion is usually accompa-
     nied by a decrease in water quantity caused by runoff losses, and by a degradation of surface water
     quality due to higher sediment loads. The useful life of dams, reservoirs and irrigation structures
     is thus reduced, and higher costs on domestic water treatment are imposed (Zurayk, 1995a).

10   A judicious reforestation policy, implemented today, could reduce water lost into the sea by 20%,
     and increase water availability in the country by 50 to 100% (MoE, 1991).

11   The Green Plan also initiated several afforestation pilot projects, reforesting a total area of
     2,000 hectares.

12   The demand for wood as a raw material (primarily for case manufacturing) has also dropped due
     to the availability of plastic for boxes.

13   Contradictions in the literature: The Ministry of the Environment (1991) and METAP (1995) state
     respectively that 34 to 35 % of Lebanon's total land area is cultivable, while Osman and Cocks
     (1992) write in Experimental Agriculture that "only 23% of the total land area in Lebanon is
     cultivable."

14   The main agricultural products commonly are: cereals, fruits (including olives), vegetables, to-
     bacco, greenhouse production, and livestock production (METAP, 1995; MoE, 1991).

15   Not considering the almost continuous, weekly Israeli bombardment of the South, the successive
     Israeli invasions and attacks (1978, 1982, 1993, and 1996) have resulted in the displacement of
     more than half a million residents from the South. In addition, 75% of the tobacco production of
     the South, as well as 140,000 livestock heads and one million poultry units have been destroyed
     (Doueiri, 1996).

16   Since 1992, the Lebanese government has initiated limited action to support the agricultural sector.
     Specifically, it has purchased 6 percent of wheat output at supportive prices and initiated more than
     25 projects in irrigation, animal production, fishery, and integrated rural development (Doueiri,
     1996). Although beneficial, further action, integrated within a comprehensive policy, is needed to
     save the sector from collapse.

17   Fish catches: 6,000 tons in 1974; an average of 1,750 tons in 1994 (1,000-2,500 tons). Working
     fishing boats: 1,000 in 1974; 986 in 1994.

18   The Israeli Navy shoots at the fishermen if they proceed beyond 1 km off the Lebanese coastline,
     and if they fish during the night.

19   Referring to sand and gravel extraction from unconsolidated tertiary and quaternary deposits

20   This is compounded by the naturally low efficiency of water recovery and use due to the steep
     slopes and local geology, which favor dissipation of water to the sea or into the groundwater.

21   Chlorination should not be the only treatment utilized, especially since it is a controversial, possibly
     disease-inducing, treatment (Bull, 1992).

22   In 1990: Nabeh el Tasseh in South Lebanon, 20 April; Tayr Debba in South Lebanon, 12-13 July;
     Bebnin in North Lebanon, 20 August; Denbo in the Akkar region, North Lebanon, 15 November
     (MoE, 1991).

23 Due to the respective mayors' opposition, asbestos-constructed water pipes will not be utilized in the neighboring villages of Hamanah and Qarnayel.

24 The average amount of domestic waste is 0.8 kg/capita/day. In practice, the real generation rate varies widely from this average figure due to seasons, incomes, and tastes.

25 Law of 10 June,1961 and decree 579 of 1 August 1956

26 The Lebanese government does, however, prohibit the importation of cars over 8 years old.

27 In 1993, 10,236,000 tons of leaded gasoline 92 Octane and 1,749,000 tons of leaded gasoline 98 Octane were imported, in comparison with only 7,000 tons of unleaded fuel (0000t) (METAP, 1995).

28 1,2,3,4,5,6-hexachlorocyclohexane

29 Law 216 on 2 April 1993 (Dean, 1994a)

30 These responsibilities are: wastewater, pollution, land use and coastal zone management, forests and agriculture, solid waste and hazardous waste, cultural heritage, industrial pollution, and water resources.

31 Ministries of Agriculture, Tourism, Housing, Hydraulic and Electrical Resources, Public Health, Urban Affairs, Public Works, and Industry and Petroleum

32 Urban Planning, Municipalities, *Mohafaza, Caza,* Council of Development and Reconstruction, Roads and Planning, Council of Grand Projects, and Department of Antiquities

33 Lebanon ratified the World Heritage Convention (3 Feb. 1983), the Barcelona Convention for the Protection of the Mediterranean Sea (18 May 1983), and the Convention on Biological Diversity (12 June 1992).

34 During the course of the project, the Lebanese government will also provide an annual support of 50 million Lebanese Lira (approximately $32,000) to each of the protected areas.

35 The three sites were chosen based upon their legislative standing, representative ecosystems, location, and level of biodiversity.

36 In addition, some established humanitarian organizations, such as Amel Association, had included environmental management and education amongst their programs.

37 Society for the Protection of Nature in Lebanon (SPNL) and Greenline are among the organizations that concentrate their attention nationally, instead of locally, and work with international NGOs.

38 One hundred twenty local and national environmental organizations is a considerable number for the small size of Lebanon. If their activities were better coordinated then the total number of organizations would decrease, especially in local areas in which several organizations strive towards the exact same purpose.

39 Foreign assistance may not always benefit the environment. Italy's assistance in Lebanon's postwar reconstruction is the official reason the Lebanese government gives for not wanting to demand that Italy decontaminate and return the toxic waste it illegally imported to Lebanon in 1987 (URI, 17 May 1996).

REFERENCES

ABU NASR, J. and R. ZANKOUL

    1992 "Industrial Pollution, Agriculture, Farming, Water Pollution, Food, Air in Lebanon." *Al-Raida.* Winter 1992, Vol. X, No. 56: 8-11.

ALOUF, N.

    1994 "L'Environment Dulcicole a Liban, Bilan et Perpectives." *Proceedings of the National Conference on Water in Lebanon,* May. (In French)

AL-KHALIDI, M. and R. ZURAYK
    1994 "The Sustainability of Internationally Funded Community Based Sanitation Projects in Lebanon." Water Environment Federation. *67th Annual Conference and Exposition.* Chicago: Illinois, October 15-19.
American University of Beirut (AUB)
    1994 Position Paper on Lebanon. Paper presented at the *Regional Workshop on the Environment in the Middle East.* Jordan University of Science and Technology: Irbid, Jordan, April.
ATALLAH, H., R. OUEIDA, and S. MORTADA
    1992 "Identification of the Sources of Industrial Pollutants on the Lebanese Coast." Friedrich Ebert Foundation, August.
AYAD, M. and A. WAY
    1993 "Fertility Decline and Population Policies in the Arab World." Prepared for *The Middle East Studies Association,* 27th Annual Meeting, November 11-14, North Carolina.
AWWA
    1986 "Are Asbestos Fibers in Drinking Water Harmful?" Roundtable.
BROWN, J.P.
    1969 *The Lebanon and Phoenicia, the physical setting and the forest.* Beirut: Centennial Publications.
BULL, R.
    1992 "Toxicology of drinking water disinfection." Lipperman, M. (ed.), *Environmental Toxicants: Human Exposures and their Health Effects.* New York: Van Nostrand Reinhold.
CHANEY, W.R. and M. BASBOUS
    1978 "The Cedars of Lebanon: Witnesses of History." *Economic Botany.* 32: 118-123.
DEAN, F.A.
    1994a *GEF Project Selection Criteria Sheet.* Lebanon—Protected Areas for Sustainable Development, 30 October.
    1994b *Wildlife Conservation for Sustainable Development in Arab Countries.* Economic and Social Commission for Western Asia (ESCWA), December.
Delphi Consulting International
    1995 *Lebanon: Above and beyond the year 2000.* Washington, DC.
DOUEIRI, D.
    1996 "Towards a comprehensive understanding of the agricultural policy in Lebanon." Ph.D. Dissertation. Department of Islamic Studies. University of California at Los Angeles.
DREGNE, H.E.
    1992 "Erosion and Soil Productivity in Asia." *Journal of Soil and Water Conservation.* 47: 8-13.
EKEN, S., P. CASHIN, S.N. ERBAS, J. MARTELINO, and A. MAZAREI
    1995 *Economic Dislocation and Recovery in Lebanon.* Occasional Paper 120. Washington, D.C.: International Monetary Fund.
EVANS, M.I.
    1994 Important Bird Areas in the Middle East. *BirdLife Conservation Series* No. 2. United Kingdom: BirdLife International.
FANAR
    1994 "The Quarries and their effects on the environment in Lebanon: Examples of "Nahr el-Mott" and the "Jurds of Hasroune." Department of Geography. Lebanese University. *Proceedings of the National Conference on Water in Lebanon,* May. (In French)
Future Television (FTV)
    15 October 1996 "Population and Housing Surveys." Beirut, Lebanon.

GOYER, R.A. and J.J. CHISOLM
  1972 "Lead." In: D. Lee (ed.), *Metallic Contaminants and Human Health*. New York: Academic Press.
Greenpeace Mediterranean
  1995 *Waste Trade in the Mediterranean. Toxic Attack Against Lebanon. Case One: Toxins From Italy*. Greenpeace Report, Malta, August.
  1995b *Toxic Waste from Italy in Lebanon: Sample Test Results 1995*. Greenpeace International Research Laboratories, Exeter University, Mediterranean Office, September.
  1996 *The Burning Truth in the Mediterranean*. A Greenpeace report on plans for incinerators and landfills in the southern Mediterranean region, and the failure of governments to implement clean production and waste prevention programs. Greenpeace Mediterranean Office, July.
Greenpeace Research Laboratories
  1996 *Heavy metal analysis of waste and environmental samples collected from industrial areas in Chekka, Selaata and Beirut, Lebanon (1995-1996)*. United Kingdom: Earth Resources Centre, University of Exeter.
HUDSON, N.W.
  1981 "Social, political and economic aspects of soil conservation." In: R.P.C. Morgan (ed.), *Soil Conservation: Problems and Prospects*. New York, N.Y.: Wiley and Sons.
HUGHES, J.D. and J.V. THIRGOOD
  1982 "Deforestation in ancient Greece and Rome." *The Ecologist* 12: 196-208.
JARJOUI, M, E. BOUTROS, J. AOUN and P. MALYCHEF
  1994 "Photocatalytic Detoxification Treatment by Solar Energy of Chemical Pollutants in Drinking Water and Catalyzed by (Ag/ZnO-TiO$_2$) Supported in SIO$_2$." *Proceedings of the National Conference on Water in Lebanon*. Conference organized by the National Council of Scientific Research and the College of Sciences, Lebanese University. Lebanese University, May.
JURDI, M.
  1992 "National Survey on Drinking Water Quality in Lebanon." *First Seminar on Water in Lebanon*, November, AUB, UNICEF. Beirut, Lebanon. (In Arabic)
KHAIR, K., N. AKER, F. HADDAD, M. JURDI, and A. HACHACH
  1994 "The Environmental Impacts of Humans on Groundwater in Lebanon." *Water, Air and Soil Pollution*, 78: 37-49.
KHALAF, G.
  1994 "Contribution to the Ecological Study of Three Lebanese Streams: Nahr Ibrahim, Nahr el-Kalb, and Nahr Antelias." *Proceedings of the National Conference on Water in Lebanon*. Conference organized by the National Council of Scientific Research and the College of Sciences, Lebanese University. Lebanese University, May. (In French)
KHAWLI, M.R.
  1994 "The Potentials of Environmental Hazards Resulting from Quarrying Operations in Lebanon." *Proceedings of the National Conference on Water in Lebanon*. Conference organized by the National Council of Scientific Research and the College of Sciences, Lebanese University. Lebanese University, May.
KOLARS, J.
  1992 "Water Resources of the Middle East." *Canadian Journal of Development Studies*. 103-119.
LAKKIS, S.
  1994 "Marine Pollution and Management of the Lebanese Coast." *Proceedings of the National Conference on Water in Lebanon*. Conference organized by the National Council of Scientific Research and the College of Sciences, Lebanese University. Lebanese University, May. (In French)

LAVE, L. and A. UPTON
    1987 "Regulating Toxic Chemicals in the Environment." In: Lave and Upton (ed.), *Toxic Chemicals, Health, and the Environment.* London: Johns Hopkins University Press.
MAHAFFEY, K.R., J. MCKINNEY and J.R. REIGART
    1992 "Lead and Compounds" Lipperman, M. (ed.), *Environmental Toxicants: Human Exposures and their Health Effects.* New York: Van Nostrand Reinhold.
MASRI, R.
    1995 *Change in the Cedar Forest of Ain Zhalta, Jabal el-Barouk, Lebanon, 1965-1994.* Duke University.
    1996a "Hunting Ban in Lebanon Until End of 1997." *Al-Jadid,* Vol. 2: 18, March.
    1996b "Three Protected Areas to be Created in Lebanon." *Al-Jadid,* Vol. 2: 18, March.
    1996c "A Chronicle of Human, Economic and Cultural Suffering." *Al-Jadid,* Vol. 2: 16-23, April.
MASRI, T. and TALIH, T.
    1996 "An integrated, holistic approach towards the protection of the *Pinus pinea* forests." Geographic Information Systems Department. National Council of Scientific Research. Unpublished.
Mediterranean Environmental Technical Assistance Program (METAP)
    1995 *Lebanon: Assessment of the State of the Environment.* Financed by the Commission of the European Communities, United Nations Development Programme, European Investment Bank, and World Bank, November.
MIKESELL, M.W.
    1969 "The Deforestation of Mount Lebanon." *The Geographical Review,* Vol. 59: 1-28.
Ministry of State for the Environment (MoE)
    1991 *National Report on the Environment and Development in Lebanon.*
NEHMEH, M.
    1978 *Wild Flowers of Lebanon.* National Council for Scientific Research, Beirut.
NADAKAVUKAREN, A.
    1986 *Man and Environment: A health perspective.* Illinois: Waveland Press, Inc.
New Scientist
    1995 "Dead in the Water." *New Scientist,* 4 February.
NRIAGU, J.O.
    1980 "Lead in the atmosphere and its effect on lead in humans." In: Singhal, R. and J. Thomas (eds), *Lead Toxicity.* Munich: Urban & Schwarzenberg.
OSMAN, A.E. and P.S. COCKS
    1992 "Prospects for improving Mediterranean Grasslands in Lebanon through seeding, fertilization, and protection from grazing." *Experimental Agriculture,* 28: 461-471.
René Moawad Foundation and Friedrich Naumann Foundation
    1994 "Coming to the aid of nature." *Conference on Environmental Problems on National and International Levels.* 23 March, Beirut, Lebanon.
Reuter
    1 September 1996 "Bardot pleads for hunting ban in Lebanon." Beirut, Lebanon.
    5 September 1996 "Bardot plea winds hunting ban in Lebanon." Beirut, Lebanon.
    13 September 1996 "Lebanon rebuffs Bardot, hunting to resume." Beirut, Lebanon.
RYAN, John
    1983 "Soil Conservation in Lebanon." *Journal of Soil and Water Conservation,* 38: 404-406.
SLIM, K.
    1993 The Current Status of the Environment in Greater Beirut During Reconstruction. *The National Seminar on Environmental Awareness,* AUB-UNESCO.

STOCKING, M.A.

1981 "Conservation strategies for less developed countries." In: R.P.C. Morgan (ed.), *Soil Conservation: Problems and Prospects*. New York, N.Y.: Wiley and Sons.

THIRGOOD, J.V.

1981 *Man and the Mediterranean Forest: a history of resource depletion*. London: Academic Press.

TOFT, P., M.E. MEEK, D.T. WIGLE, J.C. MERANGER

1984 "Asbestos in Drinking Water." *CRC Critical Review in Environmental Control*. Volume 14, Issue 2: 151-197.

TOHMÉ, G. and H. TOHMÉ

1985a *The Ecology of Lebanon: Facts and Examples*. Lebanese University Publications. Natural Science Department, Number 15, Beirut. (In Arabic)

1985b *The Wild Mammals of Lebanon*. Lebanese University Publications. Natural Science Department, Number 16, Beirut. (In French)

1986 *Birds of Lebanon*. Lebanese University Publications. Natural Science Department, Number 17, Beirut. (In Arabic)

United Nations Economic and Social Commission for Western Asia (UNESCWA)

1993 *Food and Agriculture Organization of the United Nations. Agriculture and Development in Western Asia* A joint publication of United Nations Economic and Social Commission for Western Asia and the Food and Agriculture Organization of the United Nations. December, Number 15.

UPI

17 May 1996 "Greenpeace halts Lebanon waste pact." Beirut, Lebanon.

1 April 1996 "Japan, Islamic Bank grant Lebanon loans." Beirut, Lebanon.

16 September 1996 "World Bank lends Lebanon $31 million." Washington DC.

15 October 1996 "Survey: Lebanon population 3.1 million." Beirut, Lebanon.

17 October 1996 "Lebanese poor estimated at 1 million." Beirut, Lebanon.

WEGMAN, D.

1993 "Air Pollution." In: Bertollini, R., M.D. Lebowitz, R. Saracci, and D.A. Savitz (Eds), *Environmental Epidemiology: Exposure and Disease*. Published on behalf of the World Health Organization Regional Office for Europe by Lewis Publishers.

World Conservation Monitoring Centre

1993 *1994 IUCN Red List of Threatened Animals*. The IUCN Species Survival Commission. International Union for the Conservation of Nature (IUCN), United Kingdom.

World Resources Institute

1996 *World Resources 1996-97: A guide to the global environment*. A joint publication by the World Resources Institute, the United Nations Environment Programme, the United Nations Development Programme, and the World Bank. Oxford University Press.

ZURAYK, R.

1994a "Rehabilitating the ancient terraced lands of Lebanon." *Journal of Soil and Water Conservation*, 49: 106-112.

1994b "Land degradation and mitigation in the Lebanese mountains: The breakdown of traditional systems." UNDP/DHA Disaster Management Training Programme, 29 July.

1994c "The role of the local community in the prevention and mitigation of forest fires: Case studies from Lebanon." *International Civil Defense Journal*, VII: 31-34.

1995a *The Natural Environment of Lebanon*. State of the Environment Report. World Bank-METAP and Ministry of the Environment. Beirut, Lebanon.

1995b *The Environment of Women and Children in Lebanon*. UNICEF country analysis document. UNICEF, Beirut, Lebanon.

An Imperiled Promised Land

The Antecedents of Israel's Environmental Crises and Prospects for Progress

ALON TAL*

ABSTRACT

Israel's rapid economic development has had a steep environmental price. Despite remarkable achievements in such areas as solar heating, waste water reuse and reclamation of desert lands, most environmental indicators throughout this small country reveal rapid deterioration. Degradation of water and air quality is severe and issues such as solid waste management, preservation of open spaces and pesticide usage require immediate national attention and resources. Beyond the physical causes of these problems, the article identifies the historical and cultural origins of Israel's ecological crises. A number of events converged during the 1990s, including the creation of an environmental Ministry, to produce a new era for the country's environmental movement and an attendant sense of optimism. The article proposes a number of fundamental revisions in public policy in such diverse areas as public transportation population policy, consolidation of ministerial authorities and environmental education that are necessary to move the country onto a sustainable route.

I. Introduction: Israel's Environmental Crises

THE MIRACULOUS REDEMPTION of a "barren" land has always been touted as one of Israel's most impressive achievements. Ecological criteria and environmental data, nevertheless, present a far less complimentary picture of stewardship during the third Jewish Commonwealth. Since Israel's establishment in 1948, there have indeed been notable achievements in such diverse areas as water conservation, forestry, solar energy and anti-desertification (Israel Ministry of Environment, 1992). Yet, when viewed in a broader environmental context, the first century of Zionist settlement can primarily be characterized as a non-sustainable gallop towards ecological disaster.

*   The Arava Institute for Environmental Studies, Kibbutz Ketura-D.N. Eilot 88040, Israel.

Although a small country with a total land area of 20,000 square kilometers, Israel is blessed with a geographic and biological diversity that more than matches its spiritual and historical dimensions. The southern half of the country, which is a desert region with rainfall limited to 20 to 250 mm of water annually, is a completely different landscape from the tropical and alpine environments in the north. The "Rift Valley" that dominates the eastern side of the country for 400 kilometers, encompasses the world's lowest point at the Dead Sea and offers a dramatic contrast to the limestone mountains of the Galilee in the north and the central Judean Hills. The rich landscape supports a remarkable biodiversity including 2,500 plant types (150 of which are indigenous to Israel), 350 bird species, 70 mammals and 88 reptiles/amphibians (Gabai, 1995).

Because of Israel's diminutive size, it did not take long for the full force of environmental degradation to be felt. Beginning in the 1970s, emission of most conventional air pollutants doubles every ten years, largely due to the burgeoning fleet of automobiles. The number of "exceedances" from national ambient standards has increased accordingly. During the years 1994-96, an average of 300 violations of air quality standards occurred in the Tel Aviv area alone (Israel Central Bureau of Statistics, 1995).

By 1993, Hebrew University Professor Menahem Luria, a leading expert in air quality monitoring, estimated that air pollution in Jerusalem would exceed present levels in Mexico City by the year 2010 (Luria, 1994). According to estimates of Professor Noam Gavrielli of the Technion University Medical School in Haifa, particulate emissions, only one of many problematic Israeli air pollutants, are associated with 1000 deaths each year (Gavrielli, 1995).

The water flowing in most of the country's streams and rivers is predominantly poorly-treated, putrid municipal sewage. Groundwater has become so contaminated that vast parts of the nation's largest aquifer have been disqualified, even for agricultural usage. In 1992, 30-40 percent of the wells exhibited microbial contamination (Ministry of Environment, 1992). While eutrophication in Lake Kineret (the Sea of Galilee), the country's only fresh water lake, appears to have been stemmed during the past two decades due to intensive government management activities (Berman, 1996), expanded tourism around the banks threatens the precarious equilibrium.

Green open spaces and undeveloped natural areas are being paved over to accommodate an increasingly consumerist society's appetite for automobiles, backyards and villas. The urban sprawl, once associated with the greater Tel Aviv region, stretches throughout the Central region, creating the so-called N'Ashodod (Netanya to Ashdod) coastal megalopolis. As suburban development moves eastward to the Judean Hills in Jerusalem, it devours much of Israel's natural beauty in its wake (Sagi, 1996).

There are other disturbing trends as well. Toxic and municipal solid waste is generated in growing amounts with no comprehensive policy for source reduction or treatment. Pesticides are used almost indiscriminately with one of the highest per-hectare usage rates in the world (Richter, 1994). Some ten percent of produce contains pesticide residues in excess of national standards. Factories lying in the residential areas often store considerable quantities of hazardous chemicals with no meaningful emergency response plans in place.

Leading Israeli journalist and author Amos Canaan declared recently that "Jews have caused more damage to the Holyland during the last fifty years than that cumulatively produced by a litany of conquerors during the past two thousand." As this chapter will document, such a critical view is not without empirical support.

How did the Zionist adventure, springing from an ideology that adored the land of Israel, produce such degradation? The first part of the chapter offers a cursory environmental history of Israel from the time of its independence, tracing the origins of specific environmental problems to rapid industrialization, massive population growth and government policies. In the second section it is argued that a new era of environmentalism began to emerge at the end of the 1980s with the creation of an environmental ministry and enhanced public awareness. In the final section a discussion of the requisite policy and environmental paradigm shifts will focus on the primary ideological and practical challenges facing Israeli decision makers and society. Fundamental changes are imperative if the Jewish state is to embark on a more sustainable route and return a modicum of harmony between the inhabitants and the very land Zionists came to redeem.

II. The Origins of Israel's Environmental Crises

Development and the Zionist Imperative

While Zionist visionaries in Europe dreamed about what a Jewish State might be and argued about philosophical dogma, it was a practical, energetic generation that forged Israel's physical reality (Elon, 1971). The Zionist pioneers, largely a self-selected population, preferred tangible achievements to time consuming, thorough planning. It can be argued that a pragmatic myopia emerged as the dominant approach to national development during the period prior to Israel's independence, when "creating facts on the ground" constituted a political imperative. The so-called "Stockade and Tower" settlements, created overnight to circumvent British mandatory building restrictions, remain a symbol of the efficacy and orientation of the Zionist enterprise (Ben Gurion, 1955).

These pioneers frequently perceived the natural world as a challenging, hostile wilderness to be tamed through diligent Jewish settlement. Songs extolling production, the beauty of concrete and the importance of construction became part of a nationalistic liturgy. While Israeli Zionists were certainly not unaware of the splendor of the land of Israel, the task of nation building dominated their senses (Odenheimer, 1991).

The pre-state Zionist community was also home to many figures who deviated from the dominant anthropocentric ideology, which deemed economic and political development to be paramount. The preaching of second Aliya philosopher, A.D. Gordon, as expressed in his seminal work "Man and Nature," offered a romantic and inspirational alternative (Gordon, 1951). Gordon waxed reflective about an organic rapport between the Jews and their land that would replace the Diaspora dissonance and alienation from the natural world and wrote of the edifying benefits of manual, agricultural labor. A complimentary, ecological voice can be found in the rich images penned by "Rachel", the lyrical, melancholy poet, who wrote on the banks of the Kineret Lake during the early third of this century (Blubstein, 1978). Yet their ideals, while widely admired, were never integrated into macro-decision making on physical planning and policy issues.

The almost exclusive focus of the Yishuv (The Jewish settlement in British Palestine) and later that of Israeli planners and politicians on economic and security exigencies ensured that even the most successful enterprises would give rise to severe environmental problems. Over-pumping in Tel Aviv during the 1930s and 40s led to closure of wells due to massive salt-water infiltration. The draining of the Hulah Swamp in the northern tip of Israel during the 1950s, once hailed as a visionary act of Zionist competency, today is largely considered ecological folly (Merom, 1960). Recently, a small area of the reclaimed but largely unproductive farmland was returned to wetlands.

A more recent example, the construction of Tel Aviv's Reading Dalid Power Plant in the 1960s (through a statutory circumvention of Israel's own planning law), reflects the prevailing development paradigm. The country's immediate energy needs were met with little thought to the sulfur and nitrogen dioxide levels in the surrounding metropolitan area (Laster, 1976). The prevailing, short-sighted impatience was exacerbated by a pervasive lack of national environmental consciousness. Basic concepts such as impact statements, emissions controls and endangered species were not part of the Hebrew scientific or conservational nomenclature for the first two-thirds of the twentieth century. In this sense, Israel was little different from many other western nations. But as a very small country, with minimal resources, its margin for error was, and remains perilously small.

Indeed, as long as Israel remained a sparsely populated, relatively indigent country, with an apparent surplus of basic resources, the effects of the aggressive development policy were not conspicuous. Yet, as the population grew almost tenfold between 1940 and 1996, so did the ecological damage (Ministry of Interior, 1992). The same aggressive Zionist ideology that, despite unrelenting security threats, galvanized a nation to transform swamps and deserts into a modern prosperous state left deep scars on the land of Israel.

Antiquated Paradigms in the Face of Limited Resources

Perhaps the single greatest cause of Israel's present environmental crises is the concomitant increase in population and rapid economic development (Brachya, 1996). Together, these place enormous pressures on Israel's limited and fragile resources. The symptoms emerged so rapidly that it has been difficult for decision makers to meet the challenges. When government decision-makers faced the constraints of limited national resources, hard, frequently politically unpopular decisions were required and rarely made.

It would be wrong to suggest that physical planning had no place during the initial years of statehood. A national Master Plan designed in 1950 by a team of planners headed by Arieh Sharon (no relation to the general/politician of the same name), established the physical blueprint for the Israel of today. This twenty-year plan created such landmarks as the port of Ashdod, the National Water Carrier and most development towns. Yet, the strategies for national development had no mechanism for integrating environmental considerations. Moreover, the underlying orientation and consequent objectives created environmental impacts that eventually became intolerable (Mazor, 1994).

Beyond rapid economic growth to absorb immigration, population, demographic dispersal to guarantee Jewish sovereignty was one of the Sharon Plan's paramount objectives. Professor Adam Mazor, one of Israel's most distinguished experts in physical planning, has diagnosed the prevailing orientation of early planners as "agoraphobia," or a fear of open spaces. According to this view, the major objective of planners was to fill up the country's seemingly vast empty stretches. This manifested itself in strategies that sprayed dozens of new development towns and agricultural settlements across Israel's landscape and encouraged new immigrants (with only modest success) to settle in Israel's periphery. Even within Israeli cities, high-rise buildings were relatively rare.

Within the span of a few decades, Israel was transformed from a relatively unpopulated land to one of the industrialized world's most crowded countries. While in 1948 the legitimacy of scattered and dispersed construction may have been self-evident, Mazor argues that by the 1960s, several waves of immigration made this strategy inappropriate, given Israel's diminutive size (Mazor et al., 1995).

The resulting sprawl today is bemoaned by environmentalists as "the Los Angelization" of Israel. The phenomenon has been exacerbated by an explosion of hasty development and construction during the early 1990s, exploiting an Emergency Planning Law (enacted to meet the mass immigration from the former Soviet Union) that circumvented normal approval procedures (Gouldman, 1996). The results have been profound. Mazor's recent contrast of aerial photographs between 1948 and 1993 suggest that the amount of land transformed from undeveloped or natural sites to urbanized construction increased from 3 to 17 percent.

Agriculture is another area where national policy was unable to envision the environmental ramifications of "success." The return of the "Jewish Farmer" and the greening of the desert, a central tenet of modern Zionism and modern Israeli policies, ultimately had grave ecological impacts. Heavy use of fertilizers, pesticides and waste water irrigation led to alarming deterioration in ground water quality (Mushkat, 1995).

While Israel's Water Commissioner is granted almost unrestricted authority to regulate and reduce pollution of water resources, historically, commissioners have done very little to reverse the ongoing contamination. Selected by the Minister of Agriculture, the political orientation of those holding the position has always been clear. Water prices, controlled by a powerful farm lobby (supported by their historically high representation in Israel's Knesset), reflect massive agricultural subsidies. Agriculture's share of the national water budget typically reached sixty percent (Schwartz, 1994).

As is frequently the case with subsidized commodities, water was frequently squandered, particularly by the farming sector. This often led to cases of "over-pumping" of underground aquifers and a subsequent increase in salinity levels. Until the State Comptroller issued a scathing report in 1990 castigating the irresponsible policies of the Water Commissioner (State Comptroller, 1990) however, no serious national debate about the wisdom of agriculture's water allocation occurred. Here again, deeply rooted national ideological commitments failed to accommodate the dramatic rise in population/pollution and a corresponding drop in available resources.

Present commitments to encourage access to automobiles as the primary form of transportation is yet another example of policy-makers' inability to bring old dogma in line with new ecological reality (Garb, 1996). Proactive measures to temper the impact of the geometric expansion of the domestic fleet from 70,000 vehicles in 1960 to roughly 1.5 million today were never seriously considered. Hence, the level of mass transit services deteriorated during this period, and the quality of gasoline often made the catalytic converters, that were only installed in cars during the early 1990s, largely ineffective (Tal, 1992). The associated congestion on Israeli roads, particularly during rush hours, and the pernicious air pollution levels have not yet registered with decision makers, who continue to reduce investment and subsidies for public transportation while dramatically expanding Israel's road network.

Of course the most fundamental conventional Israeli paradigm that requires rethinking in light of new ecological realities is a blind commitment to unfettered economic growth. Increasing GNP and productivity has been the raison d'être of Israel's economic policy since the country's establishment, regardless of the ruling political party. National policy assumes that the general welfare and happiness of citizens automatically improves as the economy expands. While strategies vary under Finance Ministers—from the early heavy industry emphasis of Sapir to the more recent, high-tech models of Shochat and Merridor, the pursuit of speedy, high-return projects with little or no regard to long-term impacts on the environment is consistent. By the end of the 1980s, however, the damage wrought by expanded production and consumption on the quality of Israel's air, land and water could no longer be disregarded by decision makers with impunity.

Historically, within Israeli economic circles there has been little interest in alternative paradigms. The country's many influential artists and intellectuals, so vociferous on a range of societal issues, never seriously raised questions about the limited time horizons of economic planners or industrial and agricultural producers' propensity for destroying the very resources upon which they rely. Paradoxically, while the "polluter pays" ethic, prohibiting the taking of public resources for private economic gain, increasingly found expression in Israeli environmental statutes, implementation of such principals lagged drastically (Tal, 1994).

Hence, while international awareness following the 1972 Stockholm convention caused a ripple in Israeli society, and was followed by the promulgation of the first ambient air quality standards (Abatement of Nuisances Regulations, 1972) and tough new environmental amendments to the Walter Law, 1972, (Adam Teva V'din, 1992), environmental controls, in practice, were rarely demanded from industries, particularly if they threatened short-term profits. Similarly, municipalities were not required to meet their legislative responsibility to treat sewage and dispose of garbage in a sanitary manner.

III. The Paradox of Israel's Environmental Movement

Despite the bleak picture described above, a strong environmental movement emerged in Israel during the country's first four decades (Sofer, 1991). Its efforts focused almost exclusively on nature preservation and conservation. In retrospect, it is not clear whether this narrow agenda was the result of superficial consciousness or tactical considerations (likelihood for success), given the political problems associated with tackling the powerful, vested economic interests that created the acute pollution problems. With very little environmental monitoring during this period, it may well have simply been due to a lack of understanding regarding the extent of deterioration.

Notwithstanding the inadequate attention directed towards pollution prevention, preservation efforts undertaken by the Israeli government agencies during this period are unquestionably impressive. A 1963 law established the Nature Reserves and National Park System, and it was promptly followed by an aggressive conservation plan, largely associated with the charismatic Avram Yoffe, who headed the Nature Reserves Authority. A former general, Yoffee shepherded "National Master Plan Number 8" for establishing nature reserves and parks through the bureaucracy of the Ministry of Interior. Commissioned in 1970 and submitted and approved in

1979 and 1982 respectively, the plan includes 278 sites (143 reserves and 78 parks) covering more than a million acres of land or a full quarter of the real estate lying inside pre-1967 Israel.

Numerous caveats must be mentioned when presenting Israel's Nature Reserve System (Gabai, 1995). Many of the reserves have yet to be formally declared and appear only as potential sites on the Master Plan drawing board. Other reserves are located inside firing zones and training grounds of the Israeli army, which is not duty bound by law to respect the Nature Reserve Authority. On a deeper level, it is often argued that due to centuries of human interaction with the environment and the diminutive size of the country and parks, it is practically impossible in Israel to set aside critical masses of land where nature is not only preserved, but can continue to evolve without anthropogenic disturbance.

Yet, the system of nature reserves and the attendant protection of hundreds of plants and animal species under the Nature Reserve Law's "Natural Assets Regulations" remains a very bright spot in the midst of the period's overall development fervor. The relatively few extinctions recorded this century (involving seven mammal species—including the bear and the cheetah, 14 birds—including the ostrich and field owl and two reptiles—including the crocodile) almost all predate the establishment of Israel.

Other quasi-government groups enjoyed comparable success in the area of nature conservation campaigns. The Jewish National Fund's (JNF) tree planting initiatives have led to the planting of 200,000,000 trees over hundreds of thousands of acres. Their activities received a significant boost with the recent passage of Master Plan Number 21, which will enable the JNF to double the forested lands in Israel in the future. The magnitude of the forestry activities is unprecedented internationally and a justifiable source of national pride.

Furthermore, the Society for Protection of Nature in Israel (SPNI), established in 1954, leveraged a national passion for hiking and outings to grow into the nation's largest non-government organization with thousands of members. Their highly successful educational campaign to eliminate the picking of wildflowers and expansive network of field schools is indicative of both their influence and limited focus during this period.

Ultimately, however, the national pollution problem was not addressed by either the government or the non-government sector. In the absence of an independent Environmental Ministry, limited regulatory efforts were centered at the Environmental Protection Service, established in 1973 and located for the most part in the Interior Ministry. Yet, lack of enforcement authorities and marginal influence within the Ministry placed formidable limitations on the activities of the Service's small but highly energetic professional staff.

Regulatory initiatives that did succeed (e.g., marine pollution prevention catalyzed by international efforts to protect the Mediterranean Sea) were never in response to demands by a non-governmental "green" sector that remained largely indifferent to the pollution levels spiraling out of control. The environmental movement's orientation during the 1970s and 80s led a noted Israeli environmentalist to characterize the country's environmental movement as "standing on a toxic waste dump and watching the birds."

The paradox of Israeli environmentalism through the 1980s continues to puzzle many local commentators. On the one hand, an extensive network of nature reserves, parks and field schools nurtured a remarkable culture of hiking and retreats. On the other hand, unsustainable development and an industrial sector that was rarely required to internalize pollution control costs produced unhealthy, ambient pollution levels in the cities and a parallel massive deterioration of natural resources. Ironically, the watershed event that began the changes in Israel's environmental activities had little to do with the severity of the problem.

IV. The New Era of Israeli Environmentalism

Israel's attitude towards the environment underwent a drastic change during the 1990s. While this "greening" has not yet translated into broad-based environmental gains, the political climate is finally ripe for comprehensive, environmental regulations and fundamental changes in Israeli society's attitude towards responsible ecological living. While it is difficult to single out a particular event that has led to the transition, three phenomena that served to reinforce each other are identifiable:

- the creation of the Environmental Ministry;
- the expansion of environmental activism within the non-governmental sector; and
- a dramatic expansion of environmental education and media coverage.

The 1988 elections resulted in a stalemate requiring a national unity government containing both the Labor and Likud parties. Under the coalition agreement, the two adversaries were to have an equal number of cabinet ministers. Faced with an odd number of existing portfolios, a Ministry of Environment was created to provide a cabinet entree for the talented young Likud politician (and later Mayor of Tel Aviv) Ronni Miloh. Environmentalists were ecstatic at the promise of a single, cabinet-level entity, holding the requisite authorities to confront the full range of pollution problems. They were also relieved to discover that rumors about the creation of an alternative "Sports Ministry" were unfounded.

Once established, however, the Ministry got off to a shaky start. As a "low prestige Ministry," the office itself proved to be a turnstile for ambitious politicians. During its first seven years, the Ministry has seen five different administrators at its helm from five different political parties, leading to striking inconsistencies in policy. For instance, Minister of the Environment Ora Namir (1992-93) implicitly set solid waste as her top priority and was a fervent advocate of incineration. Her successor, Yossi Sarid, became resigned to the inevitability of trash burial and to a lesser degree supported recycling, green labeling and reduced packaging. Raful Eitan, the present Minister, appears to be channeling resources to litter control and has also voiced support of incineration proposals.

Other disappointments involve budget and statutory authorities. For its first three years, the Environmental Ministry's budget was a paltry 10 million dollars (ICBS, 1990). Even when this level of appropriations increased due to Minister Sarid's extensive efforts to present four-fold level, it was still inadequate to cover the costs of highly skilled personnel, monitoring equipment, media campaigns, significant policy research and assessment. Even more problematic is the lack of substantive authority. Many key environmental areas remain largely in the hands of other government ministries. Control of mobile air pollution sources remain within the purview of the Ministry of Transportation, and public transport is even more fragmented. Sewage treatment is funded by the Ministry of Interior and monitored by the Health Ministry. Radiation is largely regulated by the Prime Minister's office. As mentioned, enforcement of water quality laws is still primarily a matter in the hands of a Ministry of Agriculture appointee, the Water Commissioner (Tal, 1993).

Nonetheless, the creation of the Ministry provided a cabinet-level advocate for environmental interests. Minister Ronni Miloh's immediate battle to impose stiff emission standards on the Haifa Oil Refineries and Electric Company, despite competing litigation by both industry and environmentalists, resulted in a compromise leading to a drastic reduction in sulfur dioxide concentrations in the Haifa area (ICBS, 1995).

The Ministry has also begun the first criminal prosecutions of municipal authorities who do not meet environmental standards. While used only sparingly, high profile prosecutions such as the trial of Eilat Mayor Raffi Hochman for illegal sewage discharges into the Red Sea, signaled that the Ministry means business (Warburg, 1993).

At the same time, the environmental movement in Israel at both the national and local level began to stir. The public, suffering from what is increasingly perceived to be unreasonable exposures, wanted activities beyond nature appreciation. The creation and subsequent aggressive activities of Adam Teva V'din, the Israel Union for Environmental Defense, a national public interest law and science group, is indicative of the growing public militancy and professional demand for better compliance with environmental laws (Silver, 1994).

The burgeoning number of effective local groups is also impressive. According to a recent survey, over 80 environmental organizations have been active over the past decade; from Kiriyat Shmoneh to Eilat, citizens across the gamut of Israeli life organized to improve the quality of their immediate environment (Bar-David, Tal, 1996). Farmers in the Jezreel valley successfully stopped a sanitary landfill in a neighboring forest; residents of the Maccabin settlement in 1994 received a

Supreme Court order enjoining construction of part of the planned Modii'n city to protect sensitive archaeological areas; in 1990, Haifa's "Citizen's Against Air Pollution" coalition, prevented the expansion of the local power plant in the country's most polluted city. Even ultra-orthodox communities such as B'nei Brak, not traditionally associated with environmental activism, have undertaken campaigns to abate pollution from small businesses, culminating in a Supreme Court petition.

Environmental education in Israel has also entered the modern age. It has been pointed out that the nature awareness approach characterizing pedagogical efforts failed to produce a broad cadre of committed environmental lawyers, economists, scientists and activists. The new environmental curriculum is more promising. By the 1990s, numerous high schools began to offer special environmental tracks with a strong science emphasis, including the opportunity for testing in high school matriculation examinations. New advanced degree programs in environmental studies were established at the Technion, Tel Aviv, Ben Gurion, Haifa and Hebrew Universities; and most recently a special Middle East regional environmental program opened at the Arava Institute for Environmental Studies. These interdisciplinary programs, relatively anomalous within Israeli academia, are appropriate given the variegated nature of the subject matter.

Formal and informal environmental education also reached new levels during the 1993-94 "Year of the Environment." Public schools introduced a mandatory environmental component in the curriculum of each grade. A series of public campaigns including battery collection, introduction of a government sponsored "green seal" for environmentally friendly products, national beach cleanup and many independent initiatives by Youth Movements and communities complemented school-room theory (Ministry of Environment, 1995).

Moreover, national environmental awareness grew as a result of expanded media coverage. In 1989, only two national newspapers, HaAretz and the Jerusalem Post had a reporter working a part-time beat to cover environmental issues. By 1994, the environment had become a major media issue, with all dailies and periodicals earmarking staff to ensure scoops and provide ongoing coverage. Environmental topics and environmentalists began to make the television "talk show" circuit and received extensive attention on the new local cable stations. Clearly, Israel's savvy press had come to believe that the public was interested in the environmental story.

Despite the concern and enthusiasm generated by educational activities, little change has been registered in environmental indicators. Not withstanding the high rainfalls during the past years and major reductions in agricultural allocation of water that returned much of the aquifers' water deficit, salinity levels in the coastal aquifer continue to rise precipitously. The number of air pollution episodes and exceedance of national standards also grew, at an even faster pace. Hazardous waste remains largely unaccounted for, and environmental regulation of pesticides is still rare. Environmentalists' future challenge involves harnessing the enhanced Israeli ecological consciousness to prompt policy changes and better enforcement on the one hand, while galvanizing a heightened commitment to environmentally responsible individual conduct on the other.

V. The Demands for a Sustainable Future

Sustainability has emerged internationally as a key ecological concept that, while vague, generally encourages development that does not degrade basic environmental resources. This requires a move from a linear approach to production and natural resources to a cyclical one. Given the country's population growth and economic boom, such an approach is long overdue in Israel. Already, much damage is irreversible.

Flora and fauna supplanted by a proliferation of urban sprawl and agricultural development probably will never return. In a recent lecture, Director of Water Quality in Israel's Ministry of Environment, Yeshayahu Bay Or, declared the coastal aquifer (a reservoir that holds a full third of Israel's fresh water supply) to be "moribund." In his pessimistic view, because of the pollutants already present in the soil that have percolated towards the groundwater and because of the high pace of the salinization process, it is only a matter of time until the entire aquifer becomes unfit for human consumption as well as agricultural use.

Much remains that can be saved. The Nature Reserve authority's Hai Bar program that returns many of the 20 animal species that have become extinct locally to their natural habitats should serve as an inspiration. If Israel is going to have an inhabitable environment for future generations, ecology must adopt an aggressive pre-emptive and restorative approach—preventing pollution and repairing the land. The recent establishment of a Rivers Administration to reclaim Israel's polluted streams constitutes just this kind of initiative. In the final analysis, business as usual is no longer sustainable, and basic values, behavior and conventions must be altered dramatically. The following are some of the essential challenges that must be on Israel's environmental agenda.

Institutional Expansion

The Ministry of Environment as mentioned is not succeeding in concentrating key powers in its hands. Water pollution, arguably Israel's number one environmental priority, is an example of where the Ministry of Environment is relegated to a secondary supporting role. The Water Commissioner's authorities must be transferred from the Ministry of Agriculture to an alternative, more independent environmental Ministry. During the present tenure of Minister Rafael Eitan, who coincidentally holds both the environment and agriculture portfolios, such an institutional transition should be remarkably easy. Similar measures are needed in other problematic areas such as pesticide registration and application. Progress cannot be expected without clear authority, wielded by a committed agency to regulate mobile source emission, radiation, mining and even the composition of petroleum products.

Environmental Planning

Israel must realize that as land becomes more scarce, it must be preserved with fanatical stinginess. In practice, this means a return from the hasty habits spawned by the Emergency Legislation of the 1990s, to the cautious and thoughtful planning process that Israel's Planning and Building Law mandates. The use of environmental impact statements needs to be expanded and should become an integral part of every major construction initiative, thus guaranteeing the public's right to know the full implications of a development project. Most important, particularly in undeveloped areas, Planning Committees must be willing to say no, even if this results in reduced tax revenues to local authorities or short-term forgone business opportunities.

Greater resources must go to expedite preservation of undeveloped lands, both for use by future generations as well as a critical mass of territory for sustaining ecologically viable food webs. A National Master Plan for preservation of open spaces should be quickly prepared to ensure that the most aesthetically and ecologically valuable lands remain unspoiled. Recommendations of Adam Mazor's long-range 2020 Program should be implemented with regards to greater efficiency in land use. This includes policies that discourage and limit development of single-story structures in the center and north of the country with corresponding incentives for construction and purchase of well-designed, attractive high-rise structures.

While new settlements have always been part of the Zionist package, it is time to freeze the map in its present state and meet population growth through expansion of existing towns. New settlements, particularly one and two-story suburban communities, serve to pave over development options for future generations. Finally, the Negev desert, a region where there is ample room for growth, should be the focus of environmentally sensitive development efforts, with Beer Sheva expanded to constitute the country's third and ultimately largest metropolis.

Public Transportation

In a country as small as Israel, there is insufficient space for a highway system that can accommodate the three million private vehicles that will serve the eight million people expected to live in Israel after the new millennium begins. Convenient, high speed public transportation is the only serious hope from both an ecological and traffic management/safety point of view. The pragmatic Israeli public will ultimately come to realize that only first-class trains and buses can break the gridlock in congested urban areas. They also offer the attendant benefits of curbing air pollution and preserving open spaces.

Existing incentives for private automobile ownership including import tax benefits for immigrants and salary perks for public servants and other employees should be replaced with public transportation subsidies. An emergency plan to implement "designated public transport lanes" should make traveling by bus faster than driving private cars. Parking freezes, additional fuel taxes, expanded pedestrian walkways, carpool incentives and bicycles lanes are solutions that must be considered, with regulation of automobile usage a last resort which may very likely become unavoidable. The remarkable success of the recently opened Rehovoth/Tel Aviv line, which without any advertising is flooded by pragmatic Israeli commuters, confounds the pessimistic conventional wisdom that Israelis are too addicted to their cars to travel by rail (Shilberg, 1996).

Enforcement

In most areas, Israel has environmental standards that are compatible with international criteria for protection of public health and welfare. For instance, the 1992 ambient air quality standards control more pollutants and are generally more stringent than the national Air Quality Criteria of the United States (Worchaizer, 1993). It is the widespread violations of these standards that serve as the primary challenge to policy makers.

Efficient and professional enforcement activities have proven successful in cleaning air and water around the world. Israel's marine pollution prevention efforts, as part of the national commitment to comply with the "Barcelona Convention" for protection of the Mediterranean, is the one area where an ongoing inspection and monitoring program has existed since the 1980s. It is therefore not coincidental that marine pollution is also the one environmental medium where pollution levels actually retreated during the 1980s. For example, tar along Israel's beaches has dropped by over 1000 percent in the period following 1975... (Whitman, 1988).

In order for enforcement efforts to be credible, however, the Attorney General and the District Attorney's offices must make prosecutions a priority. The Ministry of Environment has received authorization to prosecute violators of several environmental laws, and has hired a few private law officers on a "retainer" basis to file cases on its behalf. Yet, the number of prosecutions is marginal relative to the pervasiveness of the violations (Ministry of Environment, 1996).

A strong inspection program requires uncompromising political backing, as it inevitably leads to conflict with powerful business interest. Enforcement personnel at all levels must be ready to implement a societal decision to prefer quality of life and protection of natural resources over short-term economic profits. Israel's many environmental laws express a general legislative intent to deal rigorously with polluters, but this is not reflected in the priorities of the State or District Attorney's offices. There has always been in Israel unquestionable support for Jewish and human values. There must be similar support by the public for bold environmental actions, if the political equation regarding pollution is to be changed and environmental objectives attained.

In theory, it can be argued that Israeli environmental policies should begin to integrate economic incentives for non-polluting behavior—adding the proverbial carrot to the regulatory stick. Yet, for this theory to be compelling, certain conditions must be met. First and foremost, precise data must be available. Without accurate information about what is coming out of smoke stacks and the chemical make-up of effluents discharged by a factory into a sewage system, it is impossible to know whether a trade or tax incentive has actually helped the environment.

Experience from around the world has led to a consensus that economic incentive programs require no less supervision and enforcement than conventional "command and control" policies. In Israel, basic information and enforcement capabilities in the field are still woefully lacking. A freedom-of-information law still languishes in the Knesset, leaving the public without access to many key environmental data sets. Hence, enforcing existing Israeli standards should be seen as a prerequisite before attempting innovative pollution reduction strategies.

Population Policy

Meeting the environmental challenge honestly may call some of the fundamental beliefs of Israeli society into question. Israel's commitment to expanding its Jewish population is a so-called "sacred cow" and constitutes a public policy nonnegotiable. There are many reasons for this dynamic, including residual trauma from anti-Semitic persecution and a sense of isolation and vulnerability when faced with the hostility of the entire Arab world. Yet, when seen in a European context, the picture is very different. Today the population of Israel approaches that of Switzerland and more people speak Hebrew than Norwegian.

After fifty years of population growth at roughly one million people per decade, Israel needs to reconsider its demographic policies. While the in-gathering of the Jewish exiles will remain the raison d'être of the country, with an open immigration policy a central tenet of mainstream ideology, it is not certain that ongoing subsidies to large families make sense. While the birth rate is dropping, it remains among the highest in the Western world, despite Israel's diminutive geographic size. In the long-run, continued demographic expansion spells ecological and probably economic disaster. Sooner or later, the issue will have to be confronted—better sooner than later.

Education and Environmental Values

As the State of Israel enters the second half of its first century, its pollution profile has changed. No longer can the industrial corporate world be vilified as the

primary environmental enemy that must be unconditionally vanquished for total ecological victory. In fact, contamination is increasingly caused by hundreds of small
polluters and the seemingly banal activities of an anonymous, dispersed population.
Agriculture, automobiles, sewage treatment, dry cleaners and private home developers are at the heart of Israel's environmental crises. If Israelis seek an environmental
enemy on whom to pin their ecological distress, increasingly "it is us." In such a
context, an effective strategy for Israel's environmental movement must go beyond
symptoms to the cause of the maladies.

When so many actors are responsible for environmental problems, command
and control regulation may not offer the most efficacious control strategy, unless it
enjoys broad-based voluntary support from the public. The current educational focus
on ecological awareness must be expanded to demand individual participation—from
energy conservation to consumption patterns and environmentally-friendly shopping.
Modern Israel has increasingly come to adopt western values. Many values, such as
respect for human rights and free access to information, are ecologically neutral or
even positive. Yet, the growing materialism and emergence of a consumer society has
created a glut of solid waste, short-term economic plans and irresponsible polluting
behavior.

Polluters are ultimately tolerated because society identifies with their singular
pursuit of profits at the expense of public values and quality of life. Even though
they may be responsible for criminally high levels of pollution, they are not treated
as criminals. To enter a sustainable era, Israel must rethink its commitment to
conventional, quantitative economic measurements of success.

While no Israeli citizen should be denied a minimal level of comfort, prosperity
should not be confused with greed. In an age where emigration from Israel is an
option available to many Israelis, the decision to live in the Jewish State is largely
a matter of choice. For most citizens, a higher quality of life offers a sufficiently
compelling reason to remain and build a country, despite a modest sacrifice in
monetary standards of living.

Environmental education must therefore continue to emphasize the connection
between "quality of life" and a clean environment, with access to a healthy natural
world. While a credible case can be made in economic terms for public policies,
it is wrong to define happiness and national well-being along strict economic lines.
Expanded GNP often does not reflect expanded total utility and invariably ignores
substantial unaccounted losses of the earth's natural resources.

VI. Conclusion

Israel has proven during its brief history that it is capable of making remarkable
achievements in environmentally-related fields. It leads the world in areas such
as waste water reuse and in solar heating of water. It may be the only country

in the world where the desert is clearly in retreat and arid land reclamation has succeeded on a macro-level (Ministry of Environment, 1992). Yet, for a variety of reasons, for too long most pollution problems have "sat on the back burner" and today have reached a critical stage where irreversible damage is beginning to emerge. Environmental indicators across virtually all media are negative: the air, water and land are degrading rapidly and the unique landscape of the Holyland is spoiled by sprawl and unimaginative development.

With the advent of peace, the environmental challenges will only grow. A recent independent catalogue of proposed regional development projects likely to impact Israel's environment reached a full 53 pages (Ecopeace, 1992). Greater societal resources must focus on reducing pollution and more must be asked in revising the ecologically unfriendly lifestyles of Israeli citizens who are living in the Western world's crowded country.

As a country founded on an ideology of land reclamation, it is imperative that the State of Israel integrate modern principles of sustainability across the board in its government policies. Linear development and production patterns have left a land suffocating in the residuals. A cyclical approach to production and waste management that perceives the land, air and water as fragile and very limited resources is in fact consonant with traditional Jewish values. Israeli society meticulously preserves and nurtures the holy sites which it holds in trust for four of the world's major faiths and the generations ahead. A commitment of similar magnitude, along with true ingenuity, will be required to keep the Holyland whole.

REFERENCES

BAR, David S. and Alon TAL
    1996 "Harnessing Activism to Protect Israel's Environment: A Survey of Public Interest Activity and Potential." Tel Aviv: Adam Teva V'din.
BLUBSTEIN, Rachel and Rachel SHIRAT
    1978 Tel Aviv: Davar.
BEN GURION, David
    1955 *Israel, Years of Challenge*. Tel Aviv: Massadah.
BERMAN, T.
    1996 "Lake Kineret: Fluctuations in Ecosystem Parameters from 1970-1994." Israel: *Proceedings of the Sixth International Conference of the Israeli Society for Ecology and Environmental Quality Sciences*, 881.
BRACHYA, Valerie
    1996 "Towards Sustainable Development in Israel." Israel: *Proceedings of the Sixth International Conference of the Israeli Society for Ecology and Environmental Quality Sciences*, 350.
ECOPEACE
    1995 "Middle East Environmental NGO Forum: An Inventory of New Development Projects." Tel Aviv: Ecopeace.

ELON, Amos
    1971 *The Israelis: Founders and Sons.* New York: Holt.
FLETCHER, Elaine
    1994 "Israeli Transportation and the Environment: Learning from the European Experience." In: *Our Shared Environment.* Jerusalem: IPCRI.
GABAI, Shoshana
    1992 "The Environment in Israel." *National Report to the United Nations on Environment and Development.* Jerusalem: Israel's Ministry of the Environment.
GARB, Yaakov
    1996 "Fighting the Trans Israel Highway." Sustainable Transport.
GAVRIELLI, Noam
    1995 "New Findings on Additional Mortality as a result of Particulate Air Pollutants." *Particulate Air Pollution.* Haifa: Technion.
GORDON, A.D.
    1951 *Man and Nature.* Jerusalem: Zionist Library.
GOULDMAN, M. Dennis
    1996 "Agricultural Land and the Prevention of Urban Sprawl." Israel: *Proceedings of the Sixth International Conference of the Israeli Society for Ecology and Environmental Quality Sciences,* 332.
HADAR, Almog
    1994 "Is There an Improvement in Air Quality?" Israel: *Proceedings of the 25th Annual Conference of the Israeli Society for Ecology and Environmental Quality Sciences,* 23.
ICBS—Israel's Central Bureau of Statistics
    1995 *Statistical Abstracts of Israel,* No. 46.
    1996 *Expenditures of Public Services for Environmental Protection, 1992,* No. 46.
Israel's Ministry of Environment
    1996 *Enforcement Update*-February 29/1992 (Internal Document on file with author).
    1992 *Environmental Quality in Israel.* Annual Report 17-18 (In Hebrew) Israel: Government Printing Office.
    1995 *Environmental Quality in Israel.* Annual Report 19-20 (In Hebrew) Israel: Government Printing Office.
Israel's Ministry of Interior
    1992 *National Masterplan for Immigrant Absorption* (In Hebrew). Jerusalem.
Israel's State Comptroller
    1990 *Israel Water System* (Special Report). Jerusalem.
LASTER, Richard
    1973 "Planning and Building or Building and Then Planning?" *8 Israel Law Review,* 481.
LURIA, Menahem
    1994 "Forecast of Photochemical Pollution for the Year 2010." Israel: *Proceedings of the 25th Annual Conference of the Israeli Society for Ecology and Environmental Quality Sciences,* 26.
MAZOR, Adam et al.
    1994 *Israel in the Year 2020.* Haifa: Technion Press.
MEROM, Peter
    1960 *Song of a Dying Lake.* Tel Aviv: Yefet.
MUSHKAT, Leah
    1995 "Contamination in The Coastal Aquifer." *Our Shraed Environment Conference.* Jerusalem: IPCRI.

ODENHEIMER, M.
    1991 "Retrieving the Garden of Eden." *The Melton Journal*, Vol. 24, p. 1.
RICHTER, Eliyahu
    1994 "Sustainable Agriculture and Pesticides: Problems, Perspectives and Programs." In: *Our Shared Environment*. Jerusalem: IPCRI, 182.
SAGI, Yoav
    1996 "Open Landscape Preservation in Areas Exposed to Massive Development Pressure—the Israeli Example." Israel: *Proceedings of the Sixth International Conference of the Israeli Society for Ecology and Environmental Quality Sciences*, 335.
SCHWARTZ, Joshua
    1994 "Management of Israel's Water Resources." Isaac Shuval, Ed., *Water and Peace in the Middle East*. Amsterdam: Elsevier.
SANDRA, Postel
    1992 *Last Oasis, Facing Water Scarcity*. New York: World Watch.
SHLISBERG, Rebecca
    1996 "Why Tel Aviv Needs High-Capacity Rail Transit?" Israel: *Proceedings of the Sixth International Conference of the Israeli Society for Ecology and Environmental Quality Sciences*, 298.
SILVER, Eric
    1994 "The New Pioneers." *The Jerusalem Report*. April. Jerusalem, p. 12.
SOFER, Barbara
    1991 "A Movement Sweeps Israel." *Hadassah Magazine*, 18.
TAL, Alon
    1992 "Reform in Air Pollution Prevention from Mobile Sources, Towards the Era of the Catalytic Converter." *The Biosphere*, Vol. 22/6, 4 (In Hebrew).
    1993 "Six Reasons Behind Israel's Environmental Cries." *Politica*, Vol. 47, 48 (In Hebrew).
    1994 "Law of the Environment." *Israel, Law and Business Guide*, 341. Deventer, the Netherlands: Klluer Law and Taxation Publishers.
WARBURG, Philip
    1993 *Implementation, Enforcement and Oversight of a Gulf of Aqaba Report, Protecting the Gulf of Aqaba, A Regional Environmental Challenge*, 375. Washington, D.C.: Environmental Law Institute.
WHITMAN, Joyce
    1988 *The Environment in Israel*. Jerusalem: State of Israel.
WORCHAIZER, Susan, Ed.
    1993 *Israel's Environmental Legislation*. Jerusalem: Ministry of the Environment.

Rape of Nature

The Environmental Destruction and Ethnic Cleansing of the Sudan

DAMAZO DUT MAJAK*

ABSTRACT

This article addresses an aspect of Sudan's internal conflict to which not much attention has been given in the past: the rape of nature as it manifested itself in the systematic elimination of human life (ethnic cleansing), wildlife, deforestation and soil erosion, and destruction of grazing land. It describes vividly how the environment in Sudan has fallen prey to intractable ethnic and religious conflict, with no end in sight.

Introduction

W HAT IS BEING referred to as the rape of nature in this article is the improper treatment and destruction of the environment, genocidal killings and forceful displacement of Christian, African and non-Arab ethnic groups, and resettlement of the Muslim and Arab ethnic groups in their lands by successive Khartoum governments dominated by Muslim and Arab political leaders in the Sudan.

The British and the Protection of the Environment in the Sudan

When the British colonized the Sudan from 1899 to 1956, they protected, controlled, and managed the environment. They established rules and policies which protected wildlife, especially elephants, rhinos, leopards, cheetahs, giraffes, colobus monkeys and crocodiles, against hunting. To prevent environmental destruction, they also guarded against deforestation, overgrazing and overfishing in the Southern

---

* Loyola Marymount University, Los Angeles, CA 96045-8316, U.S.A.

One week before he died, Dr. Damazo Dut Majak sent us this paper, which he presented at the Annual Meeting of the American Historical Association, Pacific Coast Branch, on August 4-7, 1995, to be considered for inclusion in this volume. We decided to include it to perpetuate his memory. (Editors)

Sudan, Western Sudan, and Southern Blue Nile where most of the Sudan wildlife and forests were found.[1] To this end, the British Foreign Office established in 1929 the Southern Sudan Policy and the Closed Districts Ordinance to check Muslim and Arab encroachment from the Northern Sudan on the Southern Sudan, the Nuba and the Fur regions in Western Sudan, and the Ingassana in Southern Blue Nile. Mindful of nineteenth century ivory and slave trade activities of the Arab and Muslim traders which destroyed much of the wildlife and populations in these parts of the Sudan, the British officials tightened security in order to protect the environment and ethnic groups found in these regions against the Arab and Muslim intruders from the Northern and Central Sudan.

The British administration maintained security by the use of police and local chiefs. In every town or provincial headquarters, the District Commissioner or Provincial Governor invited local chiefs to meetings to discuss ways of protecting wildlife against hunters, preventing deforestation, burning of grass, and overgrazing and overfishing. They also called provincial meetings in the South or held meetings with their fellow British officials of the Northern Sudan on the borders between the South and the North to resolve environmental and ethnic conflicts along the borders.[2] As regards the environment, the officials and chiefs usually listed the animals which must not be hunted except by permits from District Commissioners and those that could be hunted without permits. The animals which required hunting permits included elephants, rhinos, giraffes, hippopotamuses, crocodiles, leopards, cheetahs and colobus monkeys. Those which did not require permits were the most numerous animals such as impalas, Thomson's gazelles, antelopes, buffaloes and others. Birds were also included in the unrestricted hunting list. While some birds were hunted year-round for meat and feathers, others were hunted at a particular time of the year. For instance, ducks and Nile geese were only hunted in October after they had laid and hatched their eggs. As regards fishing, the locals were allowed to catch any fish, but overfishing was not encouraged and colonial officials instructed local chiefs to guard against it.

While they hunted wild animals for meat, hides, skins, horns and tails, the indigenous people used traditional tools such as spears, snares, clubs, pits, nets and hooks. The British allowed these methods of hunting because they were not destructive to wildlife. They only enabled the locals to kill a few animals or catch limited numbers of fish. The use of rifles for killing animals was limited to game wardens to enable them to shoot rogue elephants when they invaded farms or villages, or lions, hippopotamuses and crocodiles that might pose a threat to human life and livestock in the savanna forests, along the rivers and in the swamps.

To further consolidate their conservation policies, the British officials established game parks and reserves in some parts of the Southern Sudan. These included the Achana and Celkou game reserves in the Bahr al-Ghazal province, the Southern National Park between Southern Bahr al-Ghazal and Western Equatoria, the Gimeza and Tindille game reserves in Equatoria province and the Buma Park in the upper Nile Province. Anyone who entered the game parks and reserves to kill animals was severely punished. Even nationals were restricted in grazing their livestock in them.

Another area of British environmental protection and conservation was forestry. During the first years of their colonial rule, the British permitted the cutting of trees, especially mahogany, for building materials. But when the demand for wood as building materials and fuel increased, they devised other ways of protecting the natural forests. They promoted the planting of teak trees in many parts of the south to provide wood for building. Teak forests were planted at Kaguli, Loka West, Rejaf, Jebel Kujur, Kajo Kaji, and in Juba Town in Equatoria and Gete and Rumbek in the Bahr al-Ghazal.[3] Saw mills were erected at Katire and Nzara in Equatoria and Gete and Pongo for the production of wood as building material. As for fuel requirements, eucalyptus and sesban trees were grown in towns and at stations for charcoal production.[4] These are fast-growing trees whose stumps resprout again when cut for use as fire wood. In addition to these artificial forests, the British encouraged the planting of trees along roads in towns and at stations to provide shade and windbreaks as well as for soil conservation. Commonly planted were mahogany, neem, mangoes and lemon trees. Gardens were also established by both the British and missionaries to provide town dwellers with fresh fruit and vegetables.[5]

The Environment in Sudan after Independence

Destruction of Wildlife

Such British environmental methods and policies were good for the protection and conservation of the environment. In fact, the colonial period witnessed a tremendous increase in wildlife and environmental protection.[6] However, following the independence of the Sudan from British colonial rule in 1956, these methods and policies were not continued by the new rulers, most of whom were Arabs and Muslims from Northern and Central Sudan. Obsessed with political domination of the Sudan as well as supporting the Arab and Muslim economic exploitation of the Southern Sudan, successive Khartoum governments deliberately ignored British environmental protection and conservation policies. Publicly these new policy-makers asserted that wildlife should be exploited to boost national economic development. Thus, with such a mind-set, they permitted hunting of wildlife in the South. Individuals and traders, most of whom were Arab and Muslim Sudanese and a few Southern Sudanese acquired rifles and licenses from the government and became legal hunters of wild animals for commercial purposes. Each of these hunters, whose numbers were unknown in public records, was permitted to kill between one and three bull elephants and a rhino for trade in tusks and horn every year.[7] Immediately after independence and as the trade in ivory and rhino horns became lucrative, government officials, soldiers and other individuals from the Northern Sudan turned into hunters of elephants, rhinos, leopards, cheetahs, giraffes, colobus monkeys, crocodiles and other animals for commercial exploitation. During the First Civil War, from 1955-1972, the Anya Nya or Southern rebel fighters also joined in hunting and killing wild animals for food and purchase of weapons. They sold ivory, rhino horns, skins, hides, tails and meat to black marketers in neighboring countries, especially Zaire which, like the Sudan, was engulfed in civil war in the 1960s.

When the First Civil War ended in 1972, one would have expected the environmental destruction to stop. However, this expectation did not materialize. Peace time, which lasted from 1972 to 1983, shockingly became the period in which the greatest damage ever was done to the environment in the southern Sudan. Some high-ranking northern Sudanese military officers who remained to serve in the south, and those who had been transferred back to the North, became involved in intensive hunting in the South.

One of these military officers was General Fadallah Hamad, a Baggara Arab from Southern Kurdufan. General Hamad was the military commander in the Southern Sudan during and immediately after the First Civil War. When the cease-fire, which brought about the end of the war, was signed in Addis Ababa in 1972, he was appointed the Chairman of the Cease-Fire Commission that supervised demobilization, disarmament and absorption of the former Anya Nya guerrilla fighters into the Sudan Army. He chaired the Commission at the time he was almost ending his service in the army. During the regime of General Jaafar al-Numairy, who ruled the Sudan as a military dictator form 1969-1985, any retiring senior military officer was given a big well-furnished house and two cars, a pension and other privileges which included appointments to positions such as minister, regional governor, or ambassador. Such privileges should have been more than satisfactory to General Hamad. However, he craved more. He turned into a game hunter whose hunting activities in the south were encouraged, condoned and defended in Khartoum by his fellow generals, including President Jaafar al-Numairy, who was himself a former general and his close associate.

Having availed himself of all kinds of weapons, including machine guns and helicopters, General Hamad ordered his hunters to hunt by helicopters and shoot elephants in the plains and swamps of the Nile and savanna forests of the Southern Sudan.[8] In one incident, a herd of about twenty-five elephants was tragically slaughtered in a single day. As he accumulated large quantities of ivory, he had it transported in 1973 from Juba airport by cargo planes through Nairobi to Singapore, Japan, Hong Kong, Taiwan, and South Korea for marketing purposes.[9] The ivory was smuggled out of Juba with the help of military and national security intelligence which was controlled by General Hamad who was still at the time the overall military commander of the Southern Sudan, and who was accountable only to the Minister of Defense in Khartoum rather than the President of the High Executive Council of the Southern Sudan. But despite his enormous influence in Khartoum, General Hamad was not insulated. When the cargo plane landed in Nairobi Airport, Kenyan intelligence intercepted the ivory and immediately informed the Southern Regional Government in Juba about the ivory smuggled out of Juba to Nairobi. The President of the High Executive Council of the Southern Sudan, who was also the second Vice President of the Republic, informed General al-Numairy, the President of the Republic, about the ivory intercepted by the Kenyan authorities. He was certain that the President of the Republic would order the dismissal of the General from the army and his subsequent arrest and trial in court. However, the President did not act that way. After summoning the General to see him in Khartoum, he advised the General to retire from military service without being punished for having illegally killed elephants and smuggling the ivory out of the country.[10] When the President of the Southern High Executive Council learned of the General's lenient treatment by the President of the Republic, he petitioned the President to reconsider punishing the General and to warn other military officers and individuals that they would be punished like General Hamad who had with impunity killed elephants in the south. The petition did not change the President's mind. In fact, the President was afraid that if he punished General Hamad, other senior army officers who had also been involved in the hunting of the wildlife in the South would plot to overthrow his government. Thus, the President did not only exonerate General Hamad, but had him appointed as Lieutenant-Governor of the Kurdufan Region in order to appease him and ensure his loyalty to the government.[11]

This failure to punish the General for his participation in the environmental destruction in the South resulted in the weakening of southern regional efforts to combat the activities of hunters in the region. Hence, from 1972-1983, many hunters penetrated Bahr al-Ghazal from Northern Sudan. In order to hide their identities from the regional government of the South, they disguised themselves as Umboro or hunters from the West African states of Chad, Niger and Nigeria.[12] But in reality, they had no connection with the people of West Africa. The capture of some of these hunters revealed that they were all Arab and Muslim hunters from northern Sudan. The majority of them were former military and men who had at one time served in the South and had thoroughly known the habitats of the wildlife in the South. Among these hunters were surrogates of some high military and civilian personnel and rich businessmen in Khartoum who had connections with companies in Singapore, Taiwan, Japan, Hong Kong and South Korea which specialized in international trafficking of ivory, rhino horns, skins and hides. Other hunters came from local Arab Baggara pastoralists in southern Kurdufan and Dar Fur.

As they were well-equipped with sophisticated weapons, the hunters penetrated Bahr al-Ghazal and Western Equatoria killing many elephants, rhinos, leopards and other animals in parks, reserves and wherever they found them in the wilderness. The slaughter of the animals by the hunters was encouraged by economic hardships which resulted from unemployment, inflation and shortage of consumer goods in the Sudan from the early 1980s onward. It was exacerbated by a hostile desert environment and chronic recent cycles of drought and famine which befell the Northern Sudan at the time.[13] Consequently, northern Sudanese who did not seek work in the oil-rich Gulf States, turned to hunting or poaching in the Southern Sudan.

In the nineteenth century, the ivory hunters who came from the northern Sudan were not as heavily armed as they were in the twentieth century. They carried with them few rifles and limited powder. They also relied on the indigenous people of the South for trade in ivory, rhino horns, skins, hides and ebony as well as supplies. But all this changed in the 1980s. Having become suspicious and mistrustful of the southern Sudanese, the northern Sudanese hunters decided not to seek help from the southern inhabitants as their predecessors had done in the past, but relied on themselves. Unlike their predecessors, they knew the wildlife habitats and where parks and reserves were located in the South. They had their own transportation which was provided by camels, donkeys, mules and bulls carrying many weapons and ammunition, food, medicines, bedding and radio equipment for contacting other hunters within the southern wilderness and their relatives and associates in the north.[14] These means of transportation and communication helped them send ivory, horns, skins and hides to the northern Sudan and from there forward to Asia for trade.

As hunting became intensified and widespread in many parts of the southern Sudan, the regional government tried to check it. It requested money from the central government in Khartoum to recruit more game wardens and buy weapons, ammunition, uniforms, vehicles and radio equipment. But the policy makers in Khartoum hesitated to send money for this purpose.[15] Having received no support from the central government, the regional government turned to the Southern Military Commander in his headquarters in Juba town, the capital of the southern Sudan, for immediate help. The Military Commander also rejected the request on the grounds that police and game wardens could deal with the illegal hunters. He argued that the role of the army was for national defense and as such, hunting for hunters or poachers who were Sudanese was not its overriding priority. Moreover, it was a regional rather than a national problem. Thus, not having been able to attain the help of the national government, the regional government ordered the ill-equipped police and game wardens to fight the hunters. However, outnumbered and outgunned by the hunters, the regional police and game wardens could not defeat them. Those who ventured lost their lives. The remaining forces became ineffective and helpless, resulting in the slaughter of many thousands of elephants and rhinos, almost to extinction. There were four hundred white rhinos in the Southern Sudan in 1980, but by the end of the decade, these had all been hunted.[16] Black rhinos, which had numbered more than the white rhinos, had been drastically reduced as a result of hunting.[17]

Destruction of Forests and Grazing Plains

Another area of environmental damage was to the artificial and natural forests and grazing plains in southern Sudan. Tree cutting for commercial reasons had caused deforestation. The wood cutters, most of whom were northern Sudanese officials and traders, cut trees for wood that was needed for building, fuel and furniture in northern Sudan. During the inter-war periods, the northern wood cutters cut down all trees which the British had planted in and around cities and sent the wood to the north for sale.[18] The soldiers contended that trees in and around towns were hideouts for the rebels at night and even during the daytime and posed security risks to them and as such had to be cut down. However, this contention was not true as forest destruction was not limited to towns. Convoys of troops cut down trees, especially mahogany, in the natural forests, and teak planted by colonial officials was cut in the countryside. They carried back the wood to the towns and from there sent it to the north by cargo and military planes for use and marketing. Moreover, southern citizens who took refuge in towns were prevented from fetching firewood and forced to buy charcoal from merchants and agents of the soldiers at higher prices. The citizens were also prevented from searching for wood outside their towns for fear that they would allegedly carry information to the rebels about the location of the army as well as providing the rebels with food and money. But in reality, this claim was not true. The Arab and Muslim officials and businessmen did not want the locals to acquire their own firewood because this would undermine the wood and charcoal trade so much coveted by soldiers and town businessmen. The cutting of trees in and around towns and nearby forests not only caused deforestation, but soil erosion as well, creating desert-like conditions in southern towns, especially in Equatoria and Bahr al-Ghazal provinces.[19] Moreover, the saw mills at Tore, Katire and Nzara in Equatoria, and Gete and Pongo in Bahr al-Ghazal were closed down as a result of the scarcity of wood.

The SPLA and the Protection of the Environment During the Second Civil War

Protection of Wildlife

Environmental destruction continued for many years, but when the Second Civil War broke out in 1983, the Sudan People's Liberation Army (SPLA) tried to protect and conserve the environment. Unlike the First Civil War in which the Southern Sudanese rebel army, the Anya Nya, was armed with lances, spears and mainly old weapons, the SPLA had quickly and heavily armed its fighters with different kinds of sophisticated modern weapons at the start of the war. It obtained weapons from a variety of sources. The first batch of weapons came from the southern troops, police and wardens who had defected to the SPLA from the Sudan Army after southern armed personnel revolted in Bor town against the Sudan government in the spring of 1983. As a result of overrunning government garrisons, the SPLA captured all types of modern weapons including artillery, tanks and ammunition.[20] When Colonel Gaddafi of Libya was upset with General Jaafar al-Numairy, the military dictator of the Sudan, for having supported the Camp David Agreement between Egypt and Israel, he sent more weapons including, SAM-6 missiles, to the SPLA through Ethiopia in order to weaken and bring about the downfall of the Numairy regime in Khartoum. Although the SPLA and Colonel Gaddafi did not have anything in common except their determination to topple President Jaafar al-Numairy's regime, the SPLA accepted the weapons from Gaddafi for the liberation of the southern Sudan.

Therefore, with the availability of weapons, the SPLA leadership decided that, while the rebellion was being staged against the Sudan government, it should continue to provide environmental protection and conservation. As a result, it forbade reckless hunting of wildlife in the South for the purpose of purchasing weapons or food as was done by the Anya Nya during the First Civil War. The SPLA instructed its forces to produce their own food by cultivating land, raising livestock and keeping poultry. The SPLA leadership also asserted that additional food would come in the form of taxes collected in kind from populations in areas under the control of the SPLA.[21] Such taxes were collected on different items, including bulls, sheep, goats, chickens, fish, sorghum, millet, corn, potatoes, cassava, and sesame.

As the SPLA forces became determined to protect, control and manage the environment, they also waged war against northern hunters who still ventured south to hunt wild animals. From 1983 to 1987, they flushed out Arab and Muslim hunters from Western Equatoria and Bahr al-Ghazal provinces. After engaging in long and bloody confrontations with the aggressive hunters from the North, the SPLA managed to gain the upper hand and provide protection for the wildlife, helping it to make a come-back despite past abuses. The number of elephants was said to have rebounded. Many elephants returned from east and central Africa to their traditional habitats in southern Sudan.[22] In order to continue its protection of wildlife against the incursions of northern Sudanese hunters, the SPLA stationed forces along the borders between Bahr al-Ghazal and southern Dar Fur and Kurdufan in the north of the country.

Protection of Grazing Fields and Forests

The last environmental problem that the SPLA had to address was overgrazing and deforestation inflicted by migrant Baggara Arab pastoralists. During the colonial period, environmental destruction was avoided in areas along the borders between northern and southern Sudan by demarcating grazing territories between the Dinka and the Baggara Arab pastoralists. This was done by involving the traditional chiefs on both sides to negotiate new administrative borders between Bahr al-Ghazal, Dar Fur, and Kurdufan Provinces in an attempt to resolve border conflicts and attendant winter grazing, fishing and hunting disagreements.[23] To enforce resolution of ethnic conflicts, the British drew a line that ran through the middle of the Kiir River from the west to the east demarcating pastoral and fishing borders, restoring the border to where it had been before British colonization of the Sudan. Police patrols on both sides of the border kept peace between African and Arab ethnic groups. However, following the independence of the Sudan, the Arab and Muslim rulers in Khartoum viewed the border demarcation as a biased colonial legacy against the Arabs and Muslims of the North. Therefore, they disregarded the status quo on the Malual Dinka-Baggara border and asserted that the separate grazing and fishing areas of the two ethnic groups must be merged.[24] The officials contended that the merger would accelerate national integration and maintenance of peace and stability on the borders.[25] Consequently, the border demarcations were abolished giving Baggara Arab pastoralists the freedom to cross the Kiir river to graze and water their livestock, and to fish and hunt with impunity in the Dinka areas of the borderlands.

The Baggara Arab pastoralists did not take part in the First Civil Conflict which took place between the South and the North from 1955 to 1972, because they considered it to be a war among riverine Arabs of the north, central and southern Sudan over political, economic, social, religious and cultural matters which did not concern them. Having decided to be neutral in the conflict, the Baggara continued to use Dinka grazing plains, fishing in Dinka pools and lagoons without problems. They also carried on with their traditional barter trade with Dinka as well as the southern Sudanese rebel forces, the Anya Nya. But when the Second Civil Conflict broke out between the South and the North in 1983, the mutually friendly relations between the Dinka and the Baggara Arabs turned into hostilities. These stemmed from the entry of many Arab and Fellata pastoralists into Dinka and Luo territories to graze their livestock during the 1980s drought. As the lack of rain resulted in the loss of livestock to the Baggara Arab and Fellata pastoralists, they entered northern Bahr al-Ghazal in large numbers with cattle, sheep, goats, horses, donkeys and camels, causing serious environmental damage to the southern Sudanese grazing plains. The Arab and Fellata influx into the territory resulted in overgrazing, overfishing, burning of grass and cutting down of valuable trees as foliage for the livestock. In addition, these pastoralists became hunters, killing small and big game in nearby forests and provoking border hostilities between the Dinka and the Baggara Arab and Fellata pastoralists.

These hostilities broke out at the time when the SPLA was flushing out northern Sudanese hunters from Bahr al-Ghazal and Western Equatoria. So, when the SPLA forces extended their operations to Dinka territories to restore the old colonial borders and protect the environment, they encountered Baggara Arab resistance in 1984 on the borders between Bahr al-Ghazal and southern Dar Fur and southern Kurdufan.

They defeated and drove away the Baggara Arab pastoralists from the borders, and established military bases. From there, they decided to increase pressure on the Sudan Army by extending their guerrilla activities to the African and non-Arab ethnic territories of the Nuba and Ingassana people in southern Kurdufan and southern Blue Nile, respectively.

The Environment and Ethnic Cleansing

Like the African and non-Arab ethnic groups in the southern Sudan, the Nuba and the Ingassana ethnic groups had also suffered from the oppressive rule of the Arabs in the Sudan. Although their regions belonged to the well-developed northern Sudan, like Southern Sudan they had been neglected by successive governments of the northern Sudan. Thus, when SPLA forces penetrated the Nuba Mountains and southern Blue Nile for recruiting and intensifying the rebellion against Arab and Muslim domination in the Sudan, many Nuba and Ingassana young men and women from urban and rural areas immediately joined the ranks of the southern Sudanese rebels. Their participation in the rebellion changed the trend of the Civil War from being a conflict between the South and the North to that between Africans both Christians and traditional believers, and other non-Arab ethnic groups, and Muslim and Arab ethnic groups. Such polarization, which had never existed before, plus the widespread rebellion in the southern and western Sudan and in the southern Blue Nile instilled fear in the Arab and Muslim rulers of the Sudan.

Traditionally, the African and non-Arab ethnic groups such as the Nuba and the Fur in the western Sudan, Ingassana in the southern Blue Nile and the Beja in the eastern Sudan provided the Sudan Army under the command of the Arab officer corps with most of its fighting men during the First Sudanese Civil War. However, the present Civil War has changed the status quo. The Nuba and the Ingassana ethnic groups regard this war as one for the total liberation of African and non-Arab ethnic groups from Arab minority rule and the restoration of their geopolitical, economic, cultural, social and religious rights in the Sudan. As a result, they have become seriously involved in the rebellion and want to have nothing to do with the Arab-dominated government in Khartoum.

Having found it difficult to recruit troops from the Nuba and the Ingassana ethnic groups as they had done in the past, the various Arab governments in Khartoum turned to recruiting most of their troops from Arab ethnic groups in both urban and rural areas. While the urban Arabs formed the core of the army, the rural Arabs, especially the pastoralists and peasants, became the militia forces of the so-called Popular Defense Forces. In order to inspire, unite and rally these forces behind them, the Khartoum rulers declared Jihad or Holy War against African and non-Arab ethnic groups, giving them freedom to kill African, and non-Arab ethnic groups, loot their wealth, turn them into slaves, expel them from strategic territories and forcefully settle Sudanese Arabs and Muslims in their lands. In short, they were intent on carrying out ethnic cleansing, which caused environmental disaster.

This new policy of ethnic cleansing was readily accepted by Arab fighters from urban and rural areas. The Arab urban elite saw it as the only way in which they could assert and continue their political, economic, religious, social and cultural domination of the Sudan. The pastoralists and peasants viewed it as the opportunity to regain their economic goals in northern Bahr al Ghazal, southern Kurdufan, Dar Fur and southern Blue Nile. It would enable them to forcefully take over the African and non-Arab lands, which they desperately needed for resettlement, grazing, farming, hunting and fishing. Hence, with these ends in mind, Arab troops and militias conducted widespread atrocities and brutalities in those African and non-Arab territories. Africans and non-Arabs were forcibly removed from their ancestral lands and replaced by Arab and Muslim merchants, troops and militia.[26]

The Baggara pastoralist militia forces operated in many areas of the southern and western Sudan. Equipped with new weapons and driven by drought, the Baggara Arab raiders surged into northern Bahr al-Ghazal and northern Upper Nile during the winter of 1983-1984.[27] They burned villages, captured livestock and enslaved men, women and children. Some older males had their Achilles tendons cut to prevent them from escaping and to keep them indoors for domestic work while children watched their parents being tortured, or their mothers and sisters raped.[28] They forces carried out raids to places as far as Waw in southern Bahr al-Ghazal and Bentiu in western Upper Nile and villages in the northern part of Malakal. Raids were conducted against Dinka villages which were considered to be SPLA bases. The use of the militias was the most efficient means of exterminating the Dinka and replacing them in northern Bahr al-Ghazal with Baggara Arabs.[29] As the Baggara were ardent supporters of the Umma Party, their resettlement in northern Bahr al-Ghazal was quickly supported by conservative forces in the Umma Party and backed by the National Islamic Front (NIF) and the Muslim Brotherhood.[30] The people displaced as the result of raids and left without food and shelter were rescued by western relief agencies. There was no assistance from the Sudan government. Despite people's starvation, the government in Khartoum made sure that no food should be given to the southern populations. Anyone among the governors in the south who did not cooperate with the government and implement its policies was immediately sacked. The notorious northern Sudanese traders known as the Jallaba hoarded supplies and sold them at prices beyond the means of the southern Sudanese. When Acting Governor Peter Mabiel, a Dinka from the Upper Nile, announced that all grain would be confiscated and sold to the public at the official price of LS85 a sack, he was swiftly removed.[31] Thus, the Muslim government in Khartoum tried to use everything at its disposal, including genocide, to convert the Christians and other southerners to Islam. For instance, when the Arab and Muslim troops and militias were campaigning against the rebels, they would force African and non-Arab ethnic peoples to carry supplies and ammunition and order them to march before them into SPLA ambushes and mine fields to ensure that the terrain was free from danger. Most of the time, the carriers died in the ambushes, usually from stepping unknowingly on mines. Those who dropped the ammunition and supplies during the SPLA ambushes and mine explosions and fled to save their lives were later rounded up by Arab troops and militiamen and executed for desertion and leaving ammunition and supplies for the enemy. Some of these victims were also accused of being a fifth column and as such were executed. Not only that, but also being Christians and traditional worshippers, they deserved no mercy and accordingly had to be eliminated to make room for the Muslims to spread Islam beyond the South.

In the western Sudan and southern Blue Nile, government troops and militia forces also carried out raids against the African and non-Arab ethnic groups. The people of the Nuba Mountains were singled out for particular repression, persecution and ethnic cleansing.[32] Many Nuba in towns and rural areas were killed. The unrestrained activities of the Sudan Army and militias in the Nuba Mountains were tantamount to genocide against the Nuba by the Sudan government.[33] The evidence about widespread atrocities in the Nuba Mountains is overwhelming. They included murder, torture, rape, enslavement and the destruction of property as well as deportation of large numbers of people from their villages to Northern Kurdufan.[34] Those who survived genocide either escaped to the SPLA or found refuge elsewhere in the Sudan. Large numbers of Nuba from southern Kurdufan joined people from southern Dar Fur, northern Bahr al-Ghazal and the western Upper Nile who were driven out of their homes by the Arab soldiers and militias and sought refuge in Khartoum and other areas in northern Sudan where they became displaced without security and sanctuary.[35] As they were forced out from their villages, towns, homes, farms and grazing areas, they were replaced by the neighboring Baggara Arab Pastoralists and Arabs who came from Northern and Central Sudan.

Moreover, the Ingassana people in the Southern Blue Nile, like the Nuba of African stock, had their land wrested from them and given to neighboring Arabs for economic projects financed by the Faisal Islamic Bank of the Sudan which is controlled by the Muslim fundamentalists. The Ingassana had to be punished for having joined other African ethnic groups in rebellion against Arab domination, injustice and repression and for having supported the creation of a new united Sudan, which would be composed of political elements from the Blue Nile, Kurdufan, Red Sea, including the Ingassana, Beja, Fur, Nuba, southern ethnic leaders and the million or more displaced southerners in Khartoum.[36]

Like their fellow Africans in the south, the Nuba and Ingassana in southern Blue Nile were terrorized for no other reason than that they refused to relinquish their own indigenous cultural heritage, geopolitical, economic, and social rights.[37] In 1990, the Ingassana rebels and people in towns and villages in southern Blue Nile supported the SPLA occupation of Kurmuk, the most important town in their region. When the government recaptured it from the SPLA, its troops and militias carried out genocidal killings of the African ethnic groups, forcing many people from their land and homes, and resettling landless Arabs in the region.

Although many people have been killed as the result of ethnic cleansing, no exact number of the dead has ever been recorded. While 1.3 million southerners have died and millions have been displaced by war and devastation,[38] the number of people who were killed by the Sudan Army and Arab militias in the western Sudan and southern Blue Nile is not yet known. The Sudan government has deliberately sealed off these territories and since 1983 to the present time, no external news media have ever been given access to them. Those who survived death and managed to escape from these territories to the outside world have alleged that hundreds of thousands of people have been killed by the army and the militias, or have died of starvation and disease.

Conclusion

As discussed in the foregoing account, the villains in the rape of nature were greedy hunters, woodcutters, pastoralists, and fishermen, most of whom were northern Sudanese. The few southern Sudanese who took part in environmental destruction also had northern connections. Some of these acted on behalf of the northern Sudanese, especially high officials in the Khartoum government and in the South. Others were northern Sudanese who were born of southern women. As they also served as surrogates for greedy Sudanese officials and businessmen, these agents engaged in extensive woodcutting degrading the environment in the South. Those who are heroes in defending against the rape of nature are southern Sudanese. They include the local chiefs, warriors, regional government officials and the SPLA who, though having limited resources, struggle to protect and preserve their ecological and cultural heritage. But when the SPLA prevented Baggara Arab pastoralists and fishermen from entering Dinka grazing and fishing areas and forests on the other side of the border between northern Bahr al-Ghazal and the northern Provinces of southern Dar Fur and Kurdufan, their attempt to protect the ecology turned into geopolitical and economic conflict on those borders.

The situation became more complicated when the SPLA in its rebellion against the rulers of the Sudan incited the Nuba, the Fur and Ingassana groups to join them in the liberation of Christian, African and non-Arab ethnic groups from Arab and Muslim rule and create a new state apart from the old Sudan. As they were afraid of being overwhelmed by these Christian, African and non-Arab ethnic groups, successive Khartoum rulers, most of whom regarded themselves as Arabs, resorted to the strategy of ethnic, cultural, religious, political, economic and social cleansing in order to consolidate their oppressive and unjust rule of the Sudan. But as dignity and security have been denied to the Christian, African and non-Arab ethnic groups, nothing short of the partition of the Sudan will bring an end to the ethnic conflict there. The enormous destruction of the environment, human lives and property will be used in the future as justification for bloodshed and atrocities, leading again to vicious acts of retaliation attended by a hopeless cycle of violence and revenge in Sudan. There will be no forgiveness and forgetting of such losses by southern Sudanese. In addition, the last four decades have shown that the northern Sudanese have been unwilling to accept equal sharing of power with the southern Sudanese, making it difficult to convince them and other marginalized African ethnic groups to continue to live with them in a united Sudan.

NOTES

1   Chief Riny Lual Dau, interview by author, tape recording, Khartoum, Sudan, July 26, 1987.
2   Ibid.
3   Dr. Oliver Duku, telephone conversation with author, Sunday, April 29, 1995.
4   Ibid.
5   Most of these gardens were established by Catholic missionaries near schools and missionary stations to provide the missionaries and students with a variety of fruits and vegetables.
6   Mr. James Bol, telephone conversation with author, Sunday, June 18, 1995.
7   Ibid.
8   Ibid.
9   Professor Ambrose Beny, telephone conversation with author, March 18, 1995.
10 Ibid.
11 Ibid.
12 Ibid.
13 *Los Angeles Times*, Tuesday, June 8, 1993, p. 6.
14 Game Officer Peter Chol Tong, conversation with author, Juba, Sudan, July 10, 1983.
15 Dr. Oliver Duku, telephone conversation with the author, Sunday, April 29, 1995.
16 Denny, Malcolm, *Rhino, the Endangered Species*. New York, 1987.
17 *Environment: The Ivory Controversy in Africa Report*, April 1995, p. 55.
18 Dr. Oliver Duku, telephone conversation with author, Sunday, April 29, 1995.
19 Ibid.
20 *Sudan Democratic Gazette*, No. 62, July 1995, p. 9.
21 Mr. Ajak Boldit, telephone conversation with author, June 26, 1995.
22 Ibid.
23 Ibid.
24 Damazo D. Majak, *The Malual Dinka-Baggara Border Conflict and the Impact on National Integration*, in the *Sudan in Northeast Africa Studies*, vol. 13, No. 1, 1991. Michigan State University, p. 75.
25 Ibid.
26 National integration which the officials wanted to achieve would result from Arabization and Islamization of the Dinka ethnic group either through intermarriage or through association with the Baggara Arab ethnic group.
27 *The New York City Sun*, June 14-20, 1995, p. 18.

28 Requiem for the Sudan, War, Drought, and Disaster on the Nile, eds. J. Millard Burr and Robert O. Collins (Boulder: Westview Press, 1955), 19.
29 Letter from the Sudan Relief and Rehabilitiation Association, Washington D.C., to the International Donors and Humanitarian Societies, December 9, 1992.
30 Requiem for the Sudan, p. 101.
31 Ibid., p. 101.
32 Ibid., p. 55.
33 *Sudan Democratic Gazette*, No. 45, Februrary, 1994, p. 1.
34 FWDP-African Documents, 4th session April, 1985.
35 *Sudan Democratic Gazette*, No. 61, June 19, 1994, p. 4.
36 Requiem for the Sudan, p. 192.
37 *The New York City Sun*, June 14-20, 1995, p. 18.
38 Requiem for the Sudan, p. 312.

Regional Instruments for the Protection of the Marine Environment in the Arabian Gulf

BADRIA A. AL-AWADHI*

ABSTRACT

This article outlines and analyses the various protocols concluded among the Arabian Gulf countries protect their marine environment from pollution and its lethal effects. It also demonstrates that a regional approach to protecting the Gulf Marine environment is desirable and promising; however, in order for this collective approach to be effective, the protocols ratified by the Gulf States for their marine environment must be entrusted to and implemented by strong regional and national agencies.

Introduction

THE GULF STATES adopted in 1978, the first instrument at Kuwait Regional Convention for Co-operation on the Protection of the Marine Environment from Pollution, and in 1989, the Emergency Protocol for regional co-operation in combating pollution caused by oil and other harmful substances. The Gulf States adopted two more regional instruments; the first, against marine pollution resulting from exploration and exploitation of the continental shelf, and the second against pollution of the marine environment from land-based sources. Both instruments were implemented on 17 February 1990, and 2 January 1993 respectively.[1] What makes these four legal instruments important is the fact that with the exception of Kuwait, Iran and Oman, the rest of the Gulf States had no specific environment laws, and in particular, no significant laws for the protection of the marine environment. This disturbing situation prompted the Gulf States to adopt a more effective regional approach for the protection of their marine environment. As a result, the Kuwait Convention's Protocols of 1978 were enacted to provide useful legal instruments for protecting the gulf marine environment from all sources of pollution. This article will outline, analyze, and assess the impact and usefulness of the main provisions of these legal instruments.

---

*   Legal and Environmental consultant. P.O. 27357 Safat, 13134 Safat, Kuwait.

A. Kuwait Regional Convention for Co-operation on the Protection of the Marine Environment from Pollution (1978)[2]

The Kuwait regional convention lists the sources of marine pollution requiring control as follows: ships, dumping, land-based sources, exploration and exploitation of the sea-bed, and pollution from other human activities.[3] The convention consists of thirty (30) articles and the following constitutes its main provisions:

1. General Obligations

Article III of the Convention which deals with the general obligations of the Contracting States specifies in paragraph (a) that: *the Contracting States shall, individually and/or jointly, take all appropriate measures in accordance with the present Convention and those protocols in force to which they are parties to prevent, abate and combat pollution of the marine environment in the sea area.* "Take all appropriate measures" requires member states to enact anti-marine pollution laws, to cooperate with each other and coordinate their national legislations for an effective protection of the gulf marine environment from serious and damaging pollution.

2. Establishment of Regional Organization for the Protection of the Marine Environment (ROPME)

Paragraph (a) of Article XVI of the Kuwait Convention provided for the establishment of a permanent regional organization for the protection of the marine environment (ROPME). It is designed to oversee the implementation of the provisions of the Convention and in particular, to promote cooperation and coordination of action among the member states to combat all sources of marine pollution. ROPME is headquartered in Kuwait and Article XVIII of the Convention outlines its functions at both the state and regional levels.

3. Technical Assistance

The participants in the Kuwait Convention knew that they lacked individually the expertise in drafting effective anti-marine pollution legislations. As a result, they made sure that the Convention provided each member state with the technical assistance needed while drafting its anti-marine pollution legislation. The participants believed that effective national legislations are crucial for successful implementation of the state obligations embodied in the Kuwait Convention and its protocols.[4]

4. Adoption of Additional Protocols

Article XIX of the Kuwait Convention provides for additional protocols to be adopted in order to strengthen the resolve of the Gulf States to combat marine pollution more effectively in the region. As a result, they adopted several protocols to provide more effective protection of the marine environment and to fill gaps in national environmental jurisdictions.

B. Marine Emergency Protocol (1978)

In their desire to avoid serious cases of marine pollution by oil and other harmful substances, the gulf states adopted the Marine Emergency Protocol in 1978 which consists of thirteen articles and provides appropriate measures to respond effectively to marine pollution emergencies. A brief discussion of the protocol's main provisions will follow:

1. Regional Action to Combat Marine Emergency

Article II of the Protocol states that: *the Contracting States shall co-operate in taking the necessary and effective measures to protect the coastlines and related interests of one or more member states from the threat and effects of pollution due to the presence of oil or other harmful substances in the marine environment resulting from marine emergencies.* Paragraph (I) provides for the need to act swiftly on a regional level in case of marine pollution emergencies. The regional approach is particularly important in preparing both the national and regional contingency plans which must be in harmony with each other. Thus, the development of an appropriate national contingency plan becomes a pre-requisite for an effective regional contingency plan to combat marine pollution in the gulf region and respond quickly to any threatening emergency.

2. Legal Assistance to Member States

In order to achieve the regional objective, Article III, sub-paragraph (b) states clearly that the main function of the Marine Emergency Mutual Aid Center (MEMAC), which was established in Bahrain in 1983 is to: *provide legal assistance to the contracting States in preparing laws and regulations concerning matters covered by this Protocol and in the establishment of appropriate authorities to tackle any emergency situation threatening the marine environment.*

3. Establishment of Appropriate Emergency Authorities

Article XII of the Protocol recognizes the importance of establishing strong and effective state authorities and provides that: *the Contracting States shall establish and maintain appropriate authorities to carry out fully their obligations under the Protocol.* By this, it is meant that the Center which was established in accordance with the provisions of the Protocol will not fulfill its functions without the support of state authorities in the member states in charge of marine pollution emergencies.

C. Protocol Concerning Marine Pollution Resulting from Exploration and Exploitation of the Continental Shelf (1989)

Exploration of the sea-bed and sub-soil of the continental shelf for mineral resources, has caused serious marine pollution in the gulf region resulting from offshore operations, such as dredging, laying pipelines and drilling. In order to minimize, or eliminate altogether the environmental problems caused by these activities, the Gulf States implemented on 17 February 1990, the Protocol Concerning Marine Pollution resulting from exploration and exploitation of the continental shelf.[5]

The Protocol is to be supplementary to the Kuwait Regional Convention of 1978 and the Protocol Concerning Regional Co-operation in Combating Pollution by Oil and Other Harmful Substances. The Protocol which consists of fifteen Articles embodies many regulations which are already implemented by the oil companies operating in the Gulf States.

While each Gulf State has its own pollution criteria, these criteria must be standardized so that a common regional anti-pollution policy can be enforced to avoid the export of pollution from one area to another in the Gulf Region. Thus, the protocol's regional instruments become crucial to preventing the pollution of the Gulf marine environment. Although the Protocol consists of fifteen articles, only some of the important provisions will be discussed below to avoid repetition of basic material included in the Kuwait Convention.

1. Supremacy of Regional Obligations

Article III of the Protocol adopted a realistic approach when *it required the Contracting parties to comply with the relevant laws and regulations issued under the authority of the State.* It also empowered the competent state authorities to take such measures as are necessary to enforce compliance therewith. It is clear from this that the Contracting States collectively shall protect the marine environment from pollution resulting from offshore operations. Under the *Protocol, their collective action will take precedence over the pollution laws of individual member states. Such obligations shall be without prejudice to the more specific obligations implied under this Protocol.* Thus, it is clear that the Contracting States have agreed that their regional obligations under this Protocol take precedence over their national legislation. It was hoped that this protocol will strengthen the regional approach to protect the marine environment.[6]

2. Co-ordination of Offshore Operator's Contingency Plan with National/Regional Contingency Plan

Article VIII, paragraph (2) of the Protocol states that the operator of offshore installations is required to co-ordinate his contingency plan with any existing national and/or regional contingency plan. This requirement will strengthen future regional contingency plans because it is clear that oil companies operating in the region have advanced contingency plans to deal with offshore marine emergencies, but without obligation to co-ordinate with national contingency plans. Article VIII will in the future overcome the lack of co-ordination between oil companies and the national/regional authorities in charge of pollution response operations.

3. Compliance with ROPME Oil Content Standard

As we have already mentioned, the provisions of the Protocol take precedence over the national legislations of the Contracting States. *"No other discharge from an offshore installation into the sea within the Protocol area, except one derived from drilling operations, shall have an oil content, whilst undiluted, greater than stipulated for the time being by the Organization. The oil content so stipulated shall not be greater than 40 mg. per liter as an average in any calendar month and shall not at any time exceed 100 mg. per liter."*

4. Observation of ROPME Guidelines

Articles XIII paragraph (2) requires the Contracting States to observe any Guidelines issued by ROPME regarding the removal of offshore installations in the protected area. This obligation specifically highlights the importance of having regional guidelines issued in the future by the Organization in order to standardize and co-ordinate the national pollution measures and procedures of individual member states which have never been implemented regionally. The regional instruments provide more effective measures and means to protect the marine environment from pollution resulting from exploration and exploitation of the continental shelf as stated clearly in the preamble of the Protocol.

D. Protocol for the Protection of the Marine Environment against Pollution from Land-Based Sources

Land-based pollution poses a serious danger to the marine environment and to human health in many of the Gulf Contracting States. The source of land-based pollution is the release of untreated, insufficiently treated, and/or inadequately disposed of domestic or industrial discharges. To combat this serious source of marine pollution, existing anti-pollution measures needed to be strengthened at both the national and regional level. The above protocol was ratified in February 1990, and implemented in January 1993. The following are the main provisions of the protocol:[7]

1. Sources of Land-Based Pollution

Article III of the Protocol outlines the protocol's application to discharges reaching the protected area from land-based sources within the territories of the Contracting States, in particular:

a. from outfalls and pipelines discharging into the sea;

b. through rivers, canals or other water sources, including underground water sources;

c. from fixed or mobile offshore facilities serving purposes other than exploration and exploitation of the seabed, the subsoil and the continental shelf; and

d. from any other land-based sources situated within the territories of the contracting states, whether through water, through the atmosphere, or directly from the coast.

2. General Obligations of Contracting States

The Protocol imposes a certain number of general obligations on the Contracting States with regard to development and adoption of regional guidelines, standards or criteria as appropriate for the proper sea water use for specific purposes. Those regional guidelines are necessary for the protection of human health, living resources and eco-system. The Protocol also calls for the regulation of waste discharged in the marine environment and the degree of treatment for all significant types of land-based sources. Moreover, subparagraph 1(c) of Article VI provides for stricter local regulations for waste discharge and/or degree of treatment for specific sources based on local pollution problems and desirable water usage considerations.

In order to ensure that the Contracting Sates fulfill their general obligations, *Paragraph 2 of Article VI stipulates that programs for implementation of the measures as defined in paragraph (1) shall be adopted and shall take into account for their progressive application, the cost of measures involved, the capacity to modify existing installations, the economic capacity of the contracting states and their need for substantial development.*

Paragraph (4) of Article VI provides that guidelines, standard criteria, as well as regulations, programs, and measures shall be developed and adopted in accordance with the provisions of Article XIV of this Protocol and periodically updated, if necessary, every two years.

3. Consideration of Particular Factors

In addition to the general obligations, Annex III, which is an integral part of the Protocol, specifies that the contracting states should be responsible for the regulation of waste discharges into the marine environment, and the specification of the degree of treatment for each pollution source. In addition, Paragraph 1 (c) of Annex III states that in this specific area, stricter local regulations should be developed. Such local regulations will apply to specific sources of marine pollution in the area under consideration.

The above measures are reasonable, and address realistically the need to protect the quality of water in the Gulf marine environment. Paragraph (d) of Annex III states that regional regulations along with the program measures and the timetable required for implementation should be developed on a priority basis, *inter alia*, for specific types of wastes:

a. Ballast water, bilges and other oily waste discharges generated by land-based reception facilities and ports through loading and repair operations.

b. Brine water and mud discharges from oil and gas drilling and extraction activities from land-based sources.

c. Oily and toxic sludge from crude oil and refined products storage facilities.

d. Effluents and emissions from petroleum refineries.

e. Effluent emissions from petrochemical and fertilizer plants.

f. Toxic effluents and emissions from industries such as chlor-alkali, primary aluminum production, pesticides, insecticides and lead recovery plants.

g. Emissions from natural gas flaring and desulphurization plants.

h. Dust emissions from major industrial sources, such as cement, lime, asphalt and concrete plants.

i. Effluents and emissions from power and desalination plants.

j. Wastes generated from coastal development activities which may have a significant impact on the marine environment.

k. Sewage and solid waste.

Conclusion

It is clear that the gulf regional instruments embodied in the Protocols have been very important milestones in the effort of the Gulf States to protect their marine environment. They have also reinforced the member states' resolve to combat marine pollution from waste discharges emitted by industrial development complexes located in the coastal zone of each contracting state. Without these regional Protocols, national efforts of individual contracting states will not be effective in protecting the region's marine environment from serious and damaging pollution.

However, it is important to note that the full implementation of regional anti-pollution legislation has been hindered by weak national institutions which have been entrusted with the implementation. Therefore, stronger implementing institutions and agencies must be put in charge of implementing clear regional anti-marine pollution policies. Without strong and effective implementing agencies, the regional anti-pollution instruments will remain weak and ineffective.

NOTES

1 The following are the eight States: Kuwait, Saudi Arabia, Bahrain, Iran, Quatar, Oman, Iraq and U.A.E.
2 In accordance with Article XXVIII, the Convention, entered into force on 30 June 1979 after deposit of five instruments of ratification by the following states: Kuwait, Bahrain, Iraq, Oman and Quatar.
3 See Articles IV, V, VI, VII and VIII of Convention.
4 Article XII.
5 Article XV of the Protocol.
6 Article IV Paragraph (b) of the Protocol states that: "In deciding to call for a environment impact and in determining its scope, the Competent State Authority shall have regard to the Guidelines issued by the Organization."
7 Paragraph (b), Article XX of the Protocol.

Managing Resources, Its Socioeconomic and Environmental Consequences
The Case of Syria

GLORIA IBRAHIM SALIBA*

ABSTRACT

Syria today is caught between the demands for economic development and its desires to preserve its natural environment. The main challenges to Syria's environment come from its limited resources, population growth, urbanization, poor agricultural management, ill-designed irrigation projects, and careless behavior in deserts and forests. Syria's resources and problems are surveyed extensively. Last, its attempts at solutions are portrayed.

S YRIA has awakened to a great interest in environment protection and conservation. However, the status of Syria's environment is seriously undermined by natural as well as human made factors. Population increase, urban sprawl, desertification, and dwindling natural resources are some of the challenges that threaten Syria's environment during the country's attempts to develop socioeconomically. In this chapter I will discuss the conflict that Syria is facing between expanding its agricultural development projects and the burden that this expansion is having on its environment and natural resources.

Geographic Regions

Syria extends from the Mediterranean sea in the west to Iraq in the east, while it borders Turkey in the north and Jordan and Palestine (Israel) in the south, and Lebanon in the west. Its total area is 18.5 million hectares, of which 6.1 million hectares (33 percent) is cultivable. The country is generally dominated by the Mediterranean climate, characterized by a rainy winter and a very long, dry summer separated by two short transitional seasons, which is especially manifested in

---

* UCLA, History Dept., Los Angeles, CA 90024, U.S.A.

western Syria, while the east is predominantly dry (Talas, 1990: 23 and El-Akhrass, 1986: 1). Adel Abdulsalam notes that "Syria can be divided into two great geographical zones, the western mountains including the Rift Valley zone and the larger eastern plateaus and inner plain zone. These two great zones can be divided into smaller divisions or regions according to different systems" (1985: 3). According to his system of "geographical regions and subregions," Syria is divided into eight major geographical regions and 23 subregions. The major geographical regions are:

1. the South-West;

2. the Syrian Desert (al-Badiyah);

3. the High Mountain;

4. the Palmyra Ranges and the Central Highlands;

5. the Orontes Valley;

6. the Coastal Plain and Mountains;

7. the Aleppo Plateau and Northern Plain; and

8. the Euphrates Region.

Population

The population growth rate in Syria is considered very high, calculated at 3.17% per annum in 1965 and 3.5% per annum in 1985 (Population Council, 1994: 248). Population size was estimated at 1.3 million in 1921; this jumped to 4.6 million in the first accurate official survey that took place in 1960, and it became 9.53 million in 1981. It is expected to reach over 17 million in the year 2000, if the population growth rate is not altered (Talas, 1990: 289).

Economy and Environment

Syria has an agriculture-based economy. Its natural assets, especially land and water, beside playing a great role in its economy, could be affected by any change in agricultural policy and methods of cultivation and irrigation. This vulnerability of natural resources to policy making in Syria is due to many factors: first, the pressure of population increase resulting in greater demand on agricultural produce; second, Syria is mostly arid; third, expanding agricultural production or even keeping it at its current level requires more water and more irrigation projects; and fourth, Syria's arable land is sandwiched between desertification and urbanization.

Mikhail Wakil of Aleppo University states that the arid region of Syria, which receives less than 250 mm of rain per annum constitutes 72% of the total area of the country. This region includes the southern and southeastern regions which form a natural extension of the Arabian steppe desert. Annual rainfall declines in this area from the northwest to the southeast, where the mean annual precipitation is less than 100 mm. The conditions prevailing in this region make it unsuitable for agriculture, unless irrigation is used. The semiarid region encompasses the rest of the country, including the coastal region and the northern plains, where the average total precipitation is more than 250 mm per annum. Conditions in these regions allow the practice of rain-fed agriculture: however, crop success is not guaranteed due to the high fluctuation in annual precipitation (Wakil, 1993: 63-64).

In a more detailed account of the relation between rainfall and agricultural regions, the Syrian Ministry of Agriculture and Agrarian Reform (1989), divides Syria into five zones of agricultural settlements based on their annual rainfall:

1. The first settlement zone, with an annual rainfall of over 350 mm., is divided into two areas:
    a. The area of annual rainfall rate of over 600 mm. where rain-fed crops can be successfully planted.
    b. The area of annual rainfall of between 350-600 mm. and not less than 300 mm. Here, on average there are two crop seasons every three years. The main crops are wheat, legumes, and summer crops. This zone consists of 269,800 hectares or 15% of the country.

2. The second settlement zone with an annual rainfall of 250-350 mm. and not less than 250 mm. Here it is possible to get two barley seasons every three years. Beside barley, wheat, legumes and summer crops could be planted. This zone comprises 2,473,000 hectares, or 13% of the country.

3. The third settlement zone with an annual rainfall of not less than 250 mm. Here it is possible to get one to two seasons each three years. Its main crop is barley, but legumes could be planted, also. This zone comprises 1,306,000 hectares, or 7% of the country.

4. The fourth settlement zone (Marginal), with an annual rainfall rate of between 200-250 mm. It is good only for barley or permanent grazing crops. It comprises 1,823,000 hectares, and 9.8% of the country.

5. The fifth settlement zone (desert and steppe) covers the rest of the country, and is not suitable for rain-fed planting. At 10,218,000 hectares, it comprises 55.1% of the country.

These facts point directly to the vulnerability of Syrian agriculture to unreliable natural factors. They also demonstrate the importance of irrigated agriculture to Syria, and consequently the importance of its water resources, especially the Euphrates river. Wakil states that the cultivable land in Syria corresponds to 33% of its total area. In 1991, 91.5% of this cultivable land was planted, of which 12% was irrigated. Most importantly, he observes that "of all cultivable land in Syria 53% is in the Euphrates basin" (1993: 63-64). This definitely justifies the great attention that several policy makers have given to the Euphrates and to the major development projects utilizing its water. It also explains the great tension among Syria, Iraq, and Turkey over this international river. Syrians believe their country's economy relies heavily on the flow of the Euphrates waters and that any threat to this flow will undermine it.

Syria has a total of sixteen rivers. The hydrologic coastal basin (Hawdh As-Sahel) is considered one of the richest hydrologic basins in Syria. Despite this fact, it suffers from water shortages which are being aggravated by increasing population and rapid growth of the coastal cities and small towns in the mountain (Abdulsalam, 1985: 18). The importance of the Euphrates stems from its volume as well as from its length of 675 km, and the location of its course which flows into the driest region of Syria, from the north to the southeast, transforming vast areas in its basin into cultivable land.

The other reason for the importance that has been given to the major irrigation projects and to the Euphrates river is the fact that Syria has already exhausted its ground water resources, because in many areas drought or scattered rain fall have necessitated their use. As well, the over-use of ground water and its mismanagement have led to soil salinization and to the loss of vast land which were once cultivable.

Irrigation Projects

Mr. Abd al Rahman Madani, the Minister of Irrigation reiterates the Syrian policy in giving priority to dam building and land reclamation as a way to achieving development and the "Agricultural Revolution." Mr. Madani suggests that the great weight that Syria is giving to its water resources was the reason for establishing the Ministry of Irrigation in 1982, and later to establish in 1983 an Institution for the Study of Water Resources. He also quotes President Assad confirming that "Syria's bright agricultural future will shine from the Euphrates Valley, which has suffered from neglect for a long time; also, we will achieve great economic prosperity leading us [syrians] in big steps towards the aspired society ... the united socialist Arab society" (Syrian Irrigation Ministry, n.d.).

Hundreds of dams have already been built all over Syria, but the Euphrates dam remains the focal point economically and even politically as a symbol of the Ba'th (the ruling party) achievements.

Since its independence, Syria has tried to utilize its share from the Euphrates to irrigate the valley extending from Aleppo to its border with Iraq. In 1966, Syria signed an agreement with the Soviet Union to build the Euphrates Dam, which was completed in 1975. The main reasons for building the dam were to provide irrigation for over 600 thousand hectares, hydro-electric power generation, and to regulate the Euphrates River (Irrigation Ministry, n.d.).

Plans for water resource development in the Euphrates basin include the construction of six dams—few are already completed—on the Euphrates and Khabur Rivers. At its completion, this development project, will have the capacity to irrigate over 7,500,000 hectares, and produce over 450 million kW of hydroelectric energy. This means that it will be able to irrigate over 50% of the irrigable land in Syria and provide over 95% of Syria's hydropower. This will definitely help the Syrian economy by boosting cropping intensity from 80% to 135%, therefore increasing agricultural production four-fold and helping to reduce the growing food deficit in Syria due to its increased population (Wakil, 1993: 68).

Such major irrigation projects, combined with such an increase in cultivation intensity, have the potential to damage the soil by causing salination, consequently transforming the area from cultivable into uncultivable land. This is the heart of the problem that developing countries, including Syria, are facing. Recently, efforts have been made to strike a balance between the objectives of development and the vulnerability of the environment and natural resources to the damage caused by rapid and ill planned development projects.

Soils

Dr. Mohamed Taweel, in his report on Syria for a conference organized by FAO, describes Syrian soil as follows:
"In terms of geology, Syria is located on a piece of different kinds of calcareous rock, where very old calcareous rocks spread to the western part, while they become more recent to the east with some Basalt lava dating from the modern ages.
In general, Syrian lands are divided into the following:

The Wet Area: The annual rainfall in this area is more than 800 mm. It is divided into two sub-groups:
Calcareous Soils also called Red Mediterranean soil: It covers the most part of the coastal mountainous areas and the coastal valley. Such soil is reddish-brown and has a high level of calcium carbonates with little organic content (about 2%).
Volcanic Soil: This soil is found in some parts of the coastal mountains stretching from the southern part of Safita to Homs, over the green rocks scattered in the northern part of Latakia, and in Quneitra Banyas, and Tartous. It is dark brown in color and almost free from calcium carbonates. It, too, has little organic content (1.5-3%).
The Semi-Wet Area: It is bounded on the west by the Coastal Mountain Ranges and ends on the east by an invisible line passing through Homs and Hama and stretching to the north up to the Taurus mountains. There is also another semi-wet area situated in the extreme north-east of Syria (Ras Al Batta). These soils are yellowish brown, brown or dark brown in color, depending on the quantity of

rainfall. They contain different rates of calcium carbonates, either originating from calcareous or volcanic rocks, with basic pH and little organic matter content.

The Semi-Arid Area: This area stretches along a narrow strip from southern to northern Syria passing through the eastern parts of Homs and Hama. This strip curves near Aleppo up to Meskaneh, then stretches to the east. The color of the soil in this area is reddish brown or light brown, and contain calcium carbonates. Its interaction is basic, with little organic matter.

The Dry Area: It forms the lands of the Syrian steppe. It is very stony, its color is light brown, and it has a high level of calcium carbonate.

Gypsiferous Lands: These are found in the dry area. Their color is light due to the high rate of gypsum and calcium carbonates (Taweel, n.d.).

As mentioned above, cultivable land in Syria is being lost due to natural desertification and dust storms. The other reason for losing land is due to land salination. Erik Eckholm estimates that in the Euphrates Valley about one-fourth to one-half of the total agricultural area has been rendered unfit for cultivation by soil salinity and saturation. This led to a drop in average cotton yields from 2.5 tons per hectare in the early fifties to about 1.5 tons per hectare by 1966. He adds that more than half of the irrigable lands of the Euphrates and Khabour Valleys, about 220,000 hectares, had been harmed or destroyed by salinity as of 1970. He concludes that this occurred in the period after the introduction of intensive, perennial cotton production and he predicts that the problem is certain to spread with the current expansion of irrigated area that will result from the Euphrates dam (1976: 125-126). In a later study, Qasim Miqdad confirmed that salinity due to ill-managed irrigation and the lack of a drainage network resulted in the loss of large areas of cultivated land. Due to this fact, in the period between 1979 to 1983, 18 thousand hectares were lost. In addition many water projects for irrigation and domestic use were forced to stop due to dwindling well waters resulting in the loss of over 27 thousand hectares of cultivable land (Miqdad, 1986: 57).

Another reason for the loss of land is ill-advised project; e.g., the Euphrates Valley lost its most fertile land to the Euphrates dam project. The region where the dam was built was considered a very fertile area that had on its banks many agricultural settlements. The residents of these settlements were transferred from that area to become known as "al-Maghmoureen" (literally, "the flooded people"). Urbanization and its encroachment on agricultural neighborhoods constitutes a constantly increasing threat. The best example on this issue is the case of al-Ghouta near Damascus, known throughout history for its orchards and pleasant atmosphere. Recently, this has been changing, thanks to the population explosion in Damascus leading to the construction of cement buildings in the green fields of al-Ghouta. Old Damascenes feel a change in the climate, they will tell you that it is getting harsher, and they will tell you why: it is the loss of trees and fields that used to surround this inland city. Nowadays, high-rise buildings replace the old trees.

It is extremely important to note that the vegetation cover in Syria in quite exceptional, for it contains an interesting and unique diversity of plants. Studies have shown that Syria and Lebanon have over 3,646 kinds of the highest grades of flora, compared to Britain, which has only 1,750 kinds (Talas, 1990: 266). Syria is an important center for the origin of plant species, especially wheat and barley. It is also one of the principal habitats of almost ten species (Taweel, n.d.: Chapter 1).

Unfortunately, Syria's plant cover is now suffering from degradation due to the following facts:

1. The spread of cultivation to new areas and the need to grow economic crops, particularly cereals, forage, and food legumes.

2. The expansion of barley cultivation to the dry and very dry (steppe) areas and the surrounding area has led to the deterioration and the removal of vegetation, which will result in soil erosion. All this is taking place in spite of the measures established by the government to prevent such cultivation.

3. Overgrazing has also increased the pressure on the steppe because of its limited area and frequent droughts. Presently, Syria has over 12 million sheep, which vastly exceeds the grazing capacity of the steppe.

4. Logging. The nomads cut trees and bushes to use as a source of energy (cooking and heating). One rarely sees the pistachio trees which were present in the steppe until early in this century.

5. The use of cars and tractors by the nomads instead of camels and other farm animals. Such vehicles have contributed, with their speed, heaviness, and easy movement, to the destruction of the upper layer of soil, reducing it to small particles. They have also contributed to vegetation degradation, thus accelerating desertification in many parts of the steppe.

6. Setting fires illegally to some parts of the forests to establish orchards in their place. Syrian laws impose heavy penalties on those who burn the forests or remove them with the purpose of utilizing the land to plant fruit trees.

7. The spread of goats in mountainous areas has contributed to the destruction of trees.

8. Accidental forest fires (Taweel, n.d.: Chapter 1).

In addition, the major development projects that Turkey is constructing on the banks of the Euphrates is causing great degradation in the water quality of the Euphrates as it flows downstream to Syria. This will consequently cause severe damage to Syrian soil, as it will increase its salination making it unsuitable for cultivation and therefore impacting negatively on the Syrian economy.

Solutions

Old policies in Syria were established to tighten its economic belt and reduce expenditures in various ways; e.g., a new car was considered a luxury item and taxed heavily. Consequently, Damascus has suffered a great deal from air pollution due to using of low-cost fuel and old cars that emit toxic fumes into the air. Air pollution from the Homs refinery has caused a lot of damage to the agriculture of this area. Ill maintained open-water canals contribute to cholera outbreaks, especially in the summer.

The Syrian government, with the support of different international organizations and centers, such as the World Bank, FAO, ICARDA, and ACSAD is trying hard to meet its challenge to develop on one hand while maintaining and preserving its natural resources on the other. Many issues result from this need to be self-sufficient and economically competitive in a competitive and already developed world market. It seems that the Syrian government is doing its best to address these issues. Its various ministries and centers are paying close attention to environmental issues and are active participants in many world conferences and agreements that encourage better environmental practices. Syria was also a founding member of the Arab Council on Environment. It issued several laws to conserve the forests and other areas, and to save animals such as deer from extinction, by preventing hunting practices. A special zoning system is in place that identifies areas in which peasants can dig wells and areas where it is forbidden. The Syrian government, in cooperation with the government of Iraq and other neighboring countries, is constantly monitoring the status of locusts at its borders.

ICARDA's Center in Aleppo reported several success stories related to Syrian wheat and barley production and government attempts to rehabilitate the Syrian steppe. A report in July, 1995, declared that in 1991, Syria, the breadbasket of the ancient world, became self-sufficient in wheat for the first time since the 1950s. Better management, irrigation and increased fertilizer use, as well as new wheat varieties, were the factors behind this success (Manners, 1995). In another report Dr. Christiansen and Dr. Ahmed Osman of ICARDA were quite excited at the improvement of a hillside that two years ago was almost totally degraded, with pasture land for sheep lost, resulting in reduced milk and meat production, and fewer lambs being weaned. In the northern Syrian village of Btajek, a family agreed with ICARDA to revegetate thirty hectares of their hill. They were provided with seeds and asked not to graze their sheep there until the seeds had germinated and set more seeds. In addition they fertilized the hill with small amounts of phosphate. Now the results are clear: " the hillside has sprung back to life." Both researchers believe that this is the way to stop the process of land degradation (Madeley, 1995). In addition, the government is cooperating with ICARDA to introduce fodder-shrub plantations for grazing by sheep and goats. In Aleppo Province alone, almost 5,800 hectares were opened for grazing in the month of April, 1995, and another 2,000 hectares will be mature for the 1996 season (ICARDA, 1995).

Conclusion

Syria's Government is highly interested in environmental issues. It is facilitating cooperation with several international organizations to achieve the objective of a well balanced and secure environment. However, the issues of environment are related to the daily life and practices of ordinary people, meaning that no matter how many treaties and agreements, or even how many institutions the government might establish (Syria has established a Ministry for Environment), environmental issues will predominantly be settled in the streets and fields of Syria. Even though the interest and the support of the government is always helpful in implementing environmental policies, still it is the citizens' awareness that will make the difference. In Syria's case there is a great need to spread this awareness among all segments and communities of people in a more effective way, in order for environmental policies to be successful. Then Syria could be considered to have met its challenge.

REFERENCES

ABDULSALAM, Adel
1986 *"The Rural Geographic Environment of the Syria Coastal Region and the Shizuoka Region, A Comparative Study of Syria and Japan."* Tokyo: ILCAA.
ECKHOLM, Erick P.
1976 *Losing Ground, Environmental Stress and World Food Prospects.* New York: W.W. Norton & Company, Inc.
EL-AKHRASS, Hisham
1986 *Syria and the CGIAR Centers, A study of their Collaboration in Agricultural Research.* Washington, D.C.: The World Bank.
ICARDA
1995 "Saving the Steppe with Saltbrush Shrubs." April, 1995. Aleppo, Syria: ICARDA.
MADELEY, John
1995 "Revegetating Degraded Land." July. Aleppo: ICARDA.
MANNERS, Guy
1995 "News Release." July. Aleppo, Syria: ICARDA Documentation and Information Services.
MIQDAD, Qasim
1986 "Water Resources and its Usage in the Syrian Region," in: ACSAD. *Conference on Water Resources and Their Usage in the Arab World.* Kuwait.
Population Council
1994 "Syria 1993: Results from the Pan Arab Project for Child Development (PAPCHILD) Survey." *Studies in Family Planning*, 25 (4).
Syrian Arab Republic
n.d. Irrigation Ministry, *Survey Report.* Damascus (post-1984).
1989 Ministry of Agriculture and Agrarian Reform, *Annual Statistical Abstract.*

TALAS, Mustafa et al.
1990 Al-Mu'Jam al-Jughrafi lil-qutr al A'rabi al-suri.
TAWEEL, Mohamed W.
n.d. *Country Report for Syria*. Geneva: FAO, International Conference and Program for Plant Genetic Resources (ICPPGR).
WAKIL, Mikhail
1993 "Sharing the Euphrates." Syria: *Research and Exploration*, V.9.

CONTRIBUTORS

Dr. Badria A. Al Awadhi specializes in the International Law of the Environment, a field in which she is well known in the Middle East. Her law practice is situated in Kuwait.

Joseph G. Jabbra is Academic Vice President at Loyola Marymount University, Los Angeles, and Professor of Political Science and International Law in the Department of Political Science. He has published extensively on the Middle East and has been the recipient of several research grants and awards. He is active in the International Association of Schools and Institutes of Administration. His current research interests include a focus on the balance between development and the quality of life, and the International Law of the Environment.

Dr. Nancy Jabbra is a social anthropologist and Director of the Women's Studies Program at Loyola Marymount University in Los Angeles, California. She previously was a member of the Sociology and Social Anthropology Department at Dalhousie University in Halifax, Canada, where she served as Director of the International Development Studies Programme and President of the Canadian Ethnic Studies Association. She carried out research on politics and gender roles in Lebanon in the 1970s and again in the 1990s, and on Lebanese immigrants in Canada during the 1980s and 1990s.

Jamil E. Jreisat is Professor of Public Administration and Political Science, Department of Government and International Affairs, at the University of South Florida, where he teaches Comparative and Development Administration, Organization Theory and Process, and Public Budgeting. He has published extensively on these subjects, and on administrative development in the Arab world in various professional journals. Dr. Jreisat's forthcoming book on *Politics without Process: Administering Development in the Arab State*, is scheduled for publication by Reinner Publishers in 1997; and his *Managing Public Organizations* is being revised for publication by Greenwood.

Joseph A. Kechichian is a consultant on the Middle East and a recognized expert on the Gulf region. He is a frequent participant on radio and television programs, a featured keynote speaker at numerous international conferences and a 1995 recipient of the Rand President's Award for Research Excellence. Dr. Kechichian was an Associate Political Scientist at Rand, a lecturer at the University of California Los Angeles, and a former Hoover Fellow at Stanford University. He received a doctorate in foreign affairs from the University of Virginia in 1985 where he also taught and assumed the Assistant Deanship in International Studies. Dr. Kechichian also writes on foreign policy issues.

Dr. Damazo Majak Kochak was born in Sudan in 1952. He received his BA and MA from the University of Khartoum and worked in a variety of capacities for the government of Sudan and the University of Juba in southern Sudan. He received his Ph.D. in history from the University of California, Santa Barbara, in 1989, and joined the Department of History at Loyola Marymount University in August of 1990. Dr. Damazo was granted tenure in 1995. He died in 1996, just two weeks after he submitted this paper for publication in this volume.

CONTRIBUTORS

Rania Masri is currently a Ph.D. candidate of Forestry at North Carolina State University. She holds a Master's Degree in Environmental Management from the Nicholas School of the Environment, Duke University. She is deeply active in humanitarian and environmental issues related to Lebanon, Iraq, and Palestine—having led seminars and presentations, organized two national conferences, and written extensively on these topics. She is a contributing editor to *Al-Jadid*, a national Arab-American magazine, and the founder and coordinator of the Iraq Action Coalition, an Internet-based organization.

Gloria Ibrahim Saliba earned her C. Phil degree in modern Middle Eastern History from the University of California, Los Angeles, where she is currently finishing her doctoral dissertation entitled, "Issues of Land and Water, Their Economic and Socio-Political Dimensions in the Agricultural Development of Syria (1958 to present)." She has been active in the Middle East Studies Association (MESA), where she regularly presents papers on Syria and the Middle East. In addition, she publishes an international electronic newsletter, "Syria-Net," which she established in May, 1995. In addition to her degree in history, Gloria Saliba holds a Master's Degree in Philosophy from Saint Joseph University in Beirut, and a Bachelor's Degree from the Lebanese University in Philosophy and Law.

Dr. Alon Tal is currently Director of the Arava Institute for Environmental Studies, a new graduate-level study center affiliated with Tel Aviv University, and formed to train Middle Eastern environmentalists. He is founding Chairman of Adam Teva V'din, the Israel Union for Environmental Defense and has appointments at the Tel Aviv University Faculty of Law and the Harvard University School of Public Health in environmental law and policy. He is a graduate of the University of North Carolina, Hebrew University Law School and Harvard University.

Seid M. Zekavat is Associate Professor of Economics at Loyola Marymount University. His research interest has been in the area of Agriculture and Sustainable Economic Development and in Environmental Economics in the Middle East, particularly in Iran. He received his law degree from University of Tehran, Iran, a B.A. in Political Science from Peperdine University, and an M.A. and a Ph.D. in Economics from the University of Southern California.